WRITING *in* PICTURES

Joseph McBride is a film historian and associate professor in the Cinema department at San Francisco State University.

His many books include *Searching for John Ford, Frank Capra: The Catastrophe of Success, Steven Spielberg: A Biography, Hawks on Hawks, Whatever Happened to Orson Welles?: A Portrait of an Independent Career*, as well as the critical studies *John Ford* (1974, with Michael Wilmington) and *Orson Welles*.

ALSO BY JOSEPH MCBRIDE

Steven Spielberg: A Biography

*What Ever Happened to Orson Welles?: A Portrait
of an Independent Career*

Searching for John Ford

Frank Capra: The Catastrophe of Success

*The Book of Movie Lists: An Offbeat, Provocative Collection
of the Best and Worst of Everything in Movies*

*High and Inside: An A-to-Z Guide
to the Language of Baseball*

Orson Welles

*Filmmakers on Filmmaking: The American Film Institute
Seminars on Motion Pictures and Television,*
Volumes I and II (editor)

Hawks on Hawks

Orson Welles: Actor and Director

Kirk Douglas

John Ford (with Michael Wilmington)

Focus on Howard Hawks (editor)

Persistence of Vision: A Collection of Film Criticism (editor)

WRITING

in

PICTURES

Screenwriting Made (Mostly) Painless

Joseph McBride

faber and faber

First published in the USA in 2012
by Vintage Books, a division of Random House, Inc., New York,
and in Canada by Random House of Canada Limited, Toronto.

First published in the UK in 2012
by Faber and Faber Ltd
Bloomsbury House
74–77 Great Russell Street
London WC1B 3DA

Printed and bound by CPI Group (UK) Ltd, Croydon, CR0 4YY

Grateful acknowledgment is made to the following
for permission to quote from published or unpublished material: *The 101
Habits of Highly Successful Screenwriters: Inside Secrets from Hollywood's
Top Writers* © 2001 by Karl Iglesias, reprinted by permission of Adams
Media, an FTW Media, Inc., co., all rights reserved; Joel and Ethan Coen,
for quotations from their screenplay *The Big Lebowski* (published by
Faber and Faber, London, 1998); Francis Ford Coppola, for quotations
from his speech to students at San Francisco State University, April 24,
2009; and excerpt from *Taxi Driver* by Paul Schrader, copyright © 1990
by Paul Schrader, reprinted by permission of Faber and Faber, Inc., an
affiliate of Farrar, Straus and Giroux, LLC.

A CIP record for this book
is available from the British Library

ISBN 978–0–571–27437–6

2 4 6 8 10 9 7 5 3 1

For Richard Parks

Contents

(vii)

Contents

WRITING *in* PICTURES

Introduction

Who Needs Another Book on Screenwriting?

You do. I imagine that you are opening this book because you haven't found the answers to the many questions you have about how to break into the field of screenwriting. The books you have looked at probably disappointed you because they laid out, in excruciating detail, a series of rules you *must* follow to write a salable script. These rules probably struck you as recipes for turning out predictable screenplays resembling too many movies you've already seen. These books may have seemed to have more in common with cookbooks than they do with the field of creative writing, encouraging standardization rather than individuality. You may also have noticed that most of the people writing these books somehow have never managed to get a script of their own produced, which probably accounts for why much of their advice may seem so vague and impractical.

At least that is what I found when I started surveying the field of books on screenwriting. When I began teaching screenwriting on a regular basis more than a decade ago, after a long career as a professional film and television writer, I naturally hoped to find a handy textbook I could use for my classes that could provide a solid framework for learning the craft. To my surprise, I couldn't find a book I thought worth using. Some seem reasonably sound but overly obvious, dull and trite in their approach to filmmaking and creative writing. Some books offer amusing comments on the field but don't offer you much practical help. You can get something out of almost any of these books, but not enough to do the job.

What I couldn't find was a book that actually gets into the nitty-gritty of what's required to learn the screenwriting craft in a systematic way and that does so concisely and without telling you how to write formulaic screenplays. I wanted a book that gives you the tools to write in your own voice. I did not want one that would tell you how to devise character "arcs" that follow standard behavior patterns for movie characters, how to include "beats" and "inciting incidents" and on what pages to put them, and how to ensure that your characters and plots are "likable" enough (meaning innocuous enough) to sell. Charlie Kaufman made wicked fun of such books in his screenplay for *Adaptation,* showing an intemperate screenwriting teacher (modeled on a certain luminary in the field) browbeating his students into following the slavish formulas pushed in his books and highly expensive seminars. Whether your ideas are truly daring and original and whether you are writing from the heart rather than just the pocketbook often seems incidental in such dogmatic approaches to the craft.

And if you are as dissatisfied as I am with such factory-style training methods, you probably share my view that what's wrong with most mainstream filmmaking today, at least in the United States, is that it follows formulas so slavishly. When you go to the theater and see a bunch of trailers (after suffering through all the ads you've paid good money to watch), you find to your distress that most of the coming attractions look alike—cars flipping over and exploding, maniacs chasing victims through shadowy houses and alleyways, slobby guys making fools of themselves pursuing impossibly pretty girls, superheroes flying through darkly painted skies, animated monsters and machines chasing tiny humans through fairytale landscapes or urban settings that look like video games—a nonstop parade of dreary clichés and tiresome (though impressively executed) special effects, all thrown together in a dizzying montage of shots lasting no more than two seconds each.

American movies that take the time and care to deal with people and their problems—such as *No Country for Old Men, Juno, Million Dollar Baby, Gran Torino, Lost in Translation, Sideways, The Good Shepherd, The Informant!, The Wrestler, Up in the Air, A Serious Man*—unfortunately seem few and far between, though audiences starved for such adult fare made most of those films popular. American movies exploring serious issues and ideas are even harder to find (with such notable exceptions as *Milk; Invictus; Bulworth; Syriana; Minority Report; Munich; Good Night, and Good Luck;* and *In the Valley of Elah*), and usually if you want to see a film about social issues, you'd better hurry before it's hustled off the screen to make room for the next CGI extravaganza. *The Hurt Locker,* a powerful human drama dealing with the Iraq War, won the best-picture Oscar for 2009 but had trouble drawing audiences to theaters. A rare example of a critically and commercially successful film dealing in an adult way with a serious social theme was *Brokeback Mountain,* which defied conventional wisdom to demonstrate that a gay love story, and a Western to boot, beautifully written (by Larry McMurtry and Diana Ossana, from the short story by Annie Proulx) and directed (by Ang Lee), could appeal to a broad audience.

But studios usually go for safer bets, films that are market-tested to appeal to the lowest common denominator. It's uncommon for a quality film to emerge from that process, although it does happen, as demonstrated by *Avatar, The Dark Knight, The Lord of the Rings: The Fellowship of the Ring, V for Vendetta, Titanic,* and Steven Soderbergh's remake of *Ocean's Eleven.* In such cases, the filmmakers found ways of overcoming genre clichés and market pressures. But someone said only half-jokingly that the ideal movie for today's marketplace would be a two-hour explosion. If you can figure out a way to write such a movie, more power to you. But if that's your goal, this is probably not the book for you. And even if it is your goal, you might well find that in trying to make that long explosion interesting, you will need a solid story structure and some well-rounded characters to inhabit the cinematic world of your imagination. This book, then, will give you the tools to tell the stories you want to tell, the ones you've been carrying around in your head, the "scenes you'd like to see" (as *Mad* magazine used to put it) but don't yet have the craft to transfer from your head to the printed page.

The New Yorker ran a cartoon a few years ago showing the screenwriting section of a chain bookstore, with a sign above the book rack proclaiming "WIN THE LOTTERY." That captures the problem with too many books about screenwriting. They assume your motivation in wanting to write screenplays is simply to get rich. Or to get famous. Or to get laid. Joe Eszterhas, in his entertaining book *The Devil's Guide to Hollywood: The Screenwriter as God!,* keeps reminding you about the time he slept with Sharon Stone, one of the perks he claims to have received for writing *Basic Instinct.* Sure, those are probably the main motivations for many people in the business. But are those really the reasons why you want to write scripts? Take a moment to ask yourself why you first wanted to get into this crazy racket.

I assume you wanted to do so because you love watching movies and telling stories. You may or may not have much experience in other forms of writing, but if you want to be a writer for the screen, you probably love words almost as much as you love pictures. The operative word here, as you notice, is "love." If you don't love what you are doing when you write screenplays and if you don't want to do it for love more than for any other reason, I'd suggest you seriously think of doing something else, because the film business is as difficult as it can be rewarding.

This book is not going to promise you that you'll get rich or win an Oscar. But if you want to take a shot at success—and let's define that as writing a script that not only sells but reaches the screen in a form reasonably similar to what you wrote—you first have to know the craft. And if you want to learn the craft, this book can show you how.

My aim here is to demystify the process. What you will get is straight talk, no mumbo jumbo or gimmicks, just a methodical, step-by-step process that walks you through the different stages of writing a screenplay. Our work together will be modeled on the development process that a screenplay undergoes in the world of professional filmmaking—from idea to outline to treatment to step outline to finished screenplay. The book will show you, with discussions and concrete examples, how each of these stages of development functions and will give you ways of correcting and polishing your own work. When you do these writing exercises, the same kind of steps that a professional writer would follow in developing a script, the end product will be a short screenplay in the professional format.

I have used this same method with hundreds of beginning screenwriting students at San Francisco State University and elsewhere, and I am happy to report that almost all of them get the hang of the process in less than three months. I can make you the same guarantee I make to them: If you learn these lessons and work diligently on your writing assignments, you will be well on your way to being a professional-quality screenwriter within ninety days or less. The only students who don't reach that goal are usually the few who skip some of the lessons or don't do all the written work. But since you are highly motivated—you've bought the book by now, I'm sure—you will escape those pitfalls and emerge ready to write your own feature-length screenplays. After that, it's up to you. Your own talent and drive will carry you into your professional career. But every professional writer has to start with the basics.

APPRENTICESHIP

How did I learn the craft? And how am I going to apply what I learned to teaching it to you? For me it started with *Citizen*

Kane. I first saw Orson Welles's masterpiece about a media tycoon when I was nineteen, one afternoon in 1966 in a film class at the University of Wisconsin–Madison. The audacity and ambition of the film, and the fact that its maker was only twenty-five, literally changed my life. I went from wanting to be a novelist to wanting to write and direct films. I started writing a critical study of Welles, completed four years later, the first of three books I've written on him and his work. By 1970, through a series of fortunate coincidences, I would be acting in a Welles film, as a film critic in *The Other Side of the Wind,* and working with the director to help write my own dialogue. That Walter Mittyish adventure was my first experience in professional filmmaking, and what a way to start!

Working with Welles for six years on that legendary, still-unfinished satire of Hollywood was my equivalent of film school. We had only two film courses at Madison, and neither was about screenwriting. But we had thirty-five film societies on campus (one of which I ran), so I was constantly studying films. The film sections of bookstores were still very skimpy in those days; although it was a good time to break into writing about film, it was a bad time to look for a book on how to write films. I also didn't have the means to go to a film school in New York or California. So I realized that I would have to teach myself the craft of screenwriting.

I was fortunate to have access to a 16 mm print of *Citizen Kane* that I watched over and over (more than sixty times in that period) to learn every aspect of cinematography, art design, editing, acting, directing, and writing. And I was even more fortunate to have access to a mimeographed original copy of the script of *Kane* at the State Historical Society of Wisconsin (now the Wisconsin Historical Society); the script was still unpublished and would not appear in print until 1971. Every day for a month, I hauled my portable manual typewriter to the Historical Society reading room to type an exact copy of that magnificent screenplay, since I couldn't afford to have it photocopied.

I took it home and studied it as my bible for the next few years, absorbing both its formatting and its content. The script of *Kane* by Herman J. Mankiewicz and Welles is a film school in itself, with its rich characters and themes, colorful and witty dialogue, brilliantly visual descriptions, and intricate flashback structure. I was pleased to learn many years later that when David Mamet was teaching himself to write plays, he similarly typed out a copy of a dramatic work he greatly admired, Tennessee Williams's *A Streetcar Named Desire*. Mamet could have taken that play out of the library, but typing it for himself made him intimately familiar with every word and line. Internalizing a play or a script in this way, to make its style second nature as you learn from your master(s), is something I'd recommend to any young writer.

And so I felt I was ready—rashly enough—to start writing scripts of my own. But how to begin?

Realizing that learning how to write in the screenplay form was challenging enough without having to come up with my own story, I sensibly decided to start with some adaptations of literary works and gradually build up to writing an original. I knew that I should start simply, by writing a short script based on a story that could be filmed without a great deal of complication. I thought of Jack London's classic short story "To Build a Fire." This story about a man's desperate attempt to survive in sub-zero Yukon cold is filled with blunt action descriptions and carries a strong emotional punch. London's storytelling is largely visual in its narrative style and free from internal monologues and other complicated literary devices. The story's elemental simplicity makes it powerful material for filming.

I studied the story carefully and turned it into an adequate blueprint for a short film. It was rather clumsy and not in the professional format, but I found that I could translate a written story into cinematic language, although I was laboring under some misapprehensions about screenwriting (more on that later). In the end I decided not to shoot the screenplay because of the practical difficulties during a Wisconsin winter of filming a man slowly freezing to death; Wisconsin may not have been as painful as the Yukon, but it was close enough.

Thus emboldened by my first experience writing a screenplay, I went on to try my hand at a feature-length script. I wrote a couple of adaptations and then ventured into writing originals. I didn't sell my first screenplay until 1977, the seventh feature-length script I had written (I had also written dozens of short film scripts and filmed several of them myself). That's one of the first lessons I will pass along to you: Don't ever stop writing. The great novelist Graham Greene wrote five novels before he found a publisher; the sheer determination involved in keeping going in such circumstances is the test of whether a writer is truly serious or not.

So I served a ten-year apprenticeship teaching myself how to write scripts before I became a professional. By then I had thoroughly learned the craft, and over the next seven years I had three features produced (including cowriting the cult classic musical *Rock 'n' Roll High School*) and six television specials. I received a Writers Guild of America Award, four other WGA nominations, a Canadian Film Awards nomination, and two Emmy nominations before I decided to concentrate full-time on writing books. But occasionally I have been lured back to work in the movie business, usually as a writer and/or producer of documentaries. I will share my varied experiences as a film and television writer to help illustrate the lessons in this book.

The methods I used to teach myself how to write screenplays proved sound, and I have replicated them in my screenwriting classes and in this book. I proved that someone can teach himself the craft if he is sufficiently dedicated to doing so and keeps challenging himself to go one step farther. But I have since come to realize that I could have saved myself several years of work if I had had some training and mentorship. I had no one to warn me about the many mistakes I would make when I landed in Hollywood, eager, knowledgeable, but largely naïve. Having a teacher guide you through the steps involved can speed up the process and save you from many false starts. And having someone who knows the business to teach you the ropes can save you years of struggling and suffering.

If you know how to write a professional-quality screenplay, whether you learn how to do so in school or do it on your own (with the help of a book), you have at least a fighting chance, as I did, to break into the business and show people what you are capable of doing.

Part I

Storytelling

1

So Why Write Screenplays?

*M*y screenwriter friend Sam Hamm, whose credits include *Batman, Batman Returns,* and the brilliantly acerbic political satire "Homecoming," often visits my classes to share his wisdom. He starts by telling the students, "If you can do anything else, do it." Sam is right. Trying to earn a living as a screenwriter, or as a writer of any kind, often resembles the Myth of Sisyphus.

If you want to be a doctor, you go to medical school. You take a series of clearly defined courses, get the required practical experience, and emerge as an M.D. The odds are strong that you will find a well-paying job with a hospital or an HMO. But in the field of screenwriting, there is no such thing as a training course that will guarantee you a well-paying job, or any other kind of job, no matter how qualified you may think you are. The odds against breaking into the field are long, and even if you do, it's hard to make a living as a screenwriter; about half of the members of the Writers Guild of America can't find work in any given year. So if you can make a living as a computer specialist or an accountant or a firefighter, the wiser course is to enter one of those saner professions.

Even if you manage to get a script before the cameras, the trouble is just beginning, because it's rare for a screenplay to survive production unscathed, without endless revisions by other writers (or anyone else on the set). And even if a miracle occurs and your script emerges from this process as a successful movie (artistically, commercially, or both), that's no guarantee you will sustain a career. A flop or two, and you may find yourself back on the unemployment line. Just about everyone in the business goes through fallow periods; managing to survive them and carve out a long career takes tremendous stamina and ingenuity, and it usually doesn't get much easier.

You can write screenplays as a means to an end, a way to move up the ladder to becoming a director. Many students admit that getting a ticket to direct is the reason they want to learn screenwriting, for being a director is generally considered a more glamorous job than being a screenwriter. Screenwriters are the Rodney Dangerfields of the film business. Directors get more respect, more publicity, more money, more of almost everything. They sometimes get their name above the title and claim that the film is "A film by Joe Doakes," much to the displeasure of the Writers Guild. But as most people in the film business know, deep down, but hate to acknowledge, the writer is the single indispensable person in the making of a film. Until the script is written, nothing can happen in front of the camera, and if the script is no good, the film doesn't have a chance of success. That fact should give great power to the writer, but it doesn't work that way. Writers are viewed as interchangeable and expendable. The industry lives in active denial of the central importance of the writer, because recognizing it would dangerously expose the insecurity of everyone else who depends on the writer's work.

Another reason writing is held in such low repute in Hollywood is that it seems that everyone who lives there wants to be a writer or describes himself or herself as a writer. People joke about how the guy bagging groceries at the local Ralphs always has a script in his back pocket to sell you, but the joke often turns out to be true. So when you tell someone in Hollywood that you're a writer, you are often met with a sneer of contempt. And in the film business, unfortunately, everyone seems to think he or she can write, so the profession is undervalued. It's not bad enough that the director and actors feel capable of improving a script. Even the star's boyfriend or girlfriend believes he or she can take a whack at the script and make it better. Few people would have the chutzpah to tell the cinematographer how to adjust the camera or set the lights, but just about everyone on the set has an opinion on how to fix the script.

Now, you may want to learn screenwriting to help you become a better cinematographer or producer or actor. That's all to the good; everyone who works in film should know from personal experience how scripts are written. A producer who has tried her hand at writing scripts will be better able to work with writers in improving the structure and style of a screenplay. An actor who has written scripts might write a good part for himself (as Sylvester Stallone famously did with *Rocky,* propelling himself from bit player to star), and an actor who knows how to write will be better able to sharpen or improvise dialogue and to evaluate the strengths and weaknesses of the scripts he is offered. A cinematographer, whose job is to tell a story with images, can benefit greatly from knowing how to conceive those images and put them into words. But choosing whether you want to be a writer or a director, or both, or whether you want to practice another filmmaking craft, is a process of learning to know yourself, your strengths, your limitations, and what gives you the most creative satisfaction. If being a screenwriter brings less recognition and offers less social activity than the life of a director, it also allows you more time to think on your own and practice your craft in blessed solitude, in complete control of the characters and story, just like a novelist or playwright—at least until you turn over your script to be filmed.

Woody Allen, one of the great writer-directors, admitted in 2009 after making the splendid romantic comedy *Vicky Cristina Barcelona,*

> I almost always feel disappointed when I see my movies. When you're conceiving them at home, it's only happening in your mind and everything's fabulous. Then you find out that Javier

and Penelope are not available, you're not gonna be able to get Buckingham Palace and the cameraman doesn't quite get the lighting exactly as you want. By the time the thing is over, between your own mistakes and the compromises and the money that you don't have to reshoot scenes, you never think, "This is amazing." Instead it's: "Oh, God, if I take it back into the editing room, cut this, put this over here and add some music, I think I can save it." You start out convinced you're gonna make *The Bicycle Thieves* and, by the time you're in the editing room, you're just fighting for survival. You've given up all your aspirations, greatness is out the window, you just don't want to embarrass yourself and for it to be coherent.

And so there are those few (I am tempted to write "those unhappy few") who just want to be screenwriters. That is a condition more to be admired than pitied. But if you take your writing seriously, you should take the craft of screenwriting seriously. Don't treat it merely as a means to an end, whether the end is status, money, fame, or anything else. Show the craft the respect it deserves. If you don't, you will be demeaning yourself by looking down on what you are doing. You should be doing it out of love for the craft and a passion to create. Only that kind of engagement and dedication will enable you to overcome all the obstacles you will face and give you a shot at a satisfying career as a screenwriter.

Once in a while someone comes along and tells the truth about how hard it is to succeed in Hollywood. George Lucas issued such a warning in 2009. Discussing the tumultuous changes that have occurred in the film industry in his lifetime, Lucas gave an interview to the *Los Angeles Times* recalling how it was in the 1980s when students considered film school and the film industry a path to riches: "I told the students then and I tell them now, if you are here to make money, you're in the wrong place. This is the place you don't want to go make money. Very few people are successful at it. You better love making movies because if you don't you will live a very miserable life. It's definitely a hard physical and mental process that you go through."

That's the same message I always give to aspiring screenwriters. I warn them about the dangers they will face so that, if they choose to plunge into the shark tank anyway, they will do so with their eyes wide open. And I do so to make sure that, before making the decision to enter this daunting profession, they ask themselves, "Do I want it badly enough, and why?"

After the old studio system collapsed in the 1960s, a new generation of writers and directors started coming into the business—the "movie brats" or "film generation," who included Lucas, Francis Ford Coppola, Steven Spielberg, Martin Scorsese, Paul Schrader, and many others. It soon became clear that more young writers wanted to write the Great American Screenplay than wanted to write the Great American Novel; someone of the caliber of Robert Towne, if he had come of age in an earlier generation, would have written *Chinatown* as a novel rather than a film, but Towne brought a masterful level of novelistic density and sophistication to the form of the original screenplay. In earlier generations, most films were based on books or plays, and original screenplays, especially ones written on "spec" (speculation), were much harder to sell. For an all-too-brief time in the 1960s and 1970s, that started to change, and movies were the better for it.

There still is a market for original screenplays today, as demonstrated by such recent Oscar-winning scripts as Mark Boal's *The Hurt Locker,* Diablo Cody's *Juno,* Dustin Lance Black's *Milk,* Michael Arndt's *Little Miss Sunshine,* Paul Haggis and Bobby Moresco's *Crash,* and Sofia Coppola's *Lost in Translation;* Florian Henckel von Donnersmarck's superb script for his Oscar-winning German film *The Lives of Others;* the Coen brothers' brilliant and diverse Oscar-nominated original scripts for such films as the zany political satire *Burn After Reading* and the existentially bleak suburban drama *A Serious Man;* Woody Allen's beautifully crafted *Midnight in Paris;* and the many fine screenplays in recent years for Pixar animated films, from the innovative *Toy Story* through the delightfully unconventional *Up*. Nevertheless, with the prevalence of remakes, sequels, and other presold properties, it's generally become much harder to interest studios in original, untested material.

"This is the toughest time for the so-called personal film I've ever seen in my life," screenwriter-director Francis Ford Coppola told our cinema students at San Francisco State University in 2009.

> Most movies are the same. When I go to the movies, if I see something I've never seen before, I just love it. *Happiness* [the 1998 film written and directed by Todd Solondz, dealing in part with pedophilia]—I said, "My God, it's the most disgusting subject, but it's one of the most beautiful films I've ever seen." How did he do it? How did he make such a unique film on such a disturbing subject matter?...If you have emotion and a heart and you're passionate about it, you just do it. You might be the Ugly Duckling who turned out to be a beautiful swan. If you do beautiful things, you'll have money. Money follows something that's original....The things that they give you lifetime achievement awards for, those are the same things that you got fired for when you were twenty. I was so raked over the coals [when I wrote] the opening of *Patton* [directed by Franklin J. Schaffner], which is where George C. Scott just comes in front of the stage and makes a whole speech to the audience as though it's his army. They *hated* that idea. Some people feel that's one of the best openings of a film ever made, and that was what I was fired for.

I've had people from outside California tell me that a screenwriter's life must be "glamorous." By that I suppose they mean hanging out with movie stars, working on sets, and attending premieres and parties. Well, if you're working in the industry, you occasionally get to meet movie stars. If the director is willing, you might be allowed to visit the set occasionally or go to the premiere. But even at the best of times, the daily life of a screenwriter is far from glamorous. When I came to Hollywood as a wide-eyed film buff in 1973, I quickly realized that the negative portraits of the town offered by screenwriters often understated its actual horrors, from its pervasive economic exploitation to its crushing of people's artistic dreams.

Oddly enough, my initial apartment was just a few blocks down the road from the dump where William Holden's struggling screenwriter Joe Gillis lived and worked in a classic film about Hollywood, Billy Wilder's 1950 *Sunset Boulevard* (which he wrote with Charles Brackett and D. M. Marshman Jr.). That caustic masterwork serves as a cautionary tale about what can happen to a hapless screenwriter, who becomes the kept man of a faded star and winds up floating dead in her swimming pool. When I interviewed Wilder in the late 1970s, I told him, "Before I came to Hollywood, I thought *Sunset Boulevard* was too cynical a depiction of the film industry. When I moved out here, I realized that it's like a documentary. Everything is totally true." Wilder replied, "It's a valentine. But it is not just the picture industry—it is every industry. You make a picture about Exxon versus Texaco versus Shell, every industry has got this kind of slush that is underneath the whole thing. *Network*. The newspaper business. Naturally."

I don't know if that's reassuring, but it helps put things in perspective. If you can minimize your illusions about screenwriting and treat it as a job like any other, as the honorable profession it is, it can be a rewarding adventure indeed. Hearing good actors speak the lines you write or seeing images you imagined come to life on-screen is thrilling. I will never forget the first time I heard an actor speak the words I wrote—Henry Fonda speaking my words honoring Jimmy Stewart for an American Film Institute Life Achievement Award tribute on CBS-TV—or the time I stood in a high school corridor watching the revolutionary chaos I conceived for *Rock 'n' Roll High School* erupting all around me. At moments like that, it's all worthwhile. It's easy to get infected by all the cynicism and corruption surrounding the movie industry and to forget that moviemaking can be fun. Somehow, to keep your head as a writer, you have to rise above the downsides of the business and keep stubborn hold of your sense of integrity, your self-respect.

That creative excitement I experienced as a young writer can happen to you if you write a script you care about and find someone with even a small amount of money who's willing to bring it to the screen. Some of the most adventurous work today is being done independently, on almost nonexistent budgets, by people who bypass the commercial system to make their own movies. Distributing your own films on DVD and over the Internet offers you a creative freedom that the writers and filmmakers of the past could only wish for. The Web offers a wealth of still-unfolding ways to get your movie seen by a worldwide audience, and you don't even have to leave home to make, distribute, and promote it, avoiding heavy advertising costs while targeting niche audiences more easily. And if you still want to take the professional route, you can quit your job as a stripper, move from the Midwest to Hollywood, write a quirky script about an unwed pregnant teenager, and win an Oscar before you turn thirty. That's how Diablo Cody (née Brook Busey), a genius at self-promotion, made her screenwriting breakthrough with *Juno*.

"If it isn't for the writing, we've got nothing," Irving Thalberg, the legendary and ruthless MGM production chief in the 1920s and 1930s, once admitted. Although Thalberg was celebrated for his skill in analyzing stories, he was an enemy of screenwriters' attempts to organize for better working conditions. Thalberg is also reported to have said, "Writers are the most important people in Hollywood. And we must never let them know it." The remark has the ring of truth, and if a screenwriter needs a mantra, it's made to order. Just keep in mind the first part of what he said and try not to think about the rest.

2

What Is Screenwriting?

I made many, many mistakes when I was teaching myself to write screenplays. But those mistakes were how I learned the craft. I pursued a process of elimination that took me closer and closer to the true nature of screenwriting.

One of the most ambitious of my early original scripts exists in two forms. The first is a screenplay of 142 pages, and the second is a three-ring binder of storyboards for the entire film, filling about three hundred pages (storyboards are cartoonlike illustrated frames roughly showing how each shot should look). I planned to direct the film myself in my own hometown, and I described every shot I wanted in the film in precise technical detail. My screenplay tells the actors exactly what to do and how to move. It tells them and the camera whether to turn left or right in every scene. And if that weren't enough, I drew every shot in the accompanying binder, leaving little up to the imagination of the director, the talents of the actors, and the spontaneity of the shooting process.

So how did I go wrong? What made me think the screenwriter's job was to direct the film on paper? If your job as writer isn't to micromanage every second on-screen, every gesture of the actors, every camera angle and visual movement, what exactly *are* you doing with the script? As screenwriter William Goldman reminds us, "Movies are story." You're grabbing people by the lapels and persuading them to go along with you on the journey. How you do that has something to do with visual suggestions but little to do with technical directions.

When the pioneer film director D. W. Griffith was asked what he considered the best course for anyone to pursue in writing for the screen, he replied, "Think in pictures!" But you have to take those pictures in your head and communicate them through words on the page, and in screenwriting terms a pencil sketch is preferable to an oil painting. A good screenplay—writing in pictures—makes the reader see the movie in his or her own head. It's something of a conjuring trick, an optical illusion. You create imagery without spelling it all out, without explaining exactly how it should look. You offer a constant stream of suggestions that, in a thousand subtle ways, enable your readers to imagine the images and actions you want them to see. Screenwriting is an art of paradoxes, and one of those is that while you shouldn't direct the movie on paper, you are still directing it in your reader's head. The subtler you are, the more effective the script will be in influencing the reader (the potential purchaser or filmmaker) to shoot it the way you are suggesting. But if you are too obvious about it, the reader will toss the script into the nearest wastebasket, the film industry's equivalent of lopping off your head.

In this chapter, we'll study what screenplays are, what function they fulfill in the filmmaking process, what makes them different from other forms of dramatic writing, and what style of writing is most effective in writing for the screen. Perhaps the best place for us to start learning what screenplays are is to consider what they are not.

WHAT SCREENPLAYS ARE NOT

Everyone who comes into the field of screenwriting is familiar with other forms of writing—books, short stories, plays, poetry—and most of us try our hand at writing stories in school long before we encounter the new and somewhat baffling screenplay format. It's understandable that some confusion results. There are similarities between films and written fiction, but the differences among these forms of storytelling are just as important, and they are crucial for a screenwriter to understand. When you come up with an idea for a film, think about why your story should be told on a movie screen rather than in a book or a play. And conceive the story for the screen; don't muddy the waters by using literary devices that won't play cinematically.

Novels come in many forms and styles, but they have certain characteristics that set them apart from screenplays. The most pervasive is their complete reliance on the medium of language. When you adapt a novel for the screen, the first thing you lose is the language of the writer. A novelist such as Jane Austen relies on the texture and wit of her prose to convey much of her meaning. A novelist also has the liberty to go into the characters' heads and describe what they are thinking and feeling. Henry James goes to great lengths in analyzing the sensibilities of his characters and their relationships with other characters and with their milieu. Leo Tolstoy devotes pages to describing and discussing the settings of the story, the sociopolitical dimensions, the historical backgrounds. The novelist can go into what screenwriters call backstory—the events that took place before the body of the story began. The novelist can easily shift voices and tenses. All of these things a novel can do with such flexibility and power are lost when you try to adapt a novel for the screen, although you can find cinematic equivalents to some of them if you want to give the viewers a similar experience.

Novels have the luxury of virtually unlimited space and time. A novelist such as Margaret Mitchell in *Gone with the Wind* can take more than a thousand pages to tell her story of the Civil War and the Reconstruction era. James Joyce can spend nearly eight hundred pages in *Ulysses* telling the story of one man's journey through Dublin on a single day in 1904. Novelists can range widely and expansively throughout the world and through the centuries. Films can range just as widely, but a feature film has to do so within the time limits of a theatrical experience.

In adapting a novel, the screenwriter is often forced to simplify both the stories and the characters, removing subplots and compressing narrative lines. Even at nearly four hours long, the film version of *Gone with the Wind* seems to rush through the Reconstruction era, and Scarlett O'Hara has only one child, instead of the three in the book. Since the advent of TV miniseries and home video, writers have been able to adapt novels at a length more comparable to the reading experience (and the writers of TV series can go on for years in unfolding their narratives, but that's another craft). Nevertheless, even a *War and Peace* running eight hours (the 1968 Russian multipart feature) or twelve hours (the 1972 BBC TV miniseries), as good as they are, must leave out reams of rich material from Tolstoy's gargantuan masterpiece. An intelligent and "faithful" adaptation of a novel may not feel like a *Classics Illustrated* comic book, as a shorter version of a long novel sometimes does, but it often suffers by contrast with the breadth, scope, and depth of the novelist's vision. So if you want that kind of narrative flexibility, the novel is the medium for you, not the screenplay.

Films are more exterior than interior; they have a harder time getting inside the heads of characters. But what they lose in that sense, they gain in immediacy and vividness. Cinema affects the viewer on a more visceral and sometimes deeper emotional level than the written word can reach. Because the film experience is dreamlike, it appeals more directly to the viewer's subconscious. A film can take the audience into another world for two hours and make that world and its people come alive. And at its best, a film can convey thought without words, through images and sounds, their rhythmical orchestration, and the expressions of the actors. Conveying thought without simply verbalizing it is perhaps the greatest challenge for a screenwriter. A good actor in a well-written part can suggest what the character is thinking in ways that can affect you more profoundly and viscerally than a novel can.

Both Alfred Hitchcock and John Ford observed that short

stories tend to make better film material than novels. A short story is characterized not so much by its page count but by the fact that it is designed to be read in one sitting, just as a feature film is designed to be viewed in one sitting. Short stories usually concentrate on the kind of compressed action and limited settings that make the screenwriter's work easier. You probably won't have to lose much from the story, unlike with a novel. Short stories are also tempting to the screenwriter because they tend to be sketchlike and allusive, offering valid incentives for fleshing out the story.

A play relies far more heavily on dialogue than a screenplay generally should do. And stage plays have an even more pervasive characteristic than their reliance on language, a trait that separates them more fully from cinema, despite their frequent use as material for movies. Most plays thrive on their artificiality—their theatricality—while film, since it is a photographic medium, tends more toward realism. A film depicts or conjures up a physically believable world. Even a fantasy film has to persuade audiences that the world it's creating actually exists. And even the most outlandish fantasy films differ from theatricality in their use of cinematic language, such as their ability to jump around at will in time and space and to move in for close-ups. Films direct the eye in a myriad of other ways that are hard, if not impossible, for theatrical productions to imitate.

And as for poetry, John Huston, perhaps the master of literary adaptation for the screen, once observed that a screenplay resembles a poem more than any other kind of writing. Every word must be chosen with great care in a poem and a screenplay. Compression is key. Allusiveness is invaluable. Both forms suggest more than they say. Both create word pictures that conjure up the images in your head. Both rely heavily on musical rhythm. And a screenplay even looks like a poem with its system of indentations and all that white space surrounding the words on the page.

The screenplays of the great Japanese director Yasujiro Ozu

and his longtime collaborator Kogo Noda resemble haiku in their eloquent simplicity. Here, from the screenplay for their classic *Tokyo Story,* is how they describe the death of the mother (Tomi, played by Chieko Higashiyama) and the reactions of her husband (Shukichi, played by Chishu Ryu) and other family members:

```
The living room. SHUKICHI comes in quietly and
sits by TOMI. With pain in his face he looks
down at her, blinking his eyes.

Daybreak—the night at Onomichi has ended. The
sky slowly brightens—it is near the time the
sun will appear. The platform at the station,
no one there; the streets, no one there. The
sea wall, quiet waves washing on the stones.

The Hirayama house. SHIGE, KOICHI, KYOKO,
NORIKO, all sit sadly. Now and then, as though
just remembering her sorrow, KYOKO wipes away
her tears. There is now a white cloth over
TOMI's face.

                  SHIGE
     Isn't life short, though...(She speaks
     sadly, and there is no answer.)
```

How the process of literary adaptation works will be the subject of much of this book, because we will be going through the steps of adapting a short story to the screen. That process will, among other things, show you in more detail how the literary and cinematic forms diverge, helping you come to a clearer practical understanding of just what a screenplay is and isn't.

ARE STORIES NECESSARY?

I should note that not everyone agrees with William Goldman that feature filmmaking is essentially a storytelling art. When director Robert Altman, one of the most influential modern filmmakers, received his honorary Academy Award in 2006, he said, "Stories don't interest me. I'm interested in behavior." Altman added, "To me, I've just made one long film."

The screenplays for Altman films were often disregarded by the director during the shooting. He tended to encourage a latitude in improvisation that helps account for the unevenness of his work and its frequent lack of creative discipline. But he was a great improviser, and much of the time he made his unusual style work triumphantly for him. His best films, such as *The Long Goodbye, Nashville, Gosford Park,* and *A Prairie Home Companion,* are more like poetic meditations or jazz riffs on themes than traditional stories. Altman's fascination with all the varieties of human behavior creates many indelible moments that reveal character and enmesh us in compellingly edgy dramatic situations.

Altman wasn't the first director to make a multicharacter film, but he popularized the multiplot story line, a technique that has since become common on television, a medium that thrives on peripatetic storytelling to keep viewers hooked and prevent them from changing channels. Altman-influenced feature films that have followed such a structure include *Do the Right Thing, Crash, Munich, L.A. Confidential, Boogie Nights, Babel, Everyone Says I Love You,* and *Love Actually.* But beginning screenwriters who attempt the multipart structure, mistakenly believing that multicharacter stories seem easier to tell, do so at their peril, because it requires much more skill to pull off than a story centering on one or two people.

Even the wooliest Altman film has some kind of story, however tenuous or eccentric his way of telling it may be. And the types of filmmaking that may seem the freest from narrative—such as the documentary and the avant-garde film and the essay film, or an experimental feature film such as Jean Renoir's sublime *The River,* which draws from all these elements—still usually need to hook the viewer with some kind of story line. A movie with little or no narrative of any kind runs the risk of seeming random or chaotic. It may work well enough as an intellectual rumination but not have much to do with the realm of emotion and drama.

"Character, story, character, story—sorry, that's what it's about," director Ridley Scott declared in 2003. "Is it my imagination, but where did the bloody writers go? There are a few, but not many. Or am I getting jaded? I don't think so. So you revisit the library. I'm now watching *The Third Man*. I can still pick up *Out of Africa,* plug it in, and be engaged for three fucking hours. I can pick up *Lawrence of Arabia* for the *sixteenth* time and be engaged."

This statement is particularly noteworthy coming from a filmmaker who is primarily known for his visual pyrotechnics in such films as *Blade Runner, Black Hawk Down,* and *Gladiator.* Even Ridley Scott realizes that the most flamboyant cinematic style needs the support of a solid narrative framework, or it will run the risk of scattering itself to the winds.

IS SCREENWRITING WRITING?

Some screenwriters would like the kind of work they do to be considered a form of literature. That is an understandable reaction to the long belittlement of their craft. While a fair number of screenplays have been published, including the works of such masters as Billy Wilder, Preston Sturges, Robert Riskin, Ingmar Bergman, Robert Towne, Woody Allen, and the Coen brothers, scripts usually don't sell well and quickly go out of print, because even the finest screenplay is incomplete on its own and, as such, takes a certain expertise to appreciate. The hard truth is that screenwriting is not literature. I once said to a veteran Hollywood writer, rather glibly and rudely, "Screenwriting isn't writing." Well, sure it is, but it's not writing in the sense of a novelist's work in creating an entire, self-sufficient world on paper, or even a playwright's work in creating a dramatic world that can be appreciated without necessarily seeing it staged and performed. A film script is a curious hybrid of words and images that lives largely to be used as a tool to sell the project, a springboard for others to start working, and a blueprint for the actual filming.

What you're writing for the screen doesn't necessarily have to be beautifully written as long as it tells the story fluidly and in a way that can be filmed. It won't hurt if your prose is enjoyable to read, told in vivid and colorful language, and you can even throw in some jokes, as Wilder and his writing partner I. A. L. Diamond liked to do in their scripts, since, after all, they were writing comedies. To give a few characteristic examples from their script of *The Apartment:* C. C. (Bud) Baxter (Jack Lemmon) encounters "a first baseman of a dame"; Bud's apartment contains "a television set (21 inches and 24 payments)"; Bud wears "a Brooks Brothers type suit, which he bought somewhere on Seventh Avenue, upstairs"; and the last line of the script reads, "And that's about it. Story-wise"—the end of a running gag mocking Madison Avenue lingo. *The Apartment* is almost as much fun to read as it is to watch. A script that is dull to read will not keep readers turning the pages.

Snappy, clever prose of the kind favored by Wilder and Diamond is fine to emulate, but if the writing gets too elaborately clever, that can be a problem. The literary style of a script is not only not the main point, it can actively interfere with the quality of the work as a clearly delineated plan for filmmaking. If the reader becomes overly engaged with admiration for the lushness of your prose and the intricacies of your syntax, you may be auditioning to be the next Marcel Proust rather than the next Diablo Cody. When Howard Hawks, in an interview for my book *Hawks on Hawks,* was explaining what makes a good screenplay, he made a gnomic, paradoxical observation that has been troubling me ever since. Hawks said, "If it reads good, it won't play good."

Many successful screenwriters are masters at writing the kind of punchy dialogue and colorful, chatty description that passes for first-rate screenwriting because it makes a script seem to play well on paper. But what I think Hawks meant is that such writing can mysteriously fall flat when a director tries to transfer it to the screen. Hawks was suggesting that a screenplay with prosaic scene description and dialogue, a script that seems flat or sketchy, can make a better film than a script that is more enjoyable to read. The kind of script to which Hawks was referring avoids self-conscious flash and dazzle to fill the more modest function of serving as a blueprint for a motion picture.

A contrary view is taken by screenwriter Ed Solomon, whose credits include *Bill & Ted's Excellent Adventure* and *Men in Black.* Solomon warns beginning writers that a script that's overly utilitarian may backfire as a reading and selling experience:

> Be careful, because the more you write a script like a final film, the more difficult it is for readers and studio executives to conceive of it as a film. What you get from a film when you watch it is a different experience than when you read a script. Edited film has a certain meaning when you watch it. The closer you get to writing a final film, the more difficult it will be to get it by the decision makers, because their gut feeling when they read the script is often different from the literal filmic translation. It is not always as satisfying when it is made into a movie.

This point is not fully understood even in the film industry. Sometimes a solid blueprint for a film may seem less exciting to a studio reader or a producer than a script that aims more to entertain with lively prose and bons mots. That may be unfortunate, but it's a fact a screenwriter has to live with. A screenplay's first job is to engage the reader.

In any case, the best descriptive language in a film script is pithy and direct. Reading Ernest Hemingway's best work, his early short stories, will show you how to describe movement and behavior with economy, precision, and grace. With his spare and punchy prose, Hemingway taught modern writers that action words are better than adjectives. One of the best lessons Ezra Pound and Gertrude Stein taught their young protégé was to cut down on adjectives and cut out adverbs, concentrating instead on nouns and verbs. That's good advice for a screenwriter as well. Hemingway tends to use short words, and he avoids long sentences and abstractions. That helped him create his terse, almost telegraphic style. His method is always to show the concrete details of "the people and the places and how the weather was."

Ironically, Hemingway's writing, despite its concentration on what we can see and hear and its general avoidance of introspective elements, usually doesn't transfer well to the screen, because so much of the meaning is in its subtext, which is difficult, though not impossible, to dramatize. But his basic writing principles can be applied directly to screenwriting. There's a wonderful phrase from Hemingway that I think captures the essence of screenwriting. He wrote in his bullfighting book *Death in the Afternoon,* "I was trying to write then and I found the greatest difficulty, aside from knowing truly what you really felt, rather than what you were supposed to feel, and had been taught to feel, was to put down what really happened in action; what the actual things were which produced the emotion that you experienced.... [B]ut the real thing, the sequence of motion and fact which made the emotion and which would be as valid in a year or in ten years or, with luck and if you stated it purely enough, always, was beyond me and I was working very hard to get it."

The sequence of motion and fact which made the emotion. That's what screenwriters must capture on the page.

YOUR NEW LANGUAGE

You need to develop the ability to see the movie in your head as you're writing it. Then it's a matter of transferring that movie to the page so the director has something to work with. And to understand how to write for the screen, you will need to learn a new language, the language of cinema. "Cinema" is a word that's more inclusive than "film," since moving images today are often on digital video or other electronic media rather than on film stock. Cinema has a grammar and syntax all its own. This language, which you need to master to become a good screen-writer, is different from the language of literature. All of us learn how to write short stories and essays at some point in grammar school or high school, but few of us receive any training in writing film scripts. Even many film critics only dimly understand the language of cinema.

Learning that language may seem daunting, but as I tell my students, it's not rocket science. Most of the cinematic terms you need to understand are relatively simple. You need to know that the basic unit of filmmaking is a *shot,* a single piece of film that is combined with other pieces of film in editing (or montage) to run through the camera as they create *sequences,* or series of shots linked in action or content. How the camera functions should be clear in your mind. You should know that a camera doesn't *pan* up, it pans horizontally ("pan" comes from the Greek word for "all," and originally a panning shot was called a "panoramic" shot, from the word meaning "to see all"). The camera may *tilt* up or down, or it may *dolly* or *track* forward and backward or laterally or in a circle.

Don't confuse these basic building blocks of filmmaking. People often conflate, for example, a *tracking shot* with a *zoom.*

A zoom uses a change in the focal length of the lens to seem to move the viewer closer to the object being filmed, while a tracking shot actually moves closer to the object, creating a more three-dimensional feeling. Being precise in your understanding of such basic tools of cinema is as important for a screenwriter as understanding the basic rules of grammar, spelling, and punctuation is for any writer.

The screenwriter doesn't have to become a thoroughgoing expert in the more arcane levels of film theory, although that wouldn't hurt as long as you don't get carried away and start putting the phrases "diegetic sound" or "extra-diegetic gaze" into your scripts. Any screenwriter, however, will need to understand the basic optical principle that underlies cinema, *persistence of vision,* the way two slightly different images projected in rapid succession will seem to move because the first one lingers briefly in the eye when the second one appears, and that superimposition creates "illusory" or "apparent" motion.

And you should know about the *Kuleshov effect,* the demonstration of another fundamental principle of cinematic storytelling. This one is related to persistence of vision but takes it a step farther. The Soviet filmmaker and theorist Lev Kuleshov filmed a single close-up of an actor's face and intercut the same shot with shots of a plate of soup, a young woman, and a dead child. As a result of the intercutting, the seemingly neutral face of the actor seemed to register, in order, hunger, sexual desire, and sorrow. All these emotions, which did not necessarily exist in the actor's face to begin with, were created by the process of juxtaposing moving images, one of the expressive properties unique to the cinema. Editing is an essential tool of filmmaking with which all writers should be familiar. I recommend watching an illuminating documentary on the subject, *The Cutting Edge,* in which top editors explain and demonstrate their craft. When you write a script, you are, in effect, doing the first edit of the film, and when the editor goes to work on the material that has been shot, he or she is doing the final draft of your screenplay.

But as much as you need to know these technical underpinnings of cinematic storytelling, you should restrain your impulse to show off that knowledge in your script. Instead be confident in the knowledge that what you are writing, and in what order, and in what style, is firmly grounded in the reality of how films are actually made and how they work on the minds and hearts of the audience. When you write, sans distracting technical mumbo jumbo, "The woman runs across a vast field, toward the mountains," the reader will know that it's a *long shot* (LS) without being told that explicitly. When you write, "She stops at the foot of the mountains and kneels to inspect a solitary bush," the reader will see a *medium shot* (MS) of the woman in the mind's eye, a shot taking in her face and much of her kneeling body. When you tell the reader, "The woman plucks a flower, lifts it to her face, and smells it," a *close-up* (CU) will instinctively come to mind. In so doing, you've created a *sequence of shots* without explicitly telling the director how to shoot the scene and while keeping the writing fluid and easy to read:

> The woman runs across a wide field, toward the mountains. She stops at the foot of the mountains and kneels to inspect a solitary bush. The woman plucks a flower, lifts it to her face, and smells it.

The marvelous thing about this kind of writing is that the person who reads it will imagine that he is thinking up the shots himself.

YOU DO YOUR JOB, THEY DO THEIRS

That lesson, which I fortunately learned early, through trial by error, is one of the essential points about screenwriting. If you try to direct the film on paper, the director not only will disregard what you tell him or her to do but may do the opposite out of spite. That's what John Ford would do when a cameraman would suggest a setup; Ford defiantly would put the camera somewhere else. It's considered intrusive to tell other creative people exactly what to do. They have their own sense of hard-won autonomy. They will respect you more if you stick to your job and let them do theirs.

When Hawks told me, "If it reads good, it won't play good," he may have been overstating his case to make a point. And as a producer and director who hired writers and worked closely with them, he was able to tailor his scripts exactly as he needed them, to serve as guides to filming. What he liked was a script that gave him plenty of leeway for working out scenes with creative input from his actors. He wasn't looking for a script that would serve as a sales job for strangers, as an average professional screenwriter will have to write. When I asked Hawks why most of his movies, even the oldest ones, look very fresh and modern today, he replied, "Most of them were well written. That's why they last. I've always been blessed with great writers. As a matter of fact, I'm such a coward that unless I get a great writer, I don't want to do a picture." But Hawks also defined precisely what a director contributes:

> They talk about "improvisation." That's one of the silliest words that's used in the motion picture industry. What the hell do they think a director *does*? How do you expect that we can go out with a story that's written up in a room, go out to the location, and do it verbatim? I have never found a writer who could imagine a thing so that you can do it like that. And somebody started saying it's "improvising." Well, I wish you could see some pictures that are *not* improvised—where they send them out and say, "We don't want you to change a word or a scene or anything."

Or as Joe Eszterhas wryly puts it from the screenwriter's point of view, "Don't do *all* of the director's work for him. Let him earn his wage by doing *something.*"

Practically speaking, not directing a movie on paper means, first of all, that you skip the technical instructions in the script. You describe Jane embracing Henry, going into some detail about their behavior and movements and the setting of the scene, but you don't tell the director where the camera should be when they are embracing. Arthur Penn, whose remarkable gift for visceral direction can be seen in films ranging from *The Miracle Worker* to *Bonnie and Clyde* and *Little Big Man,* once described film directing as "the reconstruction of processes." That marvelous phrase captures the final mental step involved in bringing alive the sequence of motion and fact suggested by the screenplay. The French call direction *"réalisation"*—that means the director is the one who "realizes" the script, not only making it real but literally realizing what it is the writer is trying to say. When Billy Wilder was asked if a director needs to know how to write, he replied, "It is not necessary for a director to know how to write. However, it helps if he knows how to read."

Wilder had some trouble with Raymond Chandler when the director invited the great detective novelist to work with him on the screenplay adaptation of James M. Cain's crime novel *Double Indemnity.* Chandler took the job so seriously that he kept trying to write all the camera directions into the script. "He didn't know the first thing about writing scripts," Wilder complained. "He only wrote about camera movements: 'The camera slips in through the keyhole and then sniffs the panties of the lady.'" What Wilder wanted in the way of visual directions was "nothing, just the scene. 'Day or night,' so that the cameraman can prepare his setup." That may sound simplistic, and it is, but such minimalism is worth emulating—up to a point. Wilder had some praise for Chandler's contribution: "We collaborated on the dialogue and defined the atmosphere."

Here is an example of effective cinematic atmosphere from their *Double Indemnity* screenplay. You'll see how they describe the entry of insurance man Walter Neff (Fred Mac-Murray) into the faux-Spanish home in the Los Feliz district of Los Angeles inhabited by the predatory Phyllis Dietrichson (Barbara Stanwyck), with whom Walter is immediately smitten in this classic film noir. The scene descriptions, in the writers' sardonic style, make us vicariously experience what Walter is feeling in this vulgar atmosphere:

```
HALLWAY - DIETRICHSON HOME

Spanish craperoo in style, as is the house
throughout. A wrought-iron staircase curves
down from the second floor. A fringed Mexican
shawl hangs down over the landing. A large
tapestry hangs on the wall....All of this,
architecture, furniture, decorations, etc., is
genuine early Leo Carrillo period.
```

Carrillo was an actor who often appeared in films and Southern California parades in stereotypical Mexican costumes. And then, after an exchange of dialogue between Walter and the maid, who sizes him up instantly as a sleaze, we have the first sight of Phyllis from Neff's point of view:

```
UPPER LANDING OF STAIRCASE - (FROM BELOW)

Phyllis Dietrichson stands looking down. She is
in her early thirties. She holds a large bath-
towel around her very appetizing torso, down
to about two inches above her knees. She wears
no stockings, no nothing. On her feet a pair of
high-heeled bedroom slippers with pom-poms. On
her left ankle a gold anklet.
```

From this colorful description, the reader gets a clear and precise word picture of the scene and the vulgar but alluring character. It's easy to imagine how it will look on the screen. But the only explicit visual direction is "(FROM BELOW)," and even that avoids the technical nature of writing "(NEFF'S POV)." The scene descriptions are economical, but they are ample enough to convey the visual feeling and quality the scene requires; beginning writers sometimes fail to do so by offering overly sketchy scene descriptions. Wilder knew he was going to direct his own script, but any good director would have had little trouble making that scene come alive on-screen.

What the writers are doing by offering such word pictures is arguably more crucial than the job of the director, because the script is the sine qua non of filmmaking. You are creating the essential blueprint for the film, designing its architecture for the builders who will come in and execute the plans. Without that document, the actors and the director and the technicians would be standing around looking lost. Even more likely, they'd be home anxiously reading the trades and waiting for their phones to ring. That's what Irving Thalberg meant when he said that writers are the most important people in the business.

3

Stories:
What They Are and How to Find Them

When I first started teaching screenwriting, I found to my surprise that some students seemed unfamiliar with the concept of stories.

Despite (or because of) our nonstop video culture, which bombards us with stories of one kind or another all day long on hundreds of channels, the old tradition of telling a story with a beginning, a middle, and an end seems in jeopardy in the twenty-first century. The fragmentation of the TV-watching experience, the influence of the Internet and YouTube, and the effect of our amped-up video culture on feature filmmaking have resulted in a style of modern filmmaking relying more on moment-by-moment sensation than on the traditional pleasures of coherent storytelling. If you've grown up with that modern style, you may find yourself becoming restless watching older movies, the kind that take their time developing characters and acclimating the audience to settings and atmosphere. But in an era when almost every shot lasts only a few seconds or less, every film starts to look alike. The culture's turning away from books in favor of the visual media in recent decades, and the related decline in reading skills, also have had a damaging effect on our storytelling skills and tastes.

But we all grew up on storybooks, and most of us have fond memories of our parents telling us stories. When we get a bit older, many of us start trying to write our own stories or put on

our own plays or make our own movies. We all absorb thousands of hours of stories on the big screen and television throughout our childhood and adolescence. So none of us is starved for
knowledge of storytelling forms; quite the contrary. Perhaps the
real problem is that we've all become too jaded by storytelling,
too inundated with it, overly accustomed to seeing the same
kinds of plots over and over again.

But we keep seeking something new and riveting amidst all the
aimless clutter. And however impatient we may sometimes seem
today with the traditional forms of yarn spinning, telling a story
is an impulse so deeply ingrained in our psyches that it will never
die but will only keep metamorphosing into newer forms. The
Internet is changing modes of storytelling even as you read this
page and reviving the old forms of short-format films and serials
as it transforms them for the electronic age. Although amateur
videos on YouTube often may seem more like anecdotes than stories, even the wildest MTV-style video, frenetic action spectacle,
or visually flamboyant TV commercial tells some kind of story.
It has to do so to grab our attention and hold us rapt throughout
its duration, whether it lasts for two hours or less than a minute.

STRUCTURE

In his book *Adventures in the Screen Trade,* William Goldman
offers

> what I believe to be the single most important lesson to be
> learned about writing for films...SCREENPLAYS ARE
> STRUCTURE. Yes, nifty dialog helps one hell of a lot; sure,
> it's nice if you can bring your characters to life. But you can
> have terrific characters spouting just swell talk to each other,
> and if the structure is unsound, forget it.

Almost every story, whether it is a drama or a comedy, and however obliquely it may be presented, follows the classical three-act

storytelling structure codified by the ancient Greeks, who seem to have thought of everything. Aristotle's *Poetics* (written in the fourth century B.C.) could be considered the earliest how-to book on screenwriting. Aristotle defines drama as

> that which has a beginning, a middle, and an end. A beginning is that which does not itself follow anything by causal necessity, but after which something naturally is or comes to be. An end, on the contrary, is that which itself naturally follows some other thing, either by necessity, or as a rule, but has nothing following it. A middle is that which follows something as some other thing follows it. A well constructed plot, therefore, must neither begin nor end at haphazard, but conform to these principles.

Aristotle would recognize the endurance of these rules in much film and television storytelling today. He goes on to offer some of the best practical advice any dramatist or screenwriter can hear about how to construct a meaningful story:

> Such an effect is best produced when the events come on us by surprise; and the effect is heightened when, at the same time, they follow as cause and effect. The tragic wonder will then be greater than if they happened of themselves or by accident; for even coincidences are most striking when they have an air of design.

You see what central emphasis Aristotle places on the three-act structure ("a beginning, a middle, and an end"), the basic form of dramatic storytelling and the foundation that keeps it standing. A good movie script has an "air of design" and a feeling of causality. But whether that design is tragic or comic, it should disguise its methodology. The artistry comes in with the underlying carpentry of the structure, which ought to be largely invisible, and with the subtle indirection involved "when the events come on us by surprise."

THE FLEXIBILITY OF A SOUND STRUCTURE

So, then, in our modern application of Aristotle to filmmaking, what constitutes a story?

1. Something happens.

2. The characters undergo change.

3. A situation or a set of relationships undergoes development and usually some kind of resolution, though some films are more "open" in their endings. Not everything has to be neatly tied up at the end.

Notice the three-act structure, slightly disguised, in that pattern. Or put another way,

Act 1. Establishes the characters and the situation

Act 2. Conflict

Act 3. Resolution

Just about every good feature film—and every bad one, for that matter—follows that kind of pattern, more or less. But it should be stressed that when it comes to structure—and to any other element of style or content—there are no hard-and-fast rules. Sometimes the best films are those that break or play with the rules (or with the "conventions" or "formulas" popular at the time). When an exasperated colleague with more traditional views of storytelling once asked the French director Jean-Luc Godard whether he thought a story should have a beginning, a middle, and an end, Godard famously replied, "Yes, but not necessarily in that order." Nevertheless, the rules of storytelling are much the same today as they always have been, and whether those rules are being followed, broken, or inflected, they demand attention from anyone trying to tell a story. A writer who knows the rules thoroughly is well on the path to both employing and breaking them creatively. But the essential three-act structure defined by Aristotle more than two millennia ago is loose enough to encompass virtually any kind of dramatic or comedic situation known to humankind.

Here's a good example of the three-act structure from a film that straddles different genres while daringly mixing violence and comedy, *Some Like It Hot*. One reason it is able to do so is that it has a three-act structure constructed as impeccably as a fine Swiss watch. Released in 1959, it begins by plunging its two main characters into the midst of notorious gangland murders. It revels in rampant sexual innuendo, including gender-bending gags about cross-dressing. Billy Wilder directed this classic film from a script he wrote with I. A. L. Diamond, from a story by Robert Thoeren and Michael Logan (previously filmed in Germany as *Fanfaren der Liebe/Fanfares of Love*):

1. Two musicians in 1929 Chicago, Joe (Tony Curtis) and Jerry (Jack Lemmon), witness the St. Valentine's Day Massacre and run for their lives, pursued by mobsters. The desperate musicians disguise themselves as women to hide out in an all-girl band headed for Miami Beach.

2. While Jerry begins to revel in his masquerade, Joe falls for the lead singer in the band, the troubled Sugar Kane (Marilyn Monroe). He disguises himself anew, as a millionaire, to try to seduce her, while Jerry is being courted by a real millionaire, Osgood Fielding III (Joe E. Brown).

3. The Chicago mobsters show up at the hotel where the band is staying and pursue the two musicians. They escape with Sugar to Osgood's yacht. Sugar and Joe wind up together, as

do Jerry and Osgood, who, when informed by Jerry, "I'm a man!" replies, "Well, nobody's perfect."

"ACTION IS CHARACTER"

How does something happen in a story?

It happens either through characters' interaction (involving such passions as love, hate, ambition, jealousy, and greed), or external forces (such as a chance meeting, a change of circumstances, a crime, a war, a disaster), or both.

For a classic definition of how these basic elements of drama apply to film, we turn from Aristotle to another great philosopher, Samuel Fuller, a hard-nosed crime reporter who went on to write and direct B movies that tear up the screen with their emotional impact. Appearing as himself in Godard's 1965 film *Pierrot le fou,* Fuller leans against a wall at a vapid French cocktail party, wearing a pair of dark glasses and holding a cigar, ignoring the idle gibble-gabble around him. Then Jean-Paul Belmondo asks him, "What, exactly, is cinema?" Fuller is roused to reply:

"A film is like a battleground. It's love—hate—action—violence—death. In one word, emotions."

When you write a screenplay, you find ways of showing people living through and acting out such emotions. Their actions convey their feelings; their faces and bodies reveal their inner states. "ACTION IS CHARACTER," F. Scott Fitzgerald wrote in his working notes for his novel about Hollywood, *The Last Tycoon.* That emphatic sentence appears at the very end of the unfinished novel. Character is enough to make a movie worth watching, even if there is not much else to look at. Frank Capra once said that if you have two skilled actors and some good dialogue, you could lower a white screen behind them and play the scene, and the audience will be rapt with attention. Even the most beautiful scenery and the most lavish action scenes won't matter much without characters who are worth watching. Charlie Chaplin was once asked why he didn't have a more interesting visual style. "*I* am interesting," he declared.

Conflict is an essential ingredient in any story. Conflict can be internal or external, or both. The most organic conflict comes from within a character and between characters. Plot situations that arise from character conflicts often seem more meaningful than plots that feel imposed on the characters, although plots in which characters struggle with unforeseen circumstances can be equally compelling, if they serve to reveal characters' inner strengths and weaknesses. In a disaster movie, the real star is the earthquake or the sinking ship, but what we hold on to for dear life are the characters we care about who are trying to survive the disaster. It all comes down to character in the end.

That's why the ordinary spectator usually goes to a movie to see a star. Most audiences drawn to *Titanic* respond primarily to the love story between two passengers from different social classes, Leonardo DiCaprio's Jack and Kate Winslet's Rose, although it wouldn't have meant as much if the ship had delivered them safely to their destination. A more sophisticated filmgoer may go to see what the director brings to the material (James Cameron's direction of *Titanic* is mesmerizing, even if his dialogue is often clunky), but a director without interesting characters and actors, even in the most cartoonish or fantastic kind of material, has a hard time making an emotional connection with an audience. The solid three-act structure Cameron's script provides (the characters meet on the ship; the "unsinkable" ship starts sinking; Jack saves Rose from the disaster and dies) ensures that we experience the sinking of the ship through an intimate personal story; recounting this familiar real-life event, whose ending we already know, through the vantage point of two "unknown" fictional passengers helps bring it alive.

The primacy of people isn't always so obvious to those who run the movie business, or even to some creative people; some directors love actors, but many fear and hate them because they are so central to the filmmaking process and not entirely controllable. As a screenwriter, you are symbiotic with your characters, and you need to learn how to write good parts for actors to play. Usually a film has a protagonist (a central character) or a pair of protagonists (such as in a love story), with an array of secondary characters rounding out the story. The antagonist— the rival or foe of the protagonist—may also be of great importance in a story. Popular filmmaking thrives on such opposition. In more melodramatic films, the antagonist is considered the "villain" or "bad guy," but the best films make all their leading characters three-dimensional human beings, whether they are the "heroes" or the "villains."

And contrary to conventional Hollywood wisdom, a protagonist does not have to be "likable" to be compelling; flaws and weaknesses, such as those displayed by George Bailey (James Stewart) in Frank Capra's *It's a Wonderful Life,* contribute to making any character come alive. The protagonist of a tragedy, however sympathetic he may be, is grievously flawed. In Shakespeare's *Othello,* the villainous Iago poisons the mind of Othello against his innocent wife, Desdemona (from somewhat mysterious motives that have kept critics and audiences debating for centuries), but the deepest fascination of the story is the awful willingness of the tragic protagonist, an otherwise admirable character, to believe the worst of his wife, despite his better judgment. Orson Welles said of his film of the play, "Jealousy is detestable, not Othello."

Even a superhero is more interesting if he has believably human flaws; Batman's dark personality is what keeps him so compelling in film after film. And why do we still enjoy watching Humphrey Bogart? Because he is such an imperfect and complicated character on-screen. If Rick in *Casablanca* were not torn between his cynicism and idealism, his actions would not be so compelling to witness, and we wouldn't be on edge waiting to see how the story will turn out, even if we've seen this World War II drama a dozen times. The human weaknesses of Oskar Schindler (Liam Neeson), his selfishness, greed, and lechery, make him all the more heroic for overcoming those flaws for the sake of selfless idealism as he rescues Jews from the Holocaust in *Schindler's List*.

Antiheroes—characters without the usual redeeming features but with a tremendous amount of charisma—often are more fascinating to audiences than traditional heroes. Marlon Brando, James Dean, and Paul Newman helped set the standard for modern acting by playing antiheroes. They didn't worry much about being "likable." Clint Eastwood's "Man with No Name" and Dirty Harry and William Munny in *Unforgiven* could have been the villains with a little rewriting, and his Walt Kowalski in *Gran Torino* is an outrageous bigot and misanthrope for much of the movie, but we identify with these characters despite as well as because of their recognizably human character flaws. Films such as these challenge our conventional moral views and make us examine our allegiances as we study the gray areas of human personality.

The lines between good and evil have become even harder to discern in the modern world. Often the villain can be so fascinating that he eclipses the hero, as Welles's charismatic Harry Lime does in *The Third Man,* opposite Joseph Cotten's hapless Holly Martins, or as Heath Ledger does as Batman's supremely twisted antagonist, the Joker, in *The Dark Knight*. Or the hero can transform himself into the villain, as Anakin Skywalker does by turning into Darth Vader in the *Star Wars* prequels or as Michael Corleone does in the *Godfather* saga.

The lasting appeal of dark, complex characters, whether they are villains or antiheroes or deeply troubled heroes, demonstrates that the virtue of "likability" is largely confined to real life, not dramatic storytelling. A writer should resist at all costs any producer, story editor, or studio executive who tells her to sandpaper off a character's rough edges to make him seem more "likable"; it's a sure way to ruin a script.

HOW DO WE GET INTO IT?

Perhaps the single most important decision a writer faces, once she has a story in mind, is deciding on where to start it. You could start almost anywhere, but there is always just one place where your story *should* start. Do you start with your central character as a girl or as a grown woman? Do you introduce her when she's middle-aged or on the last day of her life? If you're adapting a novel, do you throw out big chunks of the story to concentrate on the parts you find most compelling? Two classic films, *A Place in the Sun,* based on Theodore Dreiser's *An American Tragedy* and its stage adaptation by Patrick Kearney, and the film version of John Steinbeck's *East of Eden,* do just that. How you make this decision to begin shaping your story will govern so much of your movie. You can't put off making this critical decision; you can't begin writing the script until you narrow the possible scope of your picture. And once you know where your story should begin, you probably will begin to know where it should end. Giving the story a satisfying overall shape from beginning to end is the greater part of what Goldman calls "structure."

Coming up with a good opening might be difficult, but it might also come surprisingly easily if you have a clear sense of what you are trying to say when you are running your imagined movie in your head. A good opening makes any piece of writing flow more smoothly. If you are writing an essay and come up with an arresting opening paragraph that sets the stage for your arguments well, the rest will follow with logic and inevitability. So too with the opening scene of your screenplay. The first few minutes of your movie are your way of telling the audience how you want them to "read" your story. You are acquainting them with the setting, the characters, and your themes. You are providing a basic metaphor for the film with the images you choose to present at the beginning. Your tone of voice, your attitude toward the images and characters, tells the audience how you, and they, should view your story. This explanatory part of a work, setting out its meaning and purpose, is known as the "exposition."

John Huston once pointed out that in the first five minutes of a movie, the filmmaker can do virtually anything he wants. The audience will go along with whatever they are shown, because they don't have any other frame of reference (other than the movies they have seen before). The writer and the director can take the audience for as surprising and unconventional a ride as possible in those first few minutes while establishing the ground rules for what is to follow. This is similar to the process Walter Murch describes as an integral part of his job as a film editor, to help the audience "begin to assimilate and learn the particular language of this film." The opening minutes of a film don't even have to make obvious sense, as long as they are worth watching. This is a great liberty for a storyteller. But Huston added that after the first five minutes, the audience will quickly start demanding that the story begin to come together in a way that they can follow clearly. If it doesn't, their impatience will soon turn to anger.

It's often said that a script has only ten pages in which to hook the reader. People in the industry tend to have short attention spans and often don't much like reading. Your script most likely will be in a pile of a dozen or so scripts they have to read on a weekend. People often stop reading after the first ten pages or so if the script does not seem compelling. This is an unfortunate fact of life for screenwriters.

Still, a "compelling" opening doesn't have to mean a brawl or an explosion. One of the oddities of moviemaking today is that filmmakers often seem to think that the audience will get restless if the story doesn't start with a bang to get their attention. Perhaps this is a hangover from television, in which the audience is so quick to change channels that almost every show has to have a punchy opening or risk losing viewers within a minute or two. Some of the best dramatic and comedy writing in recent years has been done for television, however, for such series as *Law and Order, Mad Men, The Sopranos, The West Wing, Sex and the City, The Good Wife, Curb Your Enthusiasm,* and *30 Rock,* and for such miniseries and TV movies as *Band of Brothers, John Adams, Rome, Recount, Martin and Lewis,* and *The Life and Death of Peter Sellers.* Writers who want to deal with serious political or historical subjects often find that their best option is going to HBO and other cable channels rather than to the youth-dominated theatrical film market. But television has had some negative effects on feature filmmaking, and this overanxiety about needing to keep the viewer "hooked" is one of them. Compounding the film industry's chronic impatience to plunge audiences into the action, such fear doesn't entirely make sense, because people who see movies in theaters have already paid their money for the privilege and aren't going anywhere, at least for a good while, so you have some leisure to start the film any way you see fit.

"I believe in soft openings for movies," Robert Towne told students at an American Film Institute seminar. "…I think it's almost impossible to lose an audience in the first ten minutes but almost inevitable in the last if you haven't laid the groundwork of the film at the beginning. It's not television. You don't have to grab them. In a movie with a very fast opening, you end up paying for it somewhere along the way—usually by having to explain what happened in the fast and furious action. I almost like it when a movie's a little boring in the beginning because it establishes a kind of credibility that you can build on."

The animated feature *Up* (screenplay by directors Pete Docter and Bob Peterson, from a story they wrote with Thomas McCarthy) is unusual for its genre because it has an elderly protagonist. Carl Fredricksen is embittered by the loss of his wife and badly in need of human companionship, which he eventually finds with an equally lonely young boy. The film doesn't begin with Carl in old age, however, but with him as a child in the 1930s, watching a newsreel about his hero, an intrepid explorer (whom he will encounter much later in the story). We then follow the meek young Carl's discovery of a kindred spirit, a quirky little girl named Ellie, who shares his yearning for adventure. The film's placid early movement unexpectedly goes on to portray, in a wordless four-minute montage, their marriage and growth together from maturity to old age. This "soft" opening, which leads to the offscreen death of Carl's wife, is all the more moving for its quiet understatement and poignance. Gracefully serving as the prelude to the main story, it is a natural way of incorporating Carl's backstory to help us identify with the curmudgeonly old man while also providing memorable and haunting images that help determine how we will experience the rest of the story.

AND HOW DO WE GET OUT OF IT?

Endings, too, are critically important. If you leave the audience feeling satisfied, they will go out happy and tell their friends to see the movie. A good ending can make up for a myriad of flaws in the earlier parts of a film. But if the ending is forced or implausible, the audience will be unforgiving. They will feel cheated or vaguely discontented if the story is not concluded in a way that seems appropriate. Disgruntled viewers spread poor word of mouth, and box-office returns quickly fade. How satisfied viewers feel as they exit a movie usually depends on whether the ending seems inevitable and whether they think it ties together the story points satisfyingly. That doesn't mean that every thread in the story has to be neatly sewn up; leaving some aspects of a story open-ended is more realistic and allows the audience room to think about what might happen to the characters after the ending. One reason a good movie lingers in the memory is that it provides us with such mental latitude.

And contrary to Hollywood "wisdom," not every film has to

have a happy ending. Orson Welles once noted that the happy ending is such an indelible part of American culture that even a thirty-second commercial must have a happy ending. That tendency led to such notorious cinematic atrocities as the 1927 silent version of Tolstoy's *Anna Karenina, Love,* in which Anna does *not* commit suicide (the tragic ending, which does not survive, was also filmed and sent to theaters if they wanted to use it), and the 1930 John Barrymore version of Herman Melville's *Moby-Dick* in which Ahab kills the whale and returns home to his girlfriend, the preacher's daughter. The atrocious *Pearl Harbor* doesn't quite muster up the chutzpah to have the Americans repel the Japanese attack on Pearl Harbor, but it tacks on the heroic Doolittle Raid to give the film a spurious sense of uplift. There's nothing inherently wrong with a happy ending, if it is honest and fits the story you are trying to tell. But as Welles wrote in the last line of his screenplay *The Big Brass Ring,* "If you want a happy ending, that depends, of course, on where you stop your story."

Some of the biggest box-office hits in film history have had "unhappy" endings: think of *Gone with the Wind, Casablanca, E.T. The Extra-Terrestrial,* and *Titanic.* Rhett Butler finally walks out on Scarlett; Rick makes Ilsa fly off with her Resistance-leader husband; E.T. heads back to his planet after saying good-bye to Elliott; Jack slips out of Rose's hand and drowns in the icy Atlantic. In a love story, or a story of intense friendship, having the partners separate at the end may actually move the audience more deeply. And in each of those four blockbuster movies, the partner left behind, though feeling abandoned, experiences a newfound exhilaration and resolve. A bittersweet ending often feels more lifelike than one that is all one way or the other.

If you think the unhappy or (to use another Hollywood pejorative) "downbeat" ending of your screenplay is the most fitting way to conclude your story, resist any temptation or pressure to change it. Sam Fuller told me, "A director lives for the last five minutes of his movie, because that's where he makes his statement. And that's the part of the movie the studio always wants to change, so they can make it *their* statement."

And it's the writer's statement before it becomes the director's. Although it's rare for the writer to have any control over the film once it begins shooting, you can do your best to influence the form and style you want the film to have and hope that everyone involved will be so convinced by the eloquence of your screenplay that they will follow your vision.

STORIES ARE EVERYWHERE

So, how do you come up with stories? Easy. They're everywhere.

Just look in your daily newspaper (if your city still has one). Darryl F. Zanuck, the legendary studio executive who started out as a screenwriter, declared that the best way to find a story was to read the front page of your newspaper. Warner Bros. in the Depression era under Zanuck and other socially conscious executives made timely, punchy movies that were heralded as "ripped from the pages of today's headlines." The director Elia Kazan had even better advice: He said the best stories for movies are not on the front page but contained in the smaller stories inside the paper, the human-interest stories about ordinary people's problems. His 1972 film *The Visitors* was inspired by "something I'd cut out of a newspaper, the story of an ex-GI who'd brought evidence of a war crime—the rape and murder of a Vietnamese girl—against two former buddies, and how these men came looking for him at the end of the war to hold him to account." Such recent films as *The Queen, United 93, Munich, Redacted, W.,* and HBO's docudrama *Recount* have carried on the headline-ripping tradition.

Whatever page on the paper you find the stories on (or whether you find them instead on the Internet), our daily lives offer a wealth of story material for screenwriters. You don't have to write the stories exactly as they happened (and you may need to be careful about legal issues if you do). You can take a germ of a story from a newspaper clipping and run with it in any direction you want. A delightful exercise in story construction that I've often used in class is to hand out clippings of stories from the *San Francisco Chronicle*. The students form small groups, each group developing a clipping into a movie story. The wilder and freer adaptation the better. The results are often hilarious and highly imaginative, even though the students have only thirty minutes to brainstorm their stories.

Deadline pressure is helpful to both reporters and screenwriters. It helps stimulate creativity; anyone wanting to be a professional writer needs to learn to think and write fast. In a further variation of the exercise, I tell each group to adapt their story for a different genre, such as a comedy, a musical, or a sci-fi movie, or to write it for the kinds of characters who are relatively neglected in movies, such as women, African Americans, or old people. Clever and even filmable ideas often result from such an off-the-cuff exercise. One student found a story in a clipping about a social problem and went on to develop it into a haunting feature-length screenplay. Try it yourself by going through today's paper and seeing what strikes your fancy as story material. Better yet, get together with a couple of friends and try brainstorming the ideas together.

Anyone who wants to be a writer should read prodigiously. A broad knowledge of world literature will help you understand different approaches to storytelling and style. Knowing how Chekhov created characters and situations in his plays with elegant indirection will acquaint you with the state of that art. Understanding how Noël Coward perfected his own form of oblique character revelation for the stage, in a comic idiom, is indispensable for anyone trying to avoid the obvious in dialogue. Tolstoy's epic sweep as a novelist will show you how expansive a story can be while at the same time retaining its startling immediacy.

There is a danger that an aspiring writer can become intimidated by reading the masters, but if you try to draw lessons from them rather than slavishly imitating their stories and style, their influence will seep into your work in ways you can't expect or even define. A writer who doesn't know what came before him is a writer working in the dark, thinking he invented the lightbulb. That may feel satisfying, but it's not illuminating for readers who've read his (usually superior) predecessors.

Stephen King's *On Writing: A Memoir of the Craft* is a chatty how-to book that brims over with insights and generous tips for other writers. "If you want to be a writer," advises King,

> you must do two things above all others: read a lot and write a lot. There's no way around these two things that I'm aware of, no shortcut.... Every book you pick up has its own lesson or lessons, and quite often the bad books have more to teach than the good ones.... Good writing, on the other hand, teaches the learning writer about style, graceful narration, plot development, the creation of believable characters, and truth-telling.

And a knowledge of literary history can help a screenwriter find source material free of charge in works that are in the public domain. When we discuss the art of adaptation in subsequent chapters, we'll talk more about how to recognize and approach literary works that could serve as inspiration for your work and allow you to collaborate with great writers from the past.

Of course, you can also come up with stories from your life experiences and those of your family and other people you know. The most venerable cliché in writing classes is "Write what you know." Each of us is a walking library. You just need to recognize which of your experiences would make a good movie. When I was ten, my best friend, Dickie Swearingen, had a Martian as his best friend. The Martian would go around the neighborhood with us every day. I didn't believe in the Martian, but since Dickie did, I humored him. Eventually Dickie let go of that fantasy, and I forgot about it until many years later, when I saw *E.T.* I realized that I could have thought of a movie like that if only I had been smart enough to remember Dickie's Martian pal. Steven Spielberg and his writer, Melissa Mathison, were more in touch with their childhood fantasies than I was. Maybe the problem was that the Martian wasn't *my* friend, or I would have remembered him sooner.

The moral of the story: Keep your memories close and your dreams and nightmares closer. Stephen King is perhaps the most prodigiously inventive creator of stories today. It seems that he just can't stop thinking of stories. His subconscious is an open floodgate, in much the way that stories pour into all of our heads while we are dreaming, but he has found a way to keep the gate open during his working hours. My favorite inspirational story about King's imaginative abilities is one he tells in *On Writing.* King relates an experience he had at a gas station on the Pennsylvania Turnpike in the spring of 1999. After coming out of the men's room, he strolled down a slope to look at "a brawling stream full of snowmelt," slipped on a patch of snow,

> and started to slide down the embankment. I grabbed a piece of someone's old engine block and stopped myself before I got fairly started, but I realized as I got up that if I'd fallen just right, I could have slid all the way down into that stream and been swept away. I found myself wondering, had that happened, how long it would have taken the gas station attendant to call the State Police if my car, a brand-new Lincoln Navigator, just continued to stand there in front of the pumps. By the time I got back on the turnpike again, I had two things: a wet ass from my fall behind the Mobil station, and a great idea for a story.

Out of this mundane and humiliating mishap, the kind we all experience, King spun an entire novel, *From a Buick 8,* in which a

1954 Buick Roadmaster found abandoned at a gas station in western Pennsylvania turns out to have supernatural qualities.

Crafting a story for the screen from your own life experiences, or those of other people, usually involves changing it around, both "to protect the innocent" (as Jack Webb's *Dragnet* would proclaim) and to shape it artistically. It's rare that a story can be taken from life and turned into a satisfying drama or comedy without embellishment. Even if you are writing historical dramas and trying to respect the facts as much as possible, some fictional techniques inevitably come into play. Peter Morgan's screenplays for *The Queen* (about Queen Elizabeth II's reactions to the death of Princess Diana) and *Frost/Nixon* (based on his own play about TV personality David Frost interviewing the disgraced former president Richard Nixon) adroitly intermingle known facts with informed speculation and imaginative interpolation. Life tends to be messier than art, so compression is usually necessary, and giving your story some aesthetic distance is always important. As Picasso put it, "Art is a lie that makes us realize the truth."

WRITE IT DOWN

Throughout the years I was working as a Hollywood screenwriter, I kept a file of possible story ideas for films—notes, clippings, references to people and places and events, and so on. Keeping such a file, or a notebook, is invaluable for any writer. Writing down ideas, however rudimentary, helps plant them in your mind so your subconscious can go to work. Sometimes I'd come up with a story by combining one idea with another I'd been mulling over for months or years. That process of cross-fertilization often makes a slender idea seem more viable.

Maintaining a file of ideas keeps them from vanishing from your memory. There's an old Hollywood joke about a screenwriter who wakes in the middle of the night and tells his wife that he's just had the greatest idea for a movie anyone has ever had. "Quick," she says, "write it down so you won't forget it in the morning." When he gets up, he finds the note and reaches for it eagerly. It reads, "Boy meets girl."

THE PERILS OF TREND SPOTTING

Frank Capra advised young filmmakers, "Don't follow trends. *Start* trends."

Writers who chase trends are like ambulance-chasing lawyers. They may get a few jobs here and there, but the work probably won't be very significant. It's a common fallacy among beginning writers that they should study the current box-office receipts to see which movies are hits and then try to copy them. That's foolish, not only because trend following, by definition, is a secondhand way of working, but also because it's not realistic. A movie you write on spec today, if you're lucky enough to sell it, won't reach theaters for two or three years at the earliest. The movie burning up the box office today was probably developed several years ago. My former agent Jeff Berg, one of the smartest guys in the business (he's now the head of the giant talent agency ICM, International Creative Management), once told me, "A trend is over when the first project is announced. You can't be an ambulance chaser. By the time you start imitating a trend, it's going to be over anyway." That means the trend for tongue-in-cheek pirate movies or comedies about chunky male slackers losing their virginity was over months or years before you heard about it, even if you've been reading the Hollywood trade papers. Projects go through a fairly lengthy process of development before they are ready to be announced. And even then, as I calculated while working for *Variety,* only about one in four projects that are announced in the trades ever reach the screen. So there is little sense in trying to outguess the market.

This is not to say that the movie business doesn't crank out endless carbon copies of hits or that the industry's lack of originality doesn't pay some dividends. A low-budget horror movie based on a short story I wrote, *Prom Night,* became a surprise hit and helped to establish the slasher-movie subgenre; it has already spawned three sequels and a remake, none of which I have had the stomach to see (I made the mistake of selling the rights to my story without receiving credit, because I needed the money). But the people churning out the rehashes and remakes you see in your multiplex tend to be experienced hands (or hacks). Neophytes are at a serious disadvantage next to those more practiced craftsmen, for even second-rate professional writing takes a fair degree of skill. Writing a Harry Potter or James Bond or Indiana Jones knockoff isn't going to get you very far, since those actual franchises do the job better and with far bigger budgets than your facsimile could ever hope to muster. So your best chance at selling a script is to write something that you actually care about. You may or may not sell the script, but it will always be better than formulaic writing without passion and conviction. And it probably will be your best work. As Jeff Berg told me, "The material might be offbeat or it might not be ostensibly commercial, but you should weather it out. Most movies aren't set up easily. Most movies are made for all the wrong reasons."

WRITE FROM THE HEART

Writing what you care about sounds obvious, but sometimes the obvious eludes us. After some painful experiences in trying to market original screenplays during my early days in Hollywood, I'd fallen into the aspiring screenwriter's trap of trying to psych out the marketplace to determine what kinds of stories would sell to the cynical studio executives. After only two years in town, I'd become as jaded about the process of screenwriting as if I'd been there for half a lifetime. I was facing the dilemma screenwriter Joe Gillis confides to the audience in *Sunset Boulevard* as we see him pounding his typewriter in his bathrobe:

> I was living in an apartment house above Franklin and Ivar.
> Things were tough at the moment. I hadn't worked in a studio
> for a long time. So I sat there grinding out original stories,
> two a week. Only I seemed to have lost my touch. Maybe they
> weren't original enough. Maybe they were *too* original. All I
> know is they didn't sell.

Then I went to hear Mike Medavoy, at the time the senior
vice president of production for United Artists, give a talk about
screenwriting. I knew that Medavoy had the reputation of being
one of the most sophisticated studio executives in the business.
But I was surprised to find how uncynical this "suit" seemed. He
advised the audience of young screenwriters, "All you can do is
write what comes from the heart. Why else would you go to the
trouble of writing a screenplay?" Medavoy's long track record of
backing offbeat films for talented and original filmmakers (such
as *Rocky, Apocalypse Now, Raging Bull, Platoon,* and *Zodiac*)
proves he wasn't saying that just for show. I never forgot what a
salutary jolt it was to hear those words from a man who actually
green-lighted pictures.

HIGH CONCEPT

There is a terrible phrase you often hear in Hollywood and
often read in books on screenwriting: "high concept." It means
an idea for a movie that is so simple that it can be expressed in
a sentence or a few words. "A great white shark is killing people
off the coast of Martha's Vineyard." "A visionary theme-park
creator finds a way to breed actual dinosaurs, but they run amok
and destroy the park." "An 'unsinkable' ocean liner hits an iceberg and starts to sink."

There's nothing wrong with these short, simple, strong ideas; you probably enjoy *Jaws, Jurassic Park,* and *Titanic* as much as I do. But if you can train yourself to avoid any way of thinking in the movie business, try not to think of "high concept" ideas. If one occurs to you, fine, go with it. Some writers, like Stephen King or the late Michael Crichton, can't seem to help coming up with brilliant story hooks of that kind. More power to them. Director Ken Russell came up with perhaps the single greatest movie pitch when he sold United Artists on doing his 1970 Tchaikovsky biopic, *The Music Lovers,* by describing it as "the story of a homosexual who falls in love with a nymphomaniac." Irreverent as it may seem, that line actually captures the complexity of the movie and its tormented central character. But most good movie stories, most good dramas, can't be reduced to that kind of bold declarative stroke.

Try condensing *Citizen Kane* to one sentence: "An aging newspaper tycoon becomes increasingly lonely and isolated as he ostracizes his friends and mistress and goes in futile search of his childhood, looking for something he can't remember…" I tried, but the story keeps unfolding. It feels unwieldy if you try to squeeze it into so few words, perhaps because its intricate flashback structure and complex perspective on its central character would require pages to even start explaining. Nor can any of the other nine films chosen in 2002 as the best ever made in the most prestigious poll of international critics, by the British magazine *Sight & Sound,* fit comfortably into a short sound bite. Good luck doing so with *Vertigo; The Rules of the Game; The Godfather* and *The Godfather Part II; Tokyo Story; 2001: A Space Odyssey; The Battleship Potemkin; Sunrise: A Song of Two Humans; 8 1/2;* or *Singin' in the Rain.* Even *Singin' in the Rain,* which may seem the least complicated of the lot, exists on a plane of musical stylization sublimely beyond its bare-bones plot, which satirizes the transition from silent movies to talkies.

"High concept" is not what these landmarks of cinema are all about. It's as hard to boil any of them down to a mere "concept" as it would be to reduce a Van Gogh painting to a flock of crows or a bunch of sunflowers or to summarize a Beethoven symphony adequately with the names "Pastoral" or "Eroica." The complexities of genuine works of art go far beyond their *log-lines* (another simplistic term often used in books on how to sell screenplays, meaning the kind of one-line description you read in *TV Guide*).

If, on the other hand, you still want to make formulaic pictures that appeal to the lowest common denominator, keep thinking of how to come up with "high concept" ideas. I can't stop you. But if you aspire to something higher, banish that term from your vocabulary. And never forget this: The only smart way to write a script that might sell is to write one you care about, for a film you'd like to watch, and hope that other people will care about it too.

4

Ten Tips for the Road Ahead

*B*efore we move on to our practical applications and exercises, here are some of the key dos and don'ts that help define the craft of screenwriting.

1. Don't write what we can't see or hear. If I can leave you with one basic rule about screenwriting, this is it. Once you keep this point firmly in mind, you will be writing in cinematic terms. Cinema can't show the invisible, and a script should avoid nebulous concepts. So don't tell us about what happened to characters in the past (the backstory) or tell us things about them the viewer can't glean from the images or dialogue.

Beginning writers are often tempted to explain characters by telling the reader how the characters came to do what they are doing. This should be avoided. Dramatize your characters, don't explain them. Make sure your script tells the story fully without resorting to backstory. Sometimes a script will provide character biographies as prefatory material. Orson Welles included brief character bios in his script for *Touch of Evil* (originally titled *Badge of Evil,* from a novel of that title by Whit Masterson, the pseudonym of Robert Wade and H. Bill Miller), and those bios undoubtedly were helpful to the actors, but I would discourage beginning writers from relying on them, because they can be a cheat.

There are many ways to evoke the past in screenplays. Dialogue and flashbacks are the most obvious ways. The allusive use of objects to evoke emotions is a more subtle way. Sounds can create images in your mind, and sometimes hearing a voice or a bit of music or a sound will conjure up something from the past or something from another part of the story. In George Stevens's *A Place in the Sun,* written by Michael Wilson and Harry Brown, the religious upbringing of the doomed central character, George Eastman (Montgomery Clift), is masterfully evoked when he sees psalm singers proselytizing on a street corner and stares at a young boy singer who we realize reminds him of his youthful self. The brief scene serves the function of a flashback without actually necessitating a cumbersome flashback to George's youth, and at the same time reveals his melancholy adult perspective on his oppressive upbringing.

If you want to discuss abstract ideas, film generally is not the ideal medium, although characters can discuss ideas to a limited extent. And yet a central paradox about screenwriting is that it is a way of suggesting (in words) what isn't seen (on the page). And movies can evoke images that are seen only in the mind of the viewer. Cinema can find ways of drawing intellectual associations through composition, editing, and other devices (as discussed in depth in the theoretical writings of Russian filmmaker Sergei M. Eisenstein and best exemplified in his films *The Battleship Potemkin* and *October*). And as for symbolism, cinema can accommodate it quite well (see Luis Buñuel's surrealist films and the work of David Lynch), but it must be made concrete, as symbolism must be in poetry and most other forms of literature (other than the most abstractly stylized) if the writer wants it to resonate in our emotions.

2. *Don't tell us what people are thinking or feeling or remembering unless you can show it.* This is a corollary to the previous point. Descriptive passages in a script that delve deeply into a character's feelings or thoughts risk irrelevancy. They are usually a crutch for failing to dramatize your story. If a troubled man is walking through the woods, and you explain that he is

thinking about how he was abused as a child, that won't come across on-screen. How could the actor convey that backstory so specifically? And how do you convey the interior life of your character without spelling it out in dialogue or resorting to a crudely explanatory flashback? This is one of the most complex questions facing a screenwriter.

A great actor can give us a whole range of feelings and thoughts on his face. Watch Marlon Brando, as longshoreman Terry Malloy, exposing his soul in the taxicab scene in Elia Kazan's *On the Waterfront* with Rod Steiger playing his gangster brother. Terry has just realized his brother has betrayed him to the mob, and their whole relationship, from childhood naïveté to the anguished moment of truth, can be read on Brando's face. Budd Schulberg wrote the scene, providing incisive descriptions of behavior along with its memorable dialogue; this is the "I coulda been a *contender*" scene. But it would be next to impossible to describe fully the complex, moment-by-moment effect of such a scene in a script or in a work of film criticism. Still, the screenwriter needs to suggest how the characters should behave, as Schulberg does here with such parenthetical directions as "(noncommittal, sullen)," "(struggling with an unfamiliar problem of conscience and loyalties)," "(patiently, as to a stubborn child)," and "(years of abuse crying out in him)"; the actors can't begin to play the scene without that kind of foundation for their behavior. In a later chapter, we'll discuss further the crucial question of how a screenwriter should go about writing good parts for actors to play, as well as how to deal with the problem of evoking a character's interior life on-screen.

3. Don't overdo dialogue. Robert Towne advised students at the American Film Institute, "Generally speaking, the process of writing a screenplay is figuring out how to keep the dialogue as spare as possible." That is a rule I always tried to follow while writing screenplays: try to think of a scene first in visual terms and only resort to dialogue when it is truly necessary. Not that there's anything wrong with strong, colorful dialogue, as long as the narrative keeps moving. But it's too easy to fall into the trap of turning your movie into lifeless and static-looking scenes. Alfred Hitchcock complained that most movies resemble filmed plays; he scorned such works as "pictures of people talking." What he preferred—and what are hardest to create—are pictures of people *thinking*.

4. Don't underdo *dialogue.* It's unfortunate that many films today, especially action films, seem to regard actual conversation as an audience turnoff. One rationale often heard from Hollywood is that foreign audiences—which the American film industry courts aggressively, since they make up a large share of box-office gross—aren't interested in hearing characters talking. That is not only condescending but seems like a case of projection; when executives or producers disparage their audience (whether foreign or domestic) as dumb, they are rationalizing their own low tastes and standards. Characters who don't talk much can be interesting, if the talk is well chosen and expressive. But inarticulate characters can also be cartoonishly dull. Even the characters in an action movie can talk with wit and brio, as James Bond movies have been demonstrating for decades.

Because we have become so accustomed to thinking of cinema as "a visual art form" and to exalting directors over writers, we tend to downplay the importance of words in filmmaking. But there are many fine films in which characters talk in elaborate, even poetic language and do so at length. Not only some of the film adaptations of Shakespeare come to mind, but also the works of such writer-directors as Joseph L. Mankiewicz, Eric Rohmer, Woody Allen, and the Coen brothers. Allen's quintessential modern romantic comedy, *Annie Hall,* is essentially an extended dialogue between two characters (his own and Diane Keaton's), charting the ebb and flow of their romantic relationship; Rohmer's *Ma nuit chez Maud/My Night at Maud's* compresses its romantic conversation more tightly (the intensely

intellectual discussion in that film is between Jean-Louis Trinti-
gnant and Françoise Fabian). Sofia Coppola's *Lost in Translation* charms audiences partly because it revives the feeling of the
classic romantic comedies, with an offbeat courtship developed
through verbal interplay.

While it's true that some modern films—ranging from Terrence Malick's poetic sagas *The Thin Red Line* and *The New
World* to scores of action films with wall-to-wall spectacle—
play almost as silent movies (with music and effects), dialogue is
critical in such screenplays as *Synecdoche, New York* by Charlie
Kaufman; *Sideways* by Alexander Payne and Jim Taylor (based
on the novel by Rex Pickett); *Invictus* by Anthony Peckham
(based on the book *Playing the Enemy: Nelson Mandela and the
Game That Made a Nation* by John Carlin); *Do the Right Thing*
by Spike Lee; *Howards End* by Ruth Prawer Jhabvala (based
on the novel by E. M. Forster); *Gosford Park* by Julian Fellowes
(from an idea by Robert Altman and Bob Balaban); *Shakespeare in Love* by Marc Norman and Tom Stoppard; *Bulworth*
by Warren Beatty and Jeremy Pikser (from a story by Beatty);
Pulp Fiction by Quentin Tarantino (from stories he wrote with
Roger Avary); *The King's Speech* by David Seidler; and *True
Grit* by Joel and Ethan Coen (from the novel by Charles Portis).
These films revel in the glory of their language.

5. Keep scenes short (usually). When I started writing feature
screenplays, I tended to write twenty-page dramatic scenes, no
doubt influenced by the fact that I'd read a lot of stage plays
and only a few screenplays. Scenes in modern films tend to be
short—two or three minutes is a substantial length for a scene,
and some scenes can be only a few seconds long. Occasionally a
scene can run longer than a few minutes. The length of the scenes
should not always be the same, because that quickly becomes
monotonous and predictable; structure your script with a musical rhythm, varying the pace and decelerating or accelerating it
as the story demands.

It's unfortunate that today's movie audiences seem to suffer from a collective case of ADD (attention deficit disorder). You shouldn't feel the need to pander to their impatience. Still, don't have characters gab to one another at great length, especially if they are sitting around or standing around (writer-director Samuel Fuller called verbose movie dialogue "gibble-gabble"). Give characters actions to perform while they are talking and keep them moving around. Make the talk itself into a form of action. As Darryl F. Zanuck, one of Hollywood's savviest executives, liked to say, "They don't call them moving pictures because they stand still. They *move*."

6. *Don't show everything that happens in the story.* As William Goldman puts it in John Brady's interview book *The Craft of the Screenwriter,*

> Rule of thumb: You always attack a movie scene as *late* as you possibly can. You always come into the scene at the *last* possible moment, which is why when you see a scene in a movie where a person is a teacher, for instance, the scene always begins with the teacher saying, "Well, class..." and then the bell rings. And then you get into another scene because it's very dull watching a man talk to people in a room....
>
> In a book you might start with some dialogue, and then describe the room, and start with some more dialogue, and then describe your clothing, and more dialogue. The camera gets that in an *instant. Boom,* and you're on. Get on, get on. The camera is relentless. Makes you keep running.

7. *Use the helpful devices available to writers in the professional screenplay format.* Clear and creative use of scene headings keeps the script easy to follow and gives a sense of visual variety and movement. Transitional devices ("CUT TO," "DISSOLVE TO," "FADE OUT," and so on) should be used when you go from one place to another or from one time period to

another. (In a screenplay, "CUT TO" or "DISSOLVE TO" is followed with a colon, but "FADE OUT" is not.)

Though these devices may not be used by all professional screenwriters, they were not developed in some arbitrary fashion to constrain your creativity. They are some of the ways that have evolved over the years to make a screenplay a quick read. Sam Hamm says that's the first job of the screenwriter, "to keep the reader's eye moving down the page." Anything that interrupts that movement and makes the reader have to stop and reread something to figure out what's going on is potentially fatal to selling your script. You want the reader, above all, to be caught up in your story and want to keep turning the pages with excitement.

8. CLARITY! That's the virtue Alfred Hitchcock stressed most in directing. The same applies to screenwriting: If your script is not clearly written, it won't tell the story in a way the reader can follow. Clarity is the quality most conspicuously lacking in most bad writing. And screenwriting is not a medium for obscure, wooly writing, however clever you may think it is. Put a sign above your desk reading CLARITY. If a reader of your script mutters, "WTF?" that's not a hopeful sign.

9. Use good English. If your script is riddled with writing errors, the reader will quickly lose confidence in your abilities and become distracted from the story you are trying to tell. Many professional screenwriters are not the most polished writers, but there is a certain minimum standard of legibility that must be maintained in the professional world, or the script will be cast aside. Writers with poor writing mechanics like to claim that those problems don't hamper their "creativity," but that is a cop-out. How else is a writer's creativity expressed than through his writing style? Work hard to fix your writing problems; resist the temptation to create alibis for them. F. Scott Fitzgerald may have been a poor speller, but that does not mean that if you are a poor speller, you are F. Scott Fitzgerald. And even Fitzgerald could never figure out how to succeed at screenwriting.

10. Don't write an epic unless you're working for Steven Spielberg or Martin Scorsese. When I arrived in Hollywood, I found myself witnessing a strange native ritual. The first thing a producer or reader would do with a script, instinctively, was to pick it up and weigh it. Literally weigh it. Professionals develop a keen sense of how a professional script should feel in their hands. If it's too heavy, the script starts life with a strike against it. It has little chance of being read with care or read at all. Since no one had ever explained this simple lesson to me back in Wisconsin, the first script I completed after I came to Hollywood was an elegiac John Wayne Western running 182 pages. Attempting to sell a Western of any kind, let alone one built around the aging and controversial persona of John Wayne, was dodgy enough in those days, but the biggest problem was the script's inordinate length.

It took me more trial and error to learn the basic lesson that a script cannot exceed a certain length, or that it does so only at great risk. Cinema is an art form involving time—the duration of events and the manipulation of time for dramatic effect are part of its essence. Add to that the demands of the commercial marketplace, which set fairly strict boundaries on time. A writer must bear in mind that every second counts in a film or a television program (even more so in television, with its hourly schedules and commercial breaks). If you disregard this reality, you can lose your job or never sell your script.

The rule of thumb in professional screenwriting is that one page of a script equals one minute on-screen. That's for normal scenes with a mixture of dialogue and limited description of action. If a scene is all dialogue, it usually plays faster than a minute per page. If it's all action, it usually takes longer to play out on-screen. Imagine a script containing the line "Napoleon invades Russia." Those three words would take about forty-five minutes on-screen and cost maybe a hundred million dollars to film. Of course, no good screenwriter would write a battle that way. The events should be laid out in order and in careful narrative detail, with some visual color and flair; otherwise we'd have no way to imagine what we should see and in what order.

Since the standard limit for a feature film is two hours, this means that a script should be no more than 120 pages long. Billy Wilder said it could be 130, but he was Billy Wilder, and we're not. William Goldman advises making your script 130 to 135 pages "because that lets everybody be creative when they get it. That means that the producer will be able to say, 'Well, we must cut fifteen pages out of this.' ... So you have to give them a little extra to work with." I would not recommend this kind of ploy to beginning screenwriters trying to sell a script on "spec," and I would worry about doing anything to encourage people to "be creative" with your script. Give it your best shot and keep it within the standard limits of length.

There are movies these days that run over two hours, but they're usually made by important directors who have the commercial and artistic clout to get them through the system. People often complain about the self-indulgence of filmmakers who can't tell a story succinctly, but some movies need to be long— Steven Spielberg's *Schindler's List* (written by Steven Zaillian, from the book by Thomas Keneally) runs three hours and fifteen minutes, and the time is needed for that Holocaust film's epic scope and psychological depth. But as a beginning screenwriter you don't have the clout to write at such length, unless the story you are telling demands it. Conversely, if a script is too short (only 80–90 minutes), it may seem too insubstantial to make a feature film. Christopher Guest's quirky comedies, such as *Best in Show* and *Waiting for Guffman,* tend to be in that range, and the British mainstream sex film *9 Songs* runs only 69 minutes (as a gag), but those are exceptions that prove the rule.

Most directors actually are obligated in their studio contracts not to exceed 120 minutes, or the studio will take the film away from them and recut it. It's important for the writer to keep in mind the practical problems encountered when a film runs much more than two hours—not only is it more expensive to produce and harder to justify having audiences sit through, but theater owners complain that excessive length limits turnover (i.e., putting the rear ends of paying customers on chairs). Someone's overly long screenplay is threatening to everyone's livelihood. Even if such length can be justified, it's a tough sell.

To avoid problems with excessive length, it's crucial to have a sense of the film's overall shape and structure at all times. Keep a running rough estimate of how long your script will play. If your first act is taking up eighty pages, you have a problem that demands immediate attention. One of the ways professional writers keep tabs on length is by writing a step outline (i.e., laying out the story briefly in "steps"). I'll show you later how to write a step outline for the short film script we will learn to write here; the same basic principles of the screenwriting craft apply to both short and feature-length films. Writing such an outline should help ensure that your script and film have a satisfying and practical structure and length.

Part II

Adaptation

5

Breaking the Back of the Book; or, The Art of Adaptation

*T*here's another terrible phrase in Hollywood, but one that is much more useful than "high concept." This is what is known as "breaking the back of the book." It's the elegant way movie people have of explaining the delicate process of literary adaptation. It involves tearing the original work apart to see what makes it live and breathe and then finding a way to translate those qualities into cinematic terms. We'll learn how to do that in the next few chapters as I guide you through the steps involved in transforming a literary work into a screenplay. You will find that breaking the back of the work is not as cruel as it sounds, but actually a kind, if not entirely gentle, way of respecting what makes a book or story a viable idea for a film.

Now why, you may well ask, are we starting the process of learning to write a screenplay by adapting someone else's work? Why not start by writing an original?

That's a question students sometimes raise at the beginning of my introductory screenwriting courses. They naturally tend to assume that they are learning the craft so they can tell their original stories on film. While personal storytelling may indeed be the highest goal of a screenwriter, I have found that plunging headlong into writing an original screenplay is not the best way to learn the craft. It's hard enough mastering the basics of screenwriting without facing the simultaneous challenge of coming up with a usable, well-structured, original story.

When I started teaching basic screenwriting, I had my students work on original stories, but I quickly found that this was a mistake. Since they hadn't learned the craft, many of their stories were weak and inadequate as film material. Most were hardly original and often were rehashes of TV sitcom formulas. I lost track of how many times I read scripts about three college roommates having problems living together (usually two of them suspected that the third was a serial killer). Also I too often found that when one student was discussing her story, the eyes of the others would glaze over with lack of interest. The solution I came up with was to have the entire class work on an adaptation of the same published short story.

Eventually, I give them a choice of two different stories to adapt, Ernest Hemingway's "Big Two-Hearted River," a virtually wordless story of a troubled man (a World War I veteran) trying to get his head back together by fishing in the Michigan woods around 1919, or Flannery O'Connor's "A Late Encounter with the Enemy," a satirical black comedy about a senile, 104-year-old Confederate veteran approaching death in the company of his delusional granddaughter in the 1951 South. You can pick one of these to practice adapting a story to the screen or do your own adaptation of the story I will choose to adapt as a demonstration in this book (more on that later), but any other story that would make a viable short film will work as well.

By having my students at San Francisco State adapt one of two existing stories we all read, we can all go into depth on the challenges involved in cinematic adaptation, and everyone is interested, because the discussions are of direct benefit to their work. This idea has worked well in enabling students to learn the craft. It first came to me via Jean Renoir, who said in a 1961 interview with fellow director Jacques Rivette:

> I know one way we can save films, and it's extremely simple. It would be to have the producers from a place like Hollywood or Paris decide that one year everyone would do one subject.

Hollywood would decide, for example, that a certain Western would be made, that all the directors would make the same Western, and you would see the originality, the differences among the films. But instead of this, we pretend to be different by having different stories. In the end, though, we're producing exact copies. People tell a different story, but with the same faces, the same makeup, the same vocal expressions, the same emotions,... it's monotonous, don't you think?

How much truer is that today, with all the numbing monotony of most American mainstream filmmaking. When you watch trailers at the multiplex, it's remarkable how much the films resemble one another. The prevalence of sequels and remakes is part of the reason for this lack of originality, but the inflation of production budgets and ticket prices has also contributed to a stifling conservatism in the choices of films to make and see. If your film costs $200 million to produce and another $100 million to market, the temptation to homogenize the material to make it appeal to the broadest possible audience (and the lowest common denominator) is hard to resist. And you want to assure viewers who pay fourteen dollars for a ticket that they will have the safely familiar experience they seem to demand. So we are all complicit, to some degree, in this disheartening situation. And yet the films that become breakthrough hits still tend to be the ones that offer the lure of a genuine originality of approach.

By showing students how to take an existing short story, one that is well suited for filming, and turn it into a screenplay, I find that they learn how to write a screenplay much more easily than if they were writing an original. If you focus on the craft itself while using an existing story as the basis for your first script, the process becomes much clearer to follow. This also gives you the benefit of collaborating with a great writer, an inestimable advantage in your first venture into screenwriting. Your silent collaborator will give you the basic idea and structure for you to develop cinematically.

And once you've written a carefully crafted screenplay of twenty to thirty pages adapted from a short story, a script that follows the well-established professional format, you should be ready to start tackling the challenge of writing an original feature-length script. You will have the tools you need to tell the stories that come from your heart in ways that will connect with audiences most effectively. And all the lessons you will learn here about adapting a literary work into a screenplay apply just as well to transforming your own original idea into a screenplay.

But if you write an adaptation, you may ask, where does the personal element come in? "Where's my creativity?" First of all, it's a false assumption that adaptations are not creative. Every adaptation not only requires great skill but also inevitably reflects the personality of the writer who does the adapting. Even if you are "merely" trying to write a "faithful" adaptation—a problematic expression, as we shall see—you will find that you usually have to change things around considerably and invent cinematic solutions to problems of dramatization in order to reconstruct the essence of the story on-screen. And you may not *want* to be "faithful" but simply to use the germ of the story or some of its elements as the springboard for letting your creative fancies run free. Adapting a story is a way of broadening your creative horizons. Although there is some truth in "Write what you know," that adage can be too limiting for a writer with ambitions beyond her own experience. When the Nobel Prize–winning novelist Toni Morrison was asked what advice she had for a young writer, she replied, "She should not only write about what she knows but about what she doesn't know. It extends the imagination."

The way an author tells a story, the style, is inextricable from its content. Although it's not necessary to write your outline, treatment, or screenplay in a style resembling the original author's, the rhythmical ebbs and flows of the prose that inspired your adaptation, and the tone of the original, can be approximated cinematically in your imagery, the description of action, and the allocation of lengths to each scene and sequence. Of course, if you are changing a story radically in the adaptation process, you may want to come up with a much different style from the original author's way of telling it. But if you are trying to preserve at least some of the spirit of the original and not simply taking the plot as a springboard for your own ideas, coming to terms with the style of the story is a crucial step in accessing its deepest meanings and turning them into dramatic and cinematic scenes. When you find cinematic equivalents for that literary style, you are transforming the story into a genuine film adaptation.

OWNING THE IDEA

It's fascinating to watch Renoir's theory in action, to see how different people working with the same story in a screenwriting class will write scripts so utterly different in style, tone, and even theme. I encourage the aspiring screenwriters to let their imaginations loose on the stories and, if they wish, to traduce them to their hearts' content—just as long as they are writing a genuine adaptation. They are free to change the characters, settings, and time periods—making a male protagonist a woman, turning a period tale into a contemporary story, moving the action from the backwoods of Michigan to the far reaches of outer space— if they keep the essence of the story, its "spine."

"Spine" is a term borrowed from the theater; identifying it is one of the key tasks of outlining any dramatic story. As interesting as your characters are, as good as your ideas for individual scenes might be, you can't sustain dramatic interest for the length of a feature film without a solid spine, a compelling structure holding it all together. The students writing an adaptation of a short story may change a guardedly hopeful ending into a bleakly tragic conclusion, if that better expresses their own worldview, or they may add elements of comedy or whimsy, and they may attack the thematic foundations of the original. But as long as the spine is recognizably there, it's a legitimate screen adaptation. Even a seeming perversion of the original story, bending it out of shape with bold irreverence, may wind up being truer to the spirit of the original than a transcription that attempts to be slavishly faithful. In fact, it's usually the slavishly unimaginative cinematic transcription that fails most abysmally to be true to whatever it was in the original story that made it seem worth adapting to the screen in the first place.

If you become a professional screenwriter, you may be handed a book and asked to come up with a way of adapting it. Many films, of course, have been and continue to be made from literary works. With studios looking more and more for presold properties, as was also the norm in Hollywood's Golden Age, it's easier for nervous executives to commit to a project if they know it has had some degree of success in another medium. But that has never stopped filmmakers from making sweeping changes to source material, and even if you work on an original rather than an adaptation, you will face many of the same questions in considering how to make the story work on-screen.

Renoir's forty-minute adaptation of Guy de Maupassant's 1881 short story "Une partie de campagne," filmed in 1936 as *Partie de campagne/A Day in the Country,* is perhaps the finest short film ever made. Renoir is not only one of the greatest of all directors, he is also one of the most masterful screenwriters. I show *A Day in the Country* to my screenwriting students after they read the story so they can see how Renoir brought his own attitudes about nature and love to Maupassant's bittersweet story about a naïve young woman's romantic awakening. Renoir transformed Maupassant's cynical view of sexuality and the bourgeoisie with his own more generous and affectionate vision of humanity and changed Maupassant's jaundiced view of the French countryside into a rapturous ode to nature. The case could well be made that Renoir's film of *A Day in the Country* surpasses even the master of the short story in thematic complexity and stylistic richness. This did not mean that Renoir set out to attack Maupassant's story. On the contrary, he said,

> "A Day in the Country" didn't force anything on me. It only offered me an ideal framework in which to embroider....The habit of using a story already invented by someone else frees you from the unimportant aspect. What's important is the way you tell the story. If the story has already been invented by someone else, you're free to give all your attention to what is truly important, that is, the details, the development of the characters and the situations.

So when you "break the back of the book," you first figure out what the story is about (i.e., find the spine), and then you study and analyze how it works. Discovering how it is structured unlocks the secrets of the original. Outlining the original story is a helpful exercise because it makes you recognize each of its building blocks, note them down in succession, summarize them clearly and succinctly, and put them in your own words. In so doing, you will begin to see what you want to keep and what you want to change and get ideas for how your own version of the story might be structured. After the story outline, the next four logical steps in the process (which we will follow in the next few chapters) are the adaptation outline, the character biography, the treatment, and the step outline. At that point you are ready to start writing the script.

And once you start the process of putting a story in your own words, you begin to "own" the idea by virtue of internalizing it and turning it into your own stylistic expression.

TEQUILA WITH RAY BRADBURY

You don't own the story in a legal sense, of course. For the purposes of classroom exercises, it's not a problem for students to adapt copyrighted stories. And if you credit the author of a story you are adapting, it is not plagiarism. You can do the same as an exercise while practicing how to write a screenplay. If a writer actually wants to film a script based on an existing work, however, he would have to buy or option the film rights.

Sometimes authors will even be so generous as to let a young writer adapt their work for free. When I met Ray Bradbury at the American Film Institute Life Achievement Award dinner honoring Orson Welles in 1975, we went out for tequilas afterward at a Mexican restaurant with Sam Peckinpah. A mariachi band, thrilled to see the director of *The Wild Bunch,* came over to serenade us, and Peckinpah, who was completely smashed, passed out with his head on the table. Bradbury seemed both sober and amused by his friend's antics. During a break in the music, I told the writer that I loved one of his short stories ("The Utterly Perfect Murder") and wanted to adapt it as a short film but didn't have any money to buy the rights. "I have many short stories and very few lovers," he said, and he told me I could film the story for nothing. Stunned by his kindness, but not having enough money to make a film, I never took him up on the offer. The story was later filmed, with a script by Bradbury himself, for his television series *The Ray Bradbury Theater.* But my experience shows you what a wonderful thing can happen if you approach a beloved author and do so with both sincerity and chutzpah.

Another way to collaborate with a literary figure is to find a story that's in the public domain. That means the copyright has lapsed, and it is free for use in any way you want. Literary works published in the United States before January 1, 1923, are in the public domain, but you always need to make sure of the copyright status of a work you want to adapt. The copyright period in the United States used to be twenty-eight years, with an option to renew for another twenty-eight years. But in recent times, Congress, heavily lobbied by the Walt Disney Company and other film studios, has kept extending the copyright period to such lengths that works published after 1922 rarely go into the public domain, and usually only when some rights holder fails to register or renew them (as happened for a time with the 1946 film *It's a Wonderful Life*). This unfortunate situation protects corporations and writers' heirs more than it does authors, and it limits the scope of literary material freely available for reprinting and adaptation. But an industrious, well-read screenwriter can still find a vast treasure-house of books and short stories from the past that can serve as promising subject matter for films. In his June 1976 column in *American Film* magazine ("Properties, Projects, Possibilities"), the novelist, screenwriter, and bibliophile Larry McMurtry helpfully provided a lengthy list of "books I can spot on my own shelves that I think would make good movies. With very few exceptions, most of them could be acquired cheaply, and made cheaply." Look it up at the library and you will find enough stories to keep you busy for a lifetime.

If you use a public-domain story, however, you have to carefully guard your use of it so that someone else, reading your script version, might not get the bright idea to write his own script based on the same material. If that happens, you may well find yourself with a wasted effort. That's why Stanley Kubrick fiercely refused to tell anyone the title of the nineteenth-century novel he was adapting until *Barry Lyndon* was into production. He worried that if someone knew earlier what he was doing, a quickie TV movie version of *The Memoirs of Barry Lyndon, Esq.,* William Makepeace Thackeray's satire of a hapless Irish social climber, might appear before he could finish his film with his customarily painstaking methods of production. So don't run around trumpeting your literary discovery of the utterly perfect film material. In fact, as Mel Brooks advised AFI students:

Writers! Do not discuss embryo ideas! When you have coffee, don't talk to other people in the business about your ideas until they are fully written and registered. Then you can talk about them. You will not get help. You'll get envy and you'll get stealing. Also, not only will they get stolen, but you will let the vapor of creation escape when you tell it. Be a little schizophrenic, talk to yourself through the paper. It's a good exercise, and sometimes it makes money for you.

Talk about your ideas only on a strict need-to-know basis. You should register your script, outline, or treatment with the Writers Guild of America, West, Registry. The guild's registry service is available for nominal fees to both members and non-members, and material can be submitted by e-mail or regular mail or hand delivery (see www.wgawregistry.org). The guild registers more than 55,000 pieces of literary material each year (also including plays, books, short stories, and other publications), which shows how competitive the market is. Registration is valid for five years, with renewal available for another five. You can also copyright your material (usually the final draft) with the Library of Congress or send a draft to yourself by registered mail and keep the letter or package unopened (this is called "poor man's copyright").

The point of Writers Guild registration is to establish that you wrote the material by a certain date; if the material becomes the subject of a legal or WGA action, a guild employee will produce the material as evidence to prove your claim. You should list the registration number on the title page of your script. Some producers will tell you that this seems paranoid, but that's because it irritates them to be put on notice that the material is registered with the WGAW. Anything you can do to make *them* feel paranoid is all to the good. In addition, make sure there is a written record of any submission of the script or outline, including the date (an agent sends it or you send it by FedEx or fax, for example). Even that may not be enough to protect you. You can't be too paranoid about idea theft (often called "intellectual property theft"), so we will revisit this subject in more detail later in the book.

DESTROYING THE ORIGINAL
IN ORDER TO SAVE IT

So now that you're freed (at least temporarily) from what Jean Renoir calls "the unimportant aspect" of coming up with an original story, how free are you? Do you have any obligations to the original author?

When MGM made its 1935 film version of the classic Charles Dickens novel *David Copperfield,* Frank Whitbeck of the studio's advertising department was checking the credits with an executive to ensure that everyone's billing was correct. As Max Wilk tells the story in his 1971 book, *The Wit and Wisdom of Hollywood,* after they had run down the list of talent involved in the picture, Whitbeck said, "There's a lot of credit there. But one name that should get credit doesn't." "Who's that?" the executive demanded. "Probably the most important of all," Whitbeck replied. "The guy who wrote the book, Dickens." "He's dead, isn't he?" the executive asked. "Yes," conceded Whitbeck. "Well," said the executive, "screw him!"

Few authors, and usually not dead ones, retain legal control over their stories. Some raise hell about changes anyway by complaining to the film company and even to the media, but most are philosophical about the way the movies alter their material. "Let me tell you about writing for films," Ernest Hemingway said during preproduction for the film version of his novel *The Old Man and the Sea.* "You finish your book. Now, you know where the California state line is? Well, you drive right up to that line, take your manuscript, and pitch it across—No, on second thought, don't pitch it across. First, let them toss the money over. *Then* you throw it over, pick up the money, and get the hell out of there."

But while there are few legal obligations preventing a screenwriter from freely adapting a book or other literary work, once you have the rights to do so, you (and the director) may balk at altering it too much for other reasons. Some beginning writers have excessive reverence for the original author and feel so inferior that they think, "Who am I to rewrite Flannery O'Connor?" That is understandable, but try to banish such feelings. You wouldn't be trying to work in show business if you didn't have enough ego to think your contribution is worth making. Relatively obscure authors and literary works present the screenwriter with fewer anxieties and a greater sense of liberty. But if the work is so famous and so beloved that changing it would seem blasphemous to its admirers, the filmmakers have to think carefully about a possible backlash.

In his April 2009 talk at San Francisco State University, Francis Ford Coppola recalled his initial reaction when he was offered a bestselling novel to adapt early in his career: "I didn't like the book. I was shocked when I read this book. It was like an Irving Wallace, Danielle Steel type of book. It was *The Godfather*... which at first I hated the idea of doing." Coppola wasn't overly fond of the scene in Mario Puzo's novel of a studio chief waking to find a horse's head in his bed, but he felt he couldn't not include that notorious incident in the film he made three years after the book was first published. Sometimes you simply must give the audience what it wants. It's no accident that the horse's head became one of the best-remembered images in the movie. And yet Coppola felt no hesitation in discarding the tawdriest section of Puzo's novel, the part about Lucy Mancini's vagina-tightening operation, an embarrassing lapse into commercial pandering that the author should have had the sense to cut. In writing the screenplay with Puzo, Coppola said, "I just cut out the story of the woman who has the gynecological operation, which really was half the book [Coppola exaggerates for humorous effect]. It had this woman with this problem, and a plastic surgeon fixes it, and then [her regular doctor] becomes her lover. And also in the book it was the story of this man who had three sons and he was like a king, and I saw it as a kind of classical story, so I went that way." Despite the flaws of the novel, Coppola was overly harsh in his initial evaluation of the source material. Although the film deepens every aspect of the novel, the book is actually a riveting narrative filled with rich characterizations, a compelling family story, and a wealth of inside lore about the Mafia subculture.

What makes many novels so difficult to adapt are their scope and length. A screenwriter usually has to discard some of the sub-plots and minor characters and compress action throughout the story to make it fit the limitations of filming. Even though Coppola was granted an unusually long running time for the first *Godfather* film, he still had to pare down the novel's sprawling narrative to concentrate on its spine about destructive family loyalty. In so doing, he elevated the level of storytelling to epic dimensions, discarding irrelevancies and cheapness to focus on this mob family as a twisted metaphor for the American immigrant experience and their quest for a seat at the table of social power.

Paradoxically, violating the letter of the original work is often the only way to preserve its spirit. You are working in a different medium, after all, and what works for a novel may not work well for a film. Following the structure of the original as closely as possible, and trying to touch on all its dramatic highlights, may well produce a lifeless film.

William Goldman's screenplay for *All the President's Men* (based on the nonfiction book about Watergate by *Washington Post* reporters Bob Woodward and Carl Bernstein) is a model of how to adapt a book to the screen. In *Which Lie Did I Tell?: More Adventures in the Screen Trade,* Goldman writes:

> Here is one of the main rules of adaptation: you *cannot* be literally faithful to the source material.
>
> Here's another that critics never get: you *should not* be literally faithful to the source material. It is in a different form, a form that does not have the camera.
>
> Here is the most important rule of adaptation: you *must* be totally faithful to the *intention* of the source material.
>
> In *All the President's Men,* we got great credit for our faithfulness to the Woodward-Bernstein book.

Total horseshit: the movie ended *halfway through* the book. What we were faithful to was their story of a terrible hinge in American history. In other words, we didn't Hollywood-it-up.

You must feel free to reimagine the story in cinematic terms. You often have to invent new scenes and dialogue and characters as well as reshape the narrative to "create a much more rigorous structure," as Renoir advised screenwriters to do. The limitations of time come into play in filmmaking in a way that they don't in a novel, as well as the need for a story line focused more narrowly on dramatic situations than on the kind of free-flowing observations on life, lavish depictions of settings, and ruminations on ideas that distinguish many major novels. When I interviewed Anthony Minghella, the writer-director of *The English Patient,* he explained some of the challenges he faced in taking the story from one medium to another (Minghella, who died in 2008, received an Oscar as best director and was nominated for his adaptation of Michael Ondaatje's novel):

> The book can, in a single page, change voice and location and period a dozen times. You might have a chapter which is entirely about the nature of winds in the Sahara, with no reference to any particular character. The novel is a bit like a notebook, a book of ideas and thoughts and images. Parading through every page are these incredible images which arrest you, but storytelling in film is very significant, and Michael's book is anti-narrative and anti-psychology. The burden for the film was to find a story and a through-line that could collect and lasso all these images, or as many as I could collect, and make it into a film that felt coherent and had some psychological density.

The limitations of the cinematic medium—the properties that make movies what they are and what they aren't—are not necessarily a burden. "Art consists of limitation," G. K. Chesterton observed. "The most beautiful part of every picture is the frame." Sometimes those limitations can inspire you with dramatic and philosophical ideas.

Renoir's 1937 classic *La grande illusion/Grand Illusion,* which he wrote with Charles Spaak, is confined largely within the four walls of a German military prison during World War I. Conventional wisdom would consider such a claustrophobic situation "uncinematic." And yet Renoir noted that the film benefited greatly from such confinement, because "the setup is an ideal one for some discussions." In prison, as Renoir pointed out, what do prisoners mostly think about and talk about? How to escape. So that basic fact gave him an almost endless series of ideas for situations revolving around confinement and escape as metaphors for larger ideas, such as "the problem of nations, and…the racist problem, the problem of how people from different religions meet, how they can understand each other, how they cannot understand each other for some other reasons." Characters can discuss ideas more freely and naturally if the narrative line is that simple and strong: "For instance, I have a scene between [Marcel] Dalio and [Jean] Gabin when they are preparing a rope to escape. They talk, frankly, about racists. It seems that this doesn't belong to the picture, but it does. It works. I had entire scenes which were done only to express this question of origin, nation, races.... I could put fifty situations like that into the shell of my picture. You have to break the shell to find what you are filling it with."

That's another way of saying "breaking the back of the book." It is only by testing, bending, and, yes, breaking the spine of the story that you can find out where it is strongest and how to reassemble it into a playable drama. Rigorously analyzing the structure to decide what works and what doesn't, and ruthlessly discarding scenes that don't advance the story line, is the basic task of adaptation. Advancing the story line doesn't necessarily mean advancing the plot. Character scenes, moments of atmosphere, and apparent digressions (such as the kinds of discussions of ideas that Renoir cherishes) can and should move the narrative along with equal vivacity and are just as important, if not more so, than the moments when the plot mechanics are grinding. Hopefully you can disguise the mechanics and make it all seem to flow organically.

TO BUILD A SCREENPLAY

Let's start our adaptation process now by writing an outline of a story. I will show how it's done by outlining Jack London's "To Build a Fire," the story I first adapted when I was teaching myself to write screenplays (in 1967, at the age of nineteen). By approaching the story anew for this book and writing my own fresh adaptation of London with the benefit of long experience, I'll show you some good (and some not-so-good) ways to go about outlining and developing possible film material. Then we'll critique my new story outline and discuss what works for filming in London's tale, what presents problems, and how we need to change the story to make it come alive in cinematic terms. And then we will work through the rest of the adaptation process, following the standard procedures in the professional world for developing a story into a screenplay.

Along the way, I will offer what are known in the film business as "notes" on my own script—criticisms and suggestions for improvement. For professional screenwriters, this part of the process is aptly described as "development hell." Screenwriter Amy Holden Jones, whose credits include *Mystic Pizza* and *Indecent Proposal,* told Karl Iglesias in his helpful book *The 101 Habits of Highly Successful Screenwriters: Inside Secrets from Hollywood's Top Writers,* "Screenwriting is a terrible way to make a living and I always try to talk anyone out of it. Until you sit in a story meeting with the studio executives with no particular ability or actors who haven't even graduated from high school telling you exactly how to change your script, you haven't experienced what it's really like to be a screenwriter in Hollywood."

I hope I won't be as crassly interfering and idiotic with my notes on my own script as studio executives often are, and I will try to approach the task in a spirit of constructive self-criticism. With my students, rather than trying to rewrite their scripts the way I would write them, I always try to understand what they are trying to say with their story and then try to help draw it out of them. My autocritique in these pages may seem a little schizophrenic, but that should be part of the fun.

While I am demonstrating how script development works by providing concrete examples based on "To Build a Fire," I suggest that you start your own development process. Choose a story to adapt yourself for this exercise. You can pick any story you like, whether it's "To Build a Fire," one of the stories I use in my screenwriting classes, or another of your own choosing. If the story you adapt is still under copyright and you don't own the film rights, this exercise is just for your own benefit. The Jack London story, on the other hand, is in the public domain, so anybody can adapt it.

We'll discuss the London story in detail as we go through the development process together. Since we will be writing for the half-hour storytelling format, this would mean a script of between twenty and twenty-five pages. The traditional reason that a short film shouldn't run longer than half an hour is that much short-film storytelling for mass audiences is usually in the form of episodic television segments, which now tend to run for thirty minutes less eight or more minutes of commercials; though our hypothetical film adaptations aren't necessarily designed for television, that length parameter seems about right for the typical short-story subject matter. Of course, there are other, in some ways more desirable, outlets for short films today, including film festivals, which are the best venues for the uninterrupted short-film experience, and, increasingly, Internet sites that showcase films. And sometimes PBS and other TV channels will show uncut short films as filler between regular programming. Short films can be of various lengths, but if a "short" film begins to approach the one-hour mark, it is becoming more like a mini-feature.

"To Build a Fire" is so visceral in its dramatic impact, so vivid and precise in its physical detailing that this story of a man gradually losing his life-or-death struggle against nature almost reads like a screen treatment. Those qualities, and the elemental simplicity of the narrative, make it particularly useful to help demonstrate how to transform an existing story into a screenplay. London's tale has been filmed at least three times. The 1969 BBC TV adaptation that's available on DVD uses extensive narration (delivered by Orson Welles), but my new version, like the one I wrote when I was starting out, will tell the story without resorting to that distancing device. Perhaps you'll disagree with my approach to adapting "To Build a Fire" for this book and will want to go off in another direction with your adaptation of the story.

The methodical stages that will precede the writing of your script will make it much easier to begin writing the script when the time comes. The worst anxiety for any writer—facing the blank page or computer screen—will be alleviated because you will have done so much careful thinking and planning before you start writing the first scene, and so the writing will go faster.

The exercise of adapting a story will teach you how to "break the back of the book" and get the story ready for possible filming. Whether you want to follow the structure of the original you have chosen fairly closely or transform it more freely, these steps will enable you to make the story an expression of your own creative ideas. As I promised in the beginning, by the end of the process, if you follow it conscientiously and use my script adaptation of "To Build a Fire" as your model, you should be writing a professional-quality screenplay or at least be well on the way to doing so. You can find London's story in appendix B in this book; you may find it helpful to read it at this point.

Step 1

THE STORY OUTLINE

A Chinese proverb says, "A journey of a thousand miles begins with a single step." This is your first step as a screenwriter.

Write a two-page (double-spaced) outline of the story you choose. The outline should be in narrative paragraph form rather than the skeletal-outline form. Note well: This is *not* an outline of how you would adapt the short story to the screen or how you would change it. Nor is this a critical analysis of the story or a commentary on it. It is simply an outline of the original story, from beginning to end.

Don't quote the story excessively but instead put it in your own words as much as possible. Minimize quotations of dialogue in an outline. Don't start with a short summary of the story and then start telling it again in more detail, as some first-time writers anxiously feel the need to do. And don't leave out the ending; this is not a *TV Guide* teaser but an outline of the entire narrative. Don't assume the reader already knows the story; even though you and I may know it, you are writing for an "ideal reader" who needs to hear this as if for the first time. And although you are condensing the story, tell it in sufficiently clear detail so that all the key points are covered. Use present tense in telling the story ("Tom Joad walks down the highway"), not past tense. Present tense is the standard way of summarizing a dramatic story, and it is the convention for screenwriting, for a film is always happening "now," even if a scene is a flashback. If you are referring to past events in an outline or screenplay, you can use past tense sparingly, but don't do so in describing the action as it unfolds on-screen.

Make sure you establish at the beginning where and when the

story takes place. Identify the characters clearly and give brief physical descriptions, including such key details as age, gender, appearance, and ways of behaving. If you find yourself confused by anything in the story, don't guess but do some research; critical studies abound on the works of great writers. Checking historical references will enable you to understand the story's sociopolitical context. And looking at maps will help you understand the geography of the story you are outlining.

When you are outlining the key story points, give us both the exterior and interior dimensions of the story. Exterior means what the characters do and what the settings are. Interior means what the characters are thinking or feeling. An outline that neglects the interior story only skims the surface and may wind up missing the point of the story entirely.

THE IMPORTANCE OF CREDIT

Just one more thing, as Lieutenant Columbo liked to say: Don't forget to credit the author of the story you are outlining. If you were the author, think how you'd feel if your name were overlooked. Some students keep forgetting to credit the poor author, but one of the most important lessons you should learn as a screenwriter is to respect the work of other writers and never fail to give them credit. When you're a Hollywood writer sitting in your apartment in Santa Monica or a British writer living in the London district of Hoxton and toiling on a script that you hope might reach the screen, one of your most fervent wishes will be that more people would know your name.

And now start putting yourself into the mind of the author...

Outline of "To Build a Fire"

by Jack London

by Joseph McBride

It's seventy-five degrees below zero in the Yukon Territory of Canada—so cold a man's breath will freeze and crack in midair. A man is hiking on the trail one overcast morning in the early 1900s. Despite a warning from an Old-Timer that no one should venture out into the wilderness when it's colder than fifty below, the man is dangerously unimaginative about the cold. He's a red-bearded, stolid white man, a newcomer to the land, somewhere between youth and middle age, who chews tobacco that freezes into amber frost before it can fall from his face.

The man is a logger returning from a surveying trip, heading for his camp about ten miles away, where he expects to find his friends and a warm fire. Dressed in heavy winter clothes, he carries only his lunch for what he expects to be a day's journey. He is accompanied by a gray native husky who views him with careful distance because of the man's habit of addressing him brusquely. All around their small figures is a vast white emptiness.

The man heads toward a creek, occasionally registering surprise at the cold, which causes him to rub his cheeks and nose stiffly. He watches where he places his feet so he doesn't step into a hidden spring. But he dismisses his memories of the Old-Timer's warnings, even as the cold keeps encroaching. Arriving at the forks of the creek, he makes a small fire, eats his lunch, and smokes his pipe briefly before resuming his trek. The dog yearns back toward the fire before following him. He walks a while, quickening his pace.

Suddenly the man breaks through the snow and slips into a spring. He scrambles out and carefully builds another fire to start drying himself. Snow begins cascading from the tree under which he foolishly built the fire. The fire is gone. Panicking, the man goes about preparing another fire, with increasingly useless hands. Eventually he lights all his matches at once, searing his flesh but making a fire. The fire goes out again.

The cold is making the man apathetic, but he struggles to keep his wits. He lurches for the dog but cannot find a way to kill it for warmth. The man rushes wildly along the trail, falling and rising again and again. Eventually he plunges headlong in the snow and sits immobile, considering how to die with dignity. He imagines his friends finding his body—and himself moving among them as he sees it. He recalls again the Old-Timer who warned him and mumbles, "You were right, old hoss; you were right."

The man drowses off into frozen sleep. The dog sits watching. Twilight falls. The dog whines louder and louder as it catches the scent of death. Then, at night, it trots away up the trail in the direction of the camp and other providers of food and fire.

6

Research and Development

What drew me to Jack London's story "To Build a Fire" in the first place? The title. The bluntly elemental nature of this highly concrete phrase promised a flinty story of survival. At a time in my young life when I was just beginning to learn to survive on my own, that touched a nerve, as did the suggestion that the tale would deal with the precarious nature of life in a freezing climate (my native Wisconsin is not quite the Yukon, but I sometimes had to deliver newspapers when it was thirty below zero). The title implied an intense concentration on the physical. That appealed to my desire, as a fledgling screenwriter, to tell stories with visceral impact in the highly physical medium of film. The story more than lived up to the promise of its title with its meticulous detailing of a man's increasingly desperate struggle to stay alive in inhuman conditions.

And since filmmaking involves what Arthur Penn calls "the reconstruction of processes," breaking down and re-creating the process of wilderness survival in cinematic language captured my attention for my first attempt at a screenplay. When I read London's story again for this book and compared it with other stories I thought might be useful for teaching the adaptation process, I found that "To Build a Fire" had lost none of its appeal as a compelling piece of storytelling ideally suited for cinematic adaptation.

Asking yourself what drew you to the story you plan to adapt is a helpful place to begin your own work. Discovering a personal connection you have with a story, finding your own way in, is one of the secrets of successful adaptation. Answering the next logical question—What is the story about?—will enable you to begin stripping the story down to its essentials. Your outline of the original story, if well organized, will reveal its spine and the high points you need to hit as you adapt it for the screen. Having the structure in front of you in a condensed form will show you what's required to get from point A to B to C. The internal logic of the story—its psychological portraiture and thematic line of development—should stand out strongly and clearly in a brief outline. That clarity will help guide the choices you make in your cinematic adaptation.

But why only two pages for this outline? Why not three or four? You can say a lot in two pages. Lincoln's Gettysburg Address is only about 271 words long (depending on what version you count), and it manages to summarize the Civil War with unrivaled eloquence. I have to admit that when I wrote my new outline for "To Build a Fire" for this book, trying my best to keep it tightly focused on the essence of the story, my first draft came in at a little more than three pages—50 percent longer than my own assignment. Somewhat chastened as I set about cutting it down to fit, I recalled numerous instances of students telling me how hard it was to condense a story to a two-page outline (less than five hundred words). I suddenly had more empathy for what I put them through. You may find yourself running into the same problem. But writing to a set length is a valuable exercise, as is learning to write in a compressed fashion. Writing a longer initial outline defeats part of the purpose. Clearing away the underbrush to follow the narrative trail is less effective if too much brush is allowed to remain in the way. (Note: The lengths I suggest for the exercises in this book may seem somewhat at variance with those of the "typed" samples I present, but that's due to the difference in size between book pages and your own typed manuscript pages. I've kept my story outline under five hundred words.)

Time and length are always crucial elements in the art and the business of filmmaking. The aesthetics of screenwriting and directing require a careful attention to the length of individual scenes and how they fit into the whole. Having the ability to "control the time element" is critical for a filmmaker, Alfred Hitchcock told François Truffaut: "The ability to shorten or lengthen time is a primary requirement in filmmaking." And following assignments precisely is a discipline that will stand you in good stead in the professional world.

When I was teaching myself how to write screenplays, I was fortunate to come under the influence of Truffaut's *Hitchcock,* their marvelous 1966 interview book, which I still consider the best single book on the technique of filmmaking. I recommend it to you as the equivalent of a master course with two great directors; careful study of that book can save you years of film school. It may also be the best book on screenwriting, for Hitchcock is a superb teacher, drawing on a lifetime of experience collaborating with other writers (without credit after his early years), and the process he describes of conceiving and executing films is as much a process of writing as it is of directing. At some stages, the two jobs are one, even if at a certain point they radically diverge. It's important to clearly understand the differences between those two jobs as well as their points of overlap.

FINDING THE SPINE OF THE STORY

David Koepp, who has adapted such novels as Michael Crichton's *Jurassic Park* (with Crichton) and H. G. Wells's *The War of the Worlds* (with Josh Friedman) into screenplays for Steven Spielberg, explains how he begins the process of adaptation, by finding the spine of the story:

Adaptations are so much easier than an original script, of course, because you have the benefit of someone else thinking....I go back and scene-card the entire book, look at that outline, and then despair for a while that it's so un-filmlike. Then I start throwing out stuff that I've always hated, or didn't think would work in the movie, but hold on to everything that I think is cool, finding any way I possibly can to keep it, and see what interstitial material I need to write to unite it all. Then, as the drafts develop, it increasingly becomes its own story and less episodic. But you try to hold on to the stuff that made you love the book.

When I wrote my first screenplay of "To Build a Fire" at the beginning of my career, I didn't know enough to do an outline or even any research into the setting or the author of the story. Instead I just plunged in and wrote the script. The more methodical process we will follow with our adaptations will provide benefits I could have drawn from back then, if only I had had a teacher or a book like this one. This time around, I reread "To Build a Fire" three times in a book of London's collected stories before I wrote the two-page outline, and I went to the library to get books on the author. I learned about the genesis of the story and found insights into its themes and style; it was a useful process I hadn't bothered to undertake when I was starting my screenwriting career.

After reading the story repeatedly, I became thoroughly acquainted with all the nuances of its action and characterizations (there are actually two characters, a man and his dog, not counting people the man thinks about on his journey). The third time I read the story, I took a red pen and underlined key words. By then, I was thoroughly familiar with its spine, the man's foolish and desperate attempt to survive in life-threatening cold.

In the first paragraph, I underlined "exceedingly cold and gray" for the atmosphere and "the man turned aside from the main Yukon trail" for the action. Since it's always important in filmmaking to know the time of day when scenes take place and the mood that conveys, I underlined that it was "nine o'clock" (in the morning) when the action starts and that the gloom "made the day dark." Elsewhere I continued to underline action words ("There was a sharp, explosive crackle that startled him"), along with key story points ("He was a newcomer in the land, a *chechaquo*"), physical descriptions ("a crystal beard of the color and solidity of amber"), backstory ("he had come the roundabout way to take a look at the possibilities of getting out logs in the spring"), and so on.

And as Hemingway told fellow novelist John Dos Passos, "Remember to get the weather in your god damned book—weather is very important." Seldom has any story better fit that dictum than "To Build a Fire." With his earthy directness and the blunt simplicity of his style, London was a major influence on the young Hemingway when he was continuing the process of clearing away the thickets of Victorian prose. Especially important in the process of finding the spine of the London story for cinematic adaptation is identifying what Hemingway called "the real thing, the sequence of motion and fact which made the emotion," the action words that indicate important moments and transitions in the narrative.

After studying my marked-up copy of the story for a while and imprinting its elements in my memory so I could write a new screenplay, I put circled numbers in the margins to mark the key stages in the action. I numbered twenty-three stages in the action. Flagging these milestones enabled me to comprehend the shape of the narrative more easily and see its spine more clearly. Since the story includes memory scenes and some fantasies or hallucinations, I used a different kind of numbering system for those elements—1A, 2A, and so forth—to make them stand out as a separate narrative track. Later I will consider more carefully how I might incorporate such scenes.

This method of annotation is not the only way to proceed with outlining a story. Whenever I write a script (or a book), I take a yellow legal-sized notepad and summarize my thoughts in outline form, continually adding to them as I go. I make lists of ideas for scenes in a script, bits of action, and lines of dialogue and jot down information about the settings, the characters, the themes. Writing down your ideas transfers them from the somewhat nebulous region of your head into concrete form on the page. I find this process immensely helpful in crystallizing my ideas. Once you can see your thoughts, you can study, test, and embellish them. The ideas you discard will help you come gradually, by indirection, to ones that make more sense.

I mentioned earlier that it's crucial before writing a screenplay to be able to see the movie playing in your head. You can close your eyes and start having that kind of daydream. The process of taking notes on the visual elements will help you start to see that movie more vividly. When you come to write the script, it should feel like second nature to describe your internal movie. The writing will come much faster, and the images will be more vivid. You will be able to hear the characters saying the words they want to say. That's why the actual writing of the script can be the easiest part of the screenwriter's job—provided you have done enough hard work in the preliminary stages of conception when you are finding the story's spine and starting to surround it with flesh and blood. Then it will begin to live and breathe, and you'll find yourself having to keep pace with what your characters want to do. That, for me, is always the most exciting moment in the writing of a script—when the characters come alive and take over. In that sense the screenwriter is like Gandhi, who once said, "There go my people; I must hurry and catch them, for I am their leader."

GETTING TO THE HEART

Identifying the three-act structure of the story you've chosen is the next task at hand. Examining the structure of "To Build a Fire," I found that it divides clearly into these three acts:

1. A man journeying through the Yukon Territory of Canada gradually becomes fearful of the extreme cold.

2. The man falls through the ice of a hidden spring and tries to dry himself with a fire so he won't freeze.

3. The fire is extinguished by snow falling from a tree, and after failing to relight the fire, the man desperately tries to flee his advancing death.

As this structure became clear, I noticed that the first and final acts each take up 43 percent of the story, and the second act only 14 percent. This is not necessarily a problem in emphasis, for the middle act is highly dramatic. Keeping in mind what Hitchcock said about how critical it is to expand and contract time on the screen, it's worth examining ways to do so with *To Build a Fire* (I'm shifting to putting the title in italics here because I'm referring to the film adaptation I'm going to write; the title of a short story, on the other hand, goes in quotation marks). The part about the man frantically trying to dry himself by building a fire could well deserve expansion to concentrate intently on the details contained in its relatively few pages. And the first act might be worth contracting. Watching the man trek steadily along at the same pace could seem overly repetitive; a film gets its points across more quickly than a piece of literary fiction, because there is such a wealth of visual data for the audience to absorb. Much of that section of London's story is taken up with describing the man's appearance, his character, and the look and feel of the landscape. All those elements could profitably be condensed in the screenplay, and it would serve the dramatic impact of the story to concentrate more of the running time on the man's efforts to survive once his life is directly threatened.

The greatest challenge for a screenwriter in adapting "To Build a Fire" comes not in laying out the external details—which are generously and specifically provided by London—but giving equal dramatic weight to the action and to the man's internal struggle. As I mentioned in the previous chapter, and will stress again, when you outline your story, you must pay attention to both its external and internal dimensions. Without sufficient attention to what your characters are feeling and thinking, what they are doing will seem relatively uninvolving emotionally, no matter how exciting the action may be. Without understanding what drives the characters, what their conflicts are, and what they want, you won't stir the feelings of the audience. The characters' dilemmas, aspirations, and fears will be seen at too much of a distance. And as Towne puts it in the documentary "Screenwriter: Robert Towne" (part of the television series *Screenwriters: Word into Image*), "The single most important question I think that one must ask oneself about a character is, what are they really afraid of? What are they *really* afraid of? And if you ask that question, it's probably for me the single best way of getting into a character. And that, finally, is where stories are told, with a character that's real."

That advice gets to the heart of "To Build a Fire." The horrifying spectacle of a man freezing to death is the central action of the story, but the real drama is the man's growing fear of danger.

Initially he seems complacent and oblivious to the grave situation he is in. "The trouble with him was that he was without imagination," writes London. The man remembers the warning given him by the "old-timer" that no one should travel in the wilderness when it's more than fifty degrees below zero. London masterfully plays out the man's repeated memories of that warning, gradually bringing it into clearer and clearer focus as the man slowly recognizes the depths of his dilemma. At first he does not take the warning seriously: "It did not lead him to meditate upon his frailty as a creature of temperature and upon man's frailty in general...." Later he dismisses the obsessively recalled warning with smug contempt, even after he breaks through the ice: "Well, here he was; he had had the accident; he was alone; and he had saved himself. Those old-timers were rather womanish, some of them, he thought." But as events escalate out of control like a row of falling dominoes, the true dimensions of his situation force themselves into the man's consciousness, compelling him to recognize "the conjectural field of immortality and man's place in the universe."

Yes, this is the drama, but the major problem in conveying it on-screen is that the man seems somewhat opaque, at least in the early stages. Not only is he "not much given to thinking," but the cold gives him a frozen-faced appearance, with his heavy beard crusted with tobacco juice. The dog, with its keener natural instincts, senses "a vague but menacing apprehension" well ahead of the man's dawning consciousness of danger. The dog will be a useful character in drawing contrast with the man's duller wits. The screenwriter must continually find ways to emphasize the man's state of mind, from reckless complacency to chastened understanding. If filmed with sufficient depth, *To Build a Fire* can be seen as a tragedy in the true Aristotelian sense. It is a story of overweening pride leading to a fall, a story of the smugness of humankind in the face of the power of nature. To this man, with all his human failings, "comes wisdom through the awful grace of God" (as Aeschylus put it in *Agamemnon*). Such understanding lies at the heart of classical tragedy.

Dramatizing that progression from complacency to humiliated self-awareness is a challenge because of the man's relatively inexpressive nature (although his body language is more expressive than his conscious acting out of feelings) and because the story offers few opportunities for dialogue in the wilderness. The man can give commands to the dog, but having him talk much to the dog or to himself would seem like a cheat. When a solitary character does that, it usually feels as if he's actually addressing the audience. You can (as I will) use dialogue more liberally for flashback or imaginary scenes of the man with his fellow loggers at camp. But if the task of learning the craft of screenwriting is discovering how to tell a story primarily in images—as I am teaching you to do in this book—using narration to describe the man's feelings would be even more of a cheat, even if the 1969 BBC TV film version of *To Build a Fire* does so extensively.

Now that I have finished writing my script, I finally watched that version, adapted by David Cobham and Anthony Short and directed by Cobham, with Ian Hogg as "the Chechaquo." It is a well-directed, engrossing film that captures the intensity of the situation and makes us feel the man's growing desperation as he struggles against the elements. Cobham takes his time in drawing out each moment of anguish, often excruciatingly; the man's vain attempt to kill the dog for warmth is particularly gripping. But sometimes this hour-long film's leisurely pace seems to work against the mounting suspense the story should communicate. Although Orson Welles's delivery of the narration is moving, I did feel that it distances the viewer too much from the action. The narration is often redundant, telling us what we are seeing. It gives some background on the Klondike (largely unnecessary) and explores the man's thoughts and feelings, which seems an overly convenient avenue into his mind. Allowing us to watch him and *infer* his thoughts and feelings from what we see would be more powerful dramatically. Also, the fact that the narration is in the past tense, as in the short story, tends to distance us further by implying that the man's fate is sealed from the beginning and his struggles will be fruitless.

After watching this version of *To Build a Fire,* I am all the more glad I resisted the easy route of using narration for my adaptation. Doing without it makes the story feel that much more immediate and involving. And for the purposes of learning how to write a screenplay, the discipline of telling the story without relying heavily on dialogue or narration is a valuable approach to mastering the craft of "writing in pictures." After I've acquainted you with the basic elements of visual storytelling, I will discuss the art of writing dialogue in chapter 11. To think about dialogue first in screenwriting is to put the cart before the horse.

DEBATABLE CHOICES

Some of the choices I made when I was trying to eliminate parts of the story from my new outline are debatable. Some may have been mistakes. But in screenwriting, mistakes are not irrevocable.

To keep the story to its essentials, I left out some, but not all, of the man's memories of the "old-timer" warning him about the dangers of the extreme cold. And I omitted the man remembering the tale of a man who killed a steer and climbed inside to warm himself during a blizzard. That impels the man in our story to try to kill the dog. Perhaps I was simply avoiding the decision about whether the account of the steer needs to be in the film. I left out details of the dog creeping away and watching the man with wary curiosity as he thrashes his arms to try to warm himself. The dog is somewhat neglected in my outline, but he will need to be built up as an almost equal character. London refers to the dog as "it," but I've decided to make the dog male in my script, as I do in my outline, to make the character more specific. I cut down on other physical details in the outline, such as the man smashing his fingers against his leg to unfreeze them (early in the story) and becoming panicked by his inability to clutch hold of the matches (midway through the story). London's comment that the man, at the end, "entertained in his mind the conception of meeting death with dignity" also found no place in my outline.

These are not unimportant details. They convey critical stages in the man's consciousness. They should be in the film in some way, but I thought, rightly or wrongly, that the outline told the story sufficiently without them and that the missing points were implicit—the invisible part of the iceberg. But one of the advantages of doing the outline was that it forced me to consider such questions and weigh the importance of each scene. Exactly how I will incorporate the man's fantasies and memories, and to what extent, is a question that will take a lot of trial and error to answer. I also had to ask myself how I might convey on-screen, without words, that the man is entertaining the conception of meeting death with dignity. That's a tall order for a screenwriter but one that will have to be addressed.

You'll find yourself making similarly difficult choices in boiling the story you choose down to its essentials. I hope that this exercise will not prove to be too much of a Procrustean bed, but rather a helpful starting point in your decision-making process. Reassure yourself with the thought that you can put off some decisions for further mulling (as I did) and that you can lift discarded scenes from your longer outline draft (if you have the same trouble I did with length) and put them into your script. You may find that a scene you dropped must be in the film and that a scene you thought was important can be omitted or suggested in a brief image or two. It's natural in constructing scenes to elaborate on details and find space for nuances that may not have belonged in the outline. The process of conveying a clear and detailed "character arc" (a bit of jargon I try to avoid but find occasionally useful) will require painstaking care in your screenplay. How to get across what your characters are thinking at every step of the story is the toughest job you will face, and potentially the most rewarding.

So don't obsess too much about your outline; this is only the first stage of a work in progress.

HOMEWORK

You need to know enough about the period and setting of the story to get the facts straight in your outline. I find it continually surprising how many beginning screenwriters leave such basic facts out of their outlines entirely or get them confused. The social context and mood of a story are quite different depending on if it takes place in 1911, 1961, or 2011. The Michigan woods don't bear much resemblance to the hills of Afghanistan. A woman of 60 has needs and preoccupations far different from those of a woman of 20. A man of 104 won't get around in the same way as most men in their 60s. Writing your characters' ages and physical descriptions precisely requires some knowledge of life; a student once handed me a script that described its central character as "an elderly man of 41," which made me wonder how he would describe *me*.

All such salient facts need to be clearly delivered to the reader near the beginning of your outline. Sometimes beginning writers dribble out such information in the course of the outline or script, as if someone's age or where she lives is only an incidental aside. In a novel or short story, a writer can afford to be more artful or coy about identifying the people, the places, and the period; novels can be more elliptical about characterizations and conceal story points more subtly than is common in screenplays. The writer of a screenplay must give such facts right up front, in every outline and every draft of the script, and must do so explicitly and unambiguously, even at the risk of seeming heavy-handed. The people who read your script are not reading for idle curiosity but actually considering whether or not to make your film, and if they don't understand what's going on in your story, where it's taking place, or who the characters are, they won't bother guessing for more than a page or two.

A producer once told me a story of making a World War II movie with the great Japanese actor Toshirō Mifune. Mifune had actually fought in the war, and he was becoming increasingly exasperated with his young director, who, he thought, didn't know enough about the subject. As they were preparing to shoot a scene on a beach in the South Pacific, Mifune, who was short but fierce and built like a tank, suddenly ended the discussion by grabbing the director by the throat, lifting him up in the air, and shaking him up and down, screaming, "Must do homework! MUST DO HOMEWORK!"

Your homework is the research for your script. It involves

giving your script a firm grounding in historical reality—unless you're dealing in outright fantasy, and that's an even greater challenge, because then you have to make up your own reality. If your story is set in the past, you need to get out of your contemporary mind-set and reimagine the past. Period authenticity is not simply a matter of getting the physical details right; it's a matter of how the people behave. Thorough research into the period(s) of your story, by studying books, photographs, old newspapers and magazines, and documentary films, will give you endless ideas for scenes and texture. One of the key scenes in *Rock 'n' Roll High School*—the evil principal staging a burning of rock 'n' roll records on the school lawn—was suggested to me by a documentary on the 1950s that I watched for my research: it included a scene of a disk jockey burning a record he detested.

Without a solid grounding in the social and historical background of the story, your script runs the danger of being vague, inconsistent, or, at worst, embarrassingly inaccurate. I had a student screenplay that took place during the Korean War but described a soldier as walking through the jungle humming a tune by the Grateful Dead. Perhaps in a surrealistic film that would work just fine, but this was supposed to be a work of gritty realism; evidently the student was confusing Korea with Vietnam. Other students have had World War I soldiers using weapons not used until the Vietnam War; it's easy enough these days to check such information on authoritative Internet sites.

This is part of your job as a screenwriter; you are the film's initial art director. I often relied on old copies of *Life* magazine, which I would find in libraries or used-book stores. They were invaluable for pictures of how people lived in the eras I was writing about; the advertisements were particularly helpful in showing people's clothing styles, cars, and household products. For a script about the early days of Western filmmaking, I not only studied films made in that period and interviewed Allan Dwan and other silent-movie directors but also bought a reproduction of the 1908 Sears, Roebuck catalogue, which enabled me to look up any item of clothing or prop I needed to mention.

Revolutionary Road, adapted by Justin Haythe from the 1961 novel by Richard Yates and directed by Sam Mendes, looks right for its period—the mid-1950s haircuts and decor are carefully chosen, and people do a lot of smoking and drinking—but it's short on social and cultural context. The characters seem utterly uninvolved in their times (the only reference to the culture of 1955 is a scene of kids watching *Howdy Doody*). So it's no coincidence that the film's portrayal of the married couple played by Kate Winslet and Leonardo DiCaprio weirdly oscillates from clichéd notions of repressed fifties behavior to uninhibited emotional acting out of noisy desperation that would make more sense in the America of the film's year of release, 2008. In *Pearl Harbor,* a highly anachronistic 2001 film, the haircuts look too modern for 1941, nobody smokes, and all the U.S. Navy nurses act like the characters in *Sex and the City.* Such a cavalier lack of period verisimilitude would be fatal to this Michael Bay–directed monstrosity even if the two lead characters, the navy fliers played by Ben Affleck and Josh Hartnett, weren't such cardboard figures.

For contrast, look at Steven Spielberg's *Schindler's List* or *Saving Private Ryan* to see the benefit of meticulous research and careful thought by the director and his screenwriters (Steven Zaillian and Robert Rodat, respectively) about how people looked and acted during World War II. The liquidation of the Kraków ghetto in *Schindler's List* and the D-Day landing in *Saving Private Ryan* are overwhelming immersions in the realities of historical events. The fine level of evocative physical and psychological detail in these films convinces you that you are there.

It may be tempting to have your historical characters act like people you see on the street, but that defeats the purpose of setting a film in a different period. And even a contemporary screenplay requires research if you want to be accurate in the details of how people live, work, and talk. Your research into the time period will help you understand why the characters act the way they do and why their actions have such particular social consequences.

PERIOD OR MODERN?

The question of whether to keep a story in its original period or not is one of the most important issues facing writers adapting a literary work. You and I need to think about this question carefully as we go about adapting our stories for the screen. Paul Schrader, the screenwriter of *Taxi Driver,* once told me he thought there must be a very good reason to justify setting a story in period. Going to the trouble and expense of a period setting is pointless for mere nostalgia, Schrader thought; the story should only be set in period if that's the only way to tell it properly, if essential elements of the story would otherwise be lost.

Unfortunately, I was unable to follow Schrader's advice when my screenplay *Blood and Guts,* set in the 1950s, went into production in 1977. For budget reasons beyond my control, it was changed to a contemporary story. That hurt the film, because the central character lost some of his raison d'être. The aging wrestler Dandy Dan (William Smith) was loosely based on Gorgeous George, the 1940s and '50s wrestling star who affected a foppish, effete manner that outraged people in that sexually benighted era. We played on some of the same antagonisms for satirical purposes, but the effect was seriously diluted in the anything-goes atmosphere of the 1970s. (Yes, that script was something of a precursor of *The Wrestler,* the 2008 film written by Robert D. Siegel and directed by Darren Aronofsky that gives Mickey Rourke such a magnificent role.)

"To Build a Fire" is such an elemental tale of man versus nature that, on first glance, it seems its basic situation could exist in any period. However, in today's world, the man might have a radio, a cell phone, or a GPS device with him on his journey, and that equipment could save his life. He would not have to be as ignorant of the actual temperature, and he could call for help. The man would also not have to rely on a box of fragile matches to build a fire. He could carry a magnesium fire-starter device, a small piece of portable equipment that, according to Christopher Nyerges's book *How to Survive Anywhere: A Guide for Urban, Suburban, Rural, and Wilderness Environments,* is the "best, cheapest, and easiest modern fire-starting method." So it would make sense to keep *To Build a Fire* in its original period of the early 1900s, when the man would be more isolated and would have to rely on his own limited resources to survive.

But how to convey the period? In a setting away from civilization, the only details that would suggest the period would be the man's clothing and the gear he has with him. His box of matches, which already carries great symbolic weight in the story, would assume additional importance as a period indicator through its design and brand label. Images of the logging camp the man thinks about, if included in the film, would offer more extensive opportunities for capturing the time and place, however briefly.

GETTING THE ATMOSPHERE

Jack London is not known as a subtle stylist. His blunt, utilitarian approach to storytelling made him part of what was known as the social realist school of writing. London and Ernest Hemingway, whom he influenced, dealt with harsh, gritty subject matter and rebelled against the ornate style of Victorian writing. The utilitarian nature of London's prose is no detriment to his literary ability. The precision of detail in his writing, his psychological acuteness, and his close attention to action and physical processes (he advised writers to "get the atmosphere") make him not only a powerful storyteller but also an ideal collaborator for a screenwriter.

Like Hemingway, London was popular partly because of the mystique surrounding his use of personal experience to give verisimilitude to his work. London's adventures prospecting for gold in the Yukon in 1897–98 gave him material not only for "To Build a Fire" but also for other well-known stories and books, including the novel *The Call of the Wild.* The authenticity of his tales of life in the wilderness helped win him a vast following much like the one Hemingway would enjoy later with his vividly rendered accounts of the strenuous life in exotic locales. Both writers give us intense, vicarious experiences of dangerous occupations.

The first version of "To Build a Fire," published in 1902 as a juvenile story in *Youth's Companion,* stemmed from accounts London had heard of men who froze to death on the trail. "Man after man in the Klondike has died alone after getting his feet wet, through failure to build a fire," he wrote his editor at *The Century Magazine,* which published the revised version of the story in 1908. But London's first attempt flinched from that reality: the man survives with scars that always remind him of his close call. London was conscious of the commercial liability of stories that lacked happy endings. And yet, after reading a harrowing account of such a death in a 1904 book by Jeremiah Lynch, *Three Years in the Klondike,* London was emboldened to rewrite his story. He "changed the theme from one of adventure to one of tragedy," as Franklin Walker writes in *Jack London and the Klondike: The Genesis of an American Writer.* The unsparing honesty of "To Build a Fire" helps account for its lasting appeal.

The story's stark simplicity makes it relatively easy to adapt effectively to the screen in the short-film format. "I rarely handle plots, but nearly always do handle situations," London once explained. "Take the different ones of my stories which you may recollect, and you will see that they are usually built about some simple but striking human situation." No major changes need be made in "To Build a Fire" to make it accessible to a modern audience. The challenge is to bring it alive in a different medium with the same intensity London achieves in prose.

London's Darwinian view of nature is manifest in his fascination with life-or-death struggles and his theme of the survival of the fittest. While the man is fatally flawed by both hubris and inexperience, the dog, with its superior instincts, survives. The fact that the man is nameless reinforces the allegorical nature of the story, making him seem a representative of humanity in his arrogant complacency, his weakness, and the fighting courage he musters in his failed attempt to survive. But like all good allegories, "To Build a Fire" succeeds by "getting the atmosphere" and putting across its ideas with concrete imagery that makes them implicit in the action.

Step 2
THE ADAPTATION OUTLINE

Now that you've outlined the story you've chosen to adapt, write an outline of your adaptation. This two-page (double-spaced) outline should tell the story of the film you want to write, based, however loosely, on the original story. As we've discussed, you are free to change the setting, the time period, and the characters as long as what you are writing is still a valid adaptation of the story. Deviating too radically from the original—so that it is all but unrecognizable as an adaptation—would defeat the purpose of the exercise, but substantial changes can still be made within the basic thematic framework. If you want to adapt the story "faithfully," that's fine too; neither a faithful nor a freer adaptation is intrinsically superior to the other. The quality depends on the execution.

Tell your complete story in narrative paragraph form, in the present tense, including detailed character and setting descriptions and the key incidents. Be succinct, but pay attention to the themes and ideas of the story while concentrating primarily on descriptions of the action. Don't neglect the inner dramas and conflicts of your characters; dramatize them. Although you shouldn't dwell on visual details in this brief outline, it would be good to give some indication of the style of the film, especially if there are any unusual elements, such as fantasies or other stylized scenes. It's crucial to lay out the structure of your adaptation clearly. If you include flashbacks, make that clear and indicate the changes of time period as you go back and forth from the framing story to the flashbacks. Put the scenes in the order in which they will appear on-screen.

Although you are telling your story in a compressed way, don't summarize events too much. This should not read like a film review or commentary on a film, but should instead tell the story directly and in an entertaining enough way to grab the reader's interest in its potential for filming. When you give the title of your film (in italics in an outline or treatment, though not in the script itself), make sure to credit the original story and its author. If you are keeping the original title, you don't need to mention it again while crediting "the short story by…," but if you are changing the title, you should credit the source by its original title.

Now make the story your own. Have fun with it. Be imaginative!

To Build a Fire

by Joseph McBride

Based on the short story
by Jack London

The vast whiteness of the Yukon Territory
stretches, almost unbroken, to the horizon. A
faint line—a trail—points toward low rolling
snow-covered hills and a winding, frozen creek.
Eventually two specks come into view over a rise.
A man and a dog. The man is white, stocky, about
six feet tall, bearded, mittened, garbed in a
heavy woolen coat with a fur hood and clomping
along in fur-lined boots. It is a gray Canadian
morning in January 1902. The man's name is Red,
after his beard. But the tobacco he is chewing
turns his whiskers a frozen amber. The dog
following at a wary distance is a gray husky.

Red is trekking back to his logging camp ten miles away. As he slogs through the snow, he spits to test the temperature. His spittle crackles explosively in the air, surprising him. Beating his arms against his sides and chest for warmth, he thinks yearningly of the camp. A brief flashback to a few days earlier shows several lumberjacks, large and bearded, huddled around a stove in their cabin eating stew, making plans for their spring logging; Red plays "Oh, Dem Golden Slippers" on an accordion. In the wilderness, Red's stolid face creases with pain. He watches the ground carefully as he treads through the snow along Henderson Creek, fearful of stepping through hidden ice. He brusquely orders the dog to trot ahead.

A series of dissolves shows them moving through different landscapes as morning turns into afternoon. Stopping for lunch (biscuits with bacon) and a pipe over a fire, Red remembers an Old-Timer we see at the camp warning him that no one should ever travel alone when it's more than fifty below zero. Laughing hollowly, Red calls him "just an old woman." Suddenly the whiteness under his feet gives way. His legs plunge straight down into a hidden stream. Red scrambles out, alarmed. He spots a tree and runs over to grab handfuls of brush and twigs. He struggles to build a fire. His hands are numb, but he gets the fire going and starts drying his legs. He does not realize that the snowy branches of the tree are about to capsize. The fire abruptly goes out under the weight of the snow.

The dog circles fearfully as Red, agitated, tries to rebuild the fire, piling more brush away from the tree. His hands are almost useless. He yanks the whole bunch of matches from his coat and strikes them together with the heels of his bared hands. The matches burst into flame. But a piece of moss falls onto the fire, and as he clears it away, he snuffs out the fire. Red lurches for the dog, but he scurries away. Panicked, Red runs wildly along the trail. He plunges headlong into the snow. Sitting immobile, he laughs bitterly at himself. He becomes drowsy and peaceful. He begins imagining his friends finding him dead in the snow—and himself moving among them, seeing his own body. He tells the Old-Timer, "You were right, old hoss; you were right."

Reaching toward the horizon, Red drowses off into frozen sleep. The dog sits watching as twilight falls. He begins whining as he catches the scent of death. Night comes. The dog howls at the stars. Then he trots away, up the trail in the direction of camp, leaving the man's frozen corpse behind, his arms vainly outstretched.

7

The Elements of Screenwriting

So now you've written the outline for your adaptation. That wasn't so hard, was it? With the benefit of a writing collaborator, you probably found it easier than you expected to construct a good plan for a movie. The original writer's framework provided a solid foundation for your own ideas, twists, and nuances. With each successive step you take in the process, you will find yourself increasingly liberated to come up with fresh ideas. You will perform more audaciously on that creative high-wire thanks to the safety net provided by the author you've chosen to adapt.

Later in this chapter, I will discuss the pros and cons of the sample outline I've provided for my adaptation of London's "To Build a Fire" and suggest ways you can solve any story problems you might be encountering as you prepare to expand your outline into a treatment. But before I do so, I want to offer a few thoughts on the crucial importance of a sound writing style. Without clarity, which is foremost in importance for a screenwriter, what you are trying to communicate will be confusing or obscure, and your reader will have to guess at your creative intentions, which will make it hard for the reader to envision the film. The clarity of your writing is created by precision of language, cohesiveness of thought, logic in organization, and care in the employment of writing mechanics.

Poor writing mechanics are an epidemic these days. When I began teaching screenwriting in 2000, I was surprised to see what serious problems many people have with writing basic

English prose. People are reading less in this electronic age, and our educational system not only hasn't compensated for that problem but has actually made things worse by failing to ensure that everyone learns the basics of English composition. If you are already a writer of lucid English prose, someone who has mastered the fundamentals of grammar, syntax, spelling, and punctuation, good for you. Now you are ready to put those skills to use professionally. But we all have some problems with our writing, and it's a lifetime task to master the writing of English prose; the irregularities and inconsistencies of our language are what make it so fascinating, but they also are a challenge. If you lack some of the fundamentals, you must quickly get up to speed on these basic tools. Unclear, sloppy prose will cause a screenplay to be tossed aside after the first few pages.

This is not to say that every professional screenwriter writes with the graceful precision Joan Didion or Don DeLillo bring to their prose or is as fluidly gifted with visual imagery as Ray Bradbury or Stephen King. Since a screenplay is not primarily designed for publication as a self-contained work but is a utilitarian document for the use of your fellow filmmakers (screenwriter Sam Hamm wryly refers to "this odd paraliterary genre we toil in"), having an elegant style is not the sine qua non of good screenwriting. A writer may get by with a few errors, but if his script is so poorly written that it causes the reader to doubt his writing skills and intelligence, he is in trouble. If someone writes fairly well but doesn't bother cleaning up errors before submitting a script, the reader will think she lacks self-respect. Worst of all, the reader will stop paying attention to the story the writer is trying to tell. A writer only flowers when she can express her ideas with precision. Aspiring writers should banish the notion (often heard from awkward stylists) that disregarding the conventions of written English with reckless abandon is a sign of "creativity." You can only go beyond the conventions once you know how they work.

Do the reader's work for her as much as possible; be kind

to the reader so she can concentrate on your story, not on trying to figure out what you mean. Always proofread your work carefully and clean up grammatical, spelling, and punctuation errors. That will help immeasurably in making a script easier to read, and ease of reading is one of the first requisites of the screenplay form. Correct punctuation will enable your writing to flow unimpeded. Hemingway wrote his publisher in the 1920s, "My attitude toward punctuation is that it ought to be as conventional as *possible*. The game of golf would lose a good deal if croquet mallets and billiard cues were allowed on the putting green. You ought to be able to show that you can do it a good deal better than anyone else with the regular tools before you have a license to bring in your own improvements."

The best cure for writing problems is constant practice, and the quickest remedy for what ails our writing is to read *The Elements of Style* by William Strunk Jr. and E. B. White. This short (105-page) book succinctly describes and corrects the most common writing errors, as well as giving valuable tips on improving your writing style. Dorothy Parker, the poet, short-story writer, and screenwriter, once wrote, "If you have any young friends who aspire to become writers, the second-greatest favor you can do them is to present them with copies of *The Elements of Style*. The first-greatest, of course, is to shoot them now, while they're happy."

One of the handiest features of *The Elements of Style* is that it provides bad and good examples of each rule side by side. You can make your own list of some of the errors you commit most often and study the book to learn how to fix them. If you are confused about when to use commas and when not to, Strunk and White will set you straight. And if you tend to be vague in your writing, as many beginning writers are, *The Elements of Style* will teach you how to *"Use definite, specific, concrete language,"* a rule especially valuable for a screenwriter.

SITZFLEISCH; OR,
THE IMPORTANCE OF GOOD WRITING HABITS

A corollary of writing with precision is presenting your work with care. Your work represents you, and if you don't show self-respect in your presentation, the reader won't respect you or what you write. Revise everything you write carefully before submitting it. Diligently refine your prose by stripping away needless words and cleaning up any problems. Make it a firm practice never to turn in a first draft. Tennessee Williams once said that a play isn't written, it's rewritten. The same goes for screenplays. Rarely is a first draft worth submitting. Flannery O'Connor once observed that anyone's first draft looks like a chicken ran all over it. She continually rewrote her work, telling her editor, "When the grim reaper comes to get me, he'll have to give me a few extra hours to revise my last words."

It's amazing how quickly you can improve a first draft by rearranging, tightening, and polishing your prose. Having limited time is a poor excuse for submitting work that could easily be improved. Even spending half an hour proofreading and cleaning up your prose will have a substantial effect on its quality. When I worked for newspapers, I made it a rule to always do a second draft of a story, even when I was under a tight deadline. Any screenplay probably will need a lot of rewriting.

Robert Towne writes of "the pervasive tendency to underestimate the true difficulty of the screenplay form" and complains that most people don't realize "how disciplined a good script must be, and how much work goes into achieving that discipline." Towne is a notoriously painstaking writer. "You can't wing it," he says. "In the case of *Chinatown,* I was constantly trying to organize it. I wrote at least twenty different step outlines—long, long step outlines. Usually I have a pretty clear idea of where a screenplay is going, even if I don't know every step of the way." Telling his intricate story of social and personal crime through the prism of the detective-story genre, which revolves around a character searching for the truth of a mysterious situation, might have seemed a way to simplify the narrative vortex Towne faced in writing *Chinatown*. But he discovered that the complexity of the genre itself intensified his difficulties: "I was struggling through the first and second drafts simply trying to figure out the story for myself."

The kind of dogged persistence Towne exemplifies is critical to success. Writing every day, whether you feel like it or not, is the sign of a professional writer. Oddly enough, if you force yourself to write when you don't feel good, or when you don't feel "inspired," you usually will find yourself feeling better and starting to feel inspired. When I was trying to learn how to write a novel, I asked a novelist how she managed to overcome the problem I was having in getting started. "Apply your *tuchus* to the seat of the chair" was her succinct advice. If you do so, you develop what's known in the trade as *Sitzfleisch*—a Yiddish word referring to a durable ass for writing.

Beginning writers often attribute their inability to function to the specter of "writer's block." But every writer, no matter how successful, faces a form of writer's block every single day. The successful writers are those who find ways of overcoming it. Granted that there are few things more terrifying than putting pen to blank page or turning on the computer screen and facing a blank file. But the only way to deal with that terror is to confront it. W. C. Fields's cure for insomnia was "Get plenty of sleep." The cure for writer's block is "Do plenty of writing." One sure way to get started I learned from Hemingway: "The best way is always to stop when you are going good and when you know what will happen next." If you do so, you will never be at a loss to know how to begin the next day. Hemingway added that you shouldn't think about what you are writing until you resume work: "That way your subconscious will work on it all the time. But if you think about it consciously or worry about it you will kill it and your brain will be tired before you start." That advice has helped me countless times by enabling me to pick up easily from where I stopped the day before.

If you don't have any good ideas when you sit at your desk, or if your head feels groggy, just start taking random notes about your story, and eventually more cogent thoughts will begin forming themselves on the page. Or do what the novelist W. Somerset Maugham, the author of *Of Human Bondage,* would do each morning: He would start writing his name on a piece of paper and write it over and over again until he eventually started thinking of something else to write.

Another valuable piece of advice was given to students at San Francisco State University by Francis Ford Coppola. He said that after you write your pages for the day, "Turn them over and leave them. Do not read the pages. Because if you read the pages, there is a hormone injected in the glandular system of young artists that makes them hate what they're doing. Don't go back and read it until you have the whole little pile of ninety-eight pages or a hundred and five pages, and then brace yourself and sit down and really enjoy it and read it through. Then I make a little step outline and rewrite the pages." I have followed that practice religiously in my work, believing in the mantra of the great baseball pitcher Satchel Paige, "Don't look back. Something might be gaining on you."

THE FRAMEWORK

Let's break down some of the key elements of my adaptation outline to remind us of the essentials that need to be covered in outlining a film (I'll highlight those elements in boldface). They include **exposition, location, time period, characterization,** and the use of **action words** to tell the story.

In writing my adaptation outline, I tended to cut back on the fine details of the man's behavior as he becomes increasingly conscious of the extreme cold and tries to save himself with fire.

Those details are what will make the script come alive. But for the purposes of laying out the structure and making decisions about how to get from A to B to C, I didn't need as much lace-work in every scene. The Yukon terrain, such an integral part of the story, can be described with more specificity later. The man's actions can be described in excruciatingly minute detail to heighten the suspense in the screenplay. But for now, focusing on this compression is key, and more economical wording is better to sketch out the high points of the action. Following are some of the elements of screenwriting that I used to convey them.

You'll notice that I tried to give **a sense of the opening shots** of the movie in the way I described the terrain (implying a long shot, closer shots, and eventually a close-up), conveying the **exposition without using technical terms.** The story gets more quickly to the man himself, in the first sentence, and that would have worked well enough, but I wanted to give a visual idea of the vastness and indifference of nature. And as I pointed out earlier, choosing your opening images is a means of establishing your theme. With your exposition (the methodical laying out of story elements to orient the reader), you're telling the audience how to "read" your story and what's most important about it. In this case, I bore in mind London's comment that the man's lack of imagination, his fatal flaw, did not lead him to reflect on "man's frailty in general" and "man's place in the universe." This is some broad philosophy to get into a few shots, and the ideas need to be expressed in other ways throughout the film, but a visual representation of mankind's relative insignificance in nature seems a good chord to strike at the beginning of the film. A film is constructed like a symphony, in which themes are struck early, developed with variations, and brought back together by the end in a grand summation.

I was careful to identify the **location** (after checking a map of the Yukon Territory of Canada) and to specify the **time period** in a way that the story does not do explicitly. The year 1902 is the date of the story's first publication, and I chose January as the month not only because it is the one specified in the original version, but also because that intensifies the feeling of cold. And I took care to give a fairly comprehensive, though brief, word picture of the man—his clothing, his bodily appearance, his somewhat robotic way of moving. London originally named the character Tom Vincent but made him nameless in the final version. To make "the man" seem more real to the reader, and less of an allegorical abstraction, I gave him a name, Thomas "Red" McGarrity, even if we may not hear it on-screen.

Naming a man after his beard may not be the height of writerly imagination, but "Red" is a good, simple nickname and one that seems natural for the loggers' milieu. Naming a character is often a reflection of the writer's whims and experience. Billy Wilder, a sports fan, often named characters after athletes (one of his favorite and recurring character names, Sheldrake, came from Eddie Sheldrake, a guard on the UCLA basketball squad). I gave the man in *To Build a Fire* the name of a character for whom I have a sentimental fondness, the wrestling manager Red Henkel, marvelously played by Henry Beckman in my film *Blood and Guts*. Naming characters after people you know also often works well, although for legal reasons it's better not to use both first and last names of actual people for characters but to combine names from different sources.

Although I've still scanted **the character of the dog** somewhat in this outline, for which London would probably scold me, I've given some indications of his wary relationship with the man, and I intend to develop the dog fully in the screenplay, in which he will help provide dramatic tension by interacting with the man and demonstrating a superior, instinctual understanding of nature. That contrast will be helpful in elaborating on the theme of man's frailty.

I tried to use **action words** as much as possible in the outline. I found myself compressing the action of the first part of the story. Although it takes up half the outline, that part will play for less than half of the film's running time. But it is important to use sufficient space in the outline to establish the characters, the set-ting, and the situation. Making an exception to the general rule about minimizing technical terms in screenwriting, I indicated a series of dissolves to show the passage of time and the progress of the journey. That seemed the only way to get the idea across quickly, and in any case, a screenplay should indicate transitions between scenes set in different locations and times (e.g., "CUT TO," "DISSOLVE TO"). I left the details of those scenes overly vague in the outline, which is a flaw, but I was stymied by lack of space and felt compelled to start getting to the heart of the drama, the man's life-or-death battle with cold and fire. This involved coming to terms with some specific challenges in how to convey those elements.

How to deal with Red's **memories and fantasies** led me to some creative decisions in the outline. I chose to establish this separate track of reality early in the story, so it wouldn't seem to be coming out of the blue later and also because it helped set up the element of the Old-Timer who gave Red the unheeded warning about not venturing out into the snow when the temperature is colder than fifty below zero. While I was trying to figure out how to work that in, I realized I could profitably link the Old-Timer with the images of Red's friends sitting around a fire at the logging camp, by showing the old man as part of the camp. Combining such ele-ments helps streamline the story and should give opportunities for greater visual depth in the flashback scenes.

Getting in the spirit of creation, I thought of someone **playing music** and then thought, "Why not have Red be the one playing an accordion?" This gives Red a less stolid dimension, and the music could be echoed sadly later in the film. Indicating a song in a script can help convey the period and enhance the mood you seek to create. I chose "Oh, Dem Golden Slippers," a popular American song from the nineteenth century by James A. Bland, because I've heard it with pleasure in such John Ford movies as *Young Mr. Lincoln* and *My Darling Clementine* and because its lilting tune conveys the gaiety of dancing. The light-footedness, warmth, and companionship suggested by the song provide piquant counterpoint to the heavy-footed solitude experienced by Red on the frozen trail.

In *To Build a Fire,* we need **a sense of what the man is heading toward** and **the warmth of which he is deprived** through his own failure to heed the advice of a wiser comrade. This motif, used in flashbacks, would strengthen the eerie payoff at the end when his friends show up and discover the dead body in the snow, with the dead man among them in this fantasy, looking at his own corpse. London also indicates a separate vision of the Old-Timer at Sulphur Creek looking "warm and comfortable, and smoking a pipe," as the dead man admits the old man was right. I haven't yet decided whether this would work better as a last vision of warmth or whether it's just as effective, and less scattered, to have the Old-Timer among the party in the snow.

The **final image** of Red's frozen corpse with "his arms vainly outstretched" stems from my research. The account of the actual death on the trail that influenced London when he read Jeremiah Lynch's book *Three Years in the Klondike* includes such a detail:

Though only five minutes could have gone by, the terror of death was upon him. The Ice King slew him with appalling rapidity, and when his companion arrived, scarce fifteen minutes later, he found the body already cold and rigid, kneeling on the snow and ice, while the hands, partially closed together and uplifted as in adoration or prayer to God, held yet within their palms the unlighted match.... It was found impossible to remove his arms and hands from the attitude of entreaty in which they were placed, and the body was brought so to Dawson, and later buried without attempting to change their position.

London chose not to incorporate this arresting image of futile supplication, but it seems **a powerful way to end the movie,** an eloquent and melancholy image with dramatic and metaphorical significance. I didn't specifically mention that the man might have been praying but chose to leave his attitude ambiguous.

Perhaps I will embellish this image more in the screenplay and add the detail of the unlighted match in the man's hand. The ghastliness of the image, so suited to expressing the terrible nature of death by freezing, also reminded me of Stanley Kubrick's image of the death of Jack Torrance (Jack Nicholson) in *The Shining,* his ferocious face in the snowy maze mocked by frozen immobility. Providing explicit film "homages" is sometimes distracting, but this would be a more subtle reference, and the image of Red reaching for something greater than himself, or simply reaching for help that never came, conveys quite a different emotion from Kubrick's bleakly horrific image.

So take the outline for your adaptation and study it with the same kind of critical eye I've tried to apply to my outline for *To Build a Fire.* When you question a choice you've made, other possible choices may appear. Try them out and see what happens. As Yogi Berra says, "When you get to a fork in the road, take it." If that fork proves mistaken, you can always go back and take the original road. But quite likely you will find a better one. Paul Schrader once told me that when he gets stuck in a script, he arbitrarily does the opposite of what he's been doing—changes a man to a woman, or has a gunshot victim fire the shot himself—and the alternative always seems to work better. You need to feel free to change your work and not become overly wedded to your first effort. Rewriting can be fun once you give yourself the license to practice it.

Step 3
THE CHARACTER BIOGRAPHY

The new frontier in film style is character. They've pushed film style so far that there's no sense trying to change these music video and film school kids. You go back to basics....

That's what it's about. Particularly on a lower budget, the only things you can compete on are dialogue and story. You can beat the hell out of them in those categories.

—*Screenwriter-director Paul Schrader, 1996*

A character description should be included the first time the character appears in your script. You need to describe the way the character (particularly the central character) looks and behaves, without going into unfilmable backstory (telling about events in the character's past without showing them). A good way to learn how to write vivid character description is to study the work of master novelists and screenwriters and to see how they go about providing physical descriptions of their characters. A novel's description when a character first appears tends to be longer than most screenplays take to introduce their characters, but a script can afford to take some space to do so as well.

Here is one of my favorite character descriptions in a novel. This is the introduction to the title character in Joseph Conrad's *Lord Jim,* the story of a coward's redemption:

> He was an inch, perhaps two, under six feet, powerfully built, and he advanced straight at you with a slight stoop of the shoulders, head forward, and a fixed from-under stare which made you think of a charging bull. His voice was deep, loud, and his manner displayed a kind of dogged self-assertion which had nothing aggressive in it. It seemed a necessity, and it was directed apparently as much at himself as at anybody else. He was spotlessly neat, apparelled in immaculate white from shoes to hat, and in the various Eastern ports where he got his living as ship-chandler's water-clerk he was very popular.

Notice how Conrad defines Jim right from the beginning as someone who strives for but fails to live up to a high standard, both physical and moral. This description captures the essence of the man in sharply drawn detail and lays out the problems and conflicts the novel will explore.

Paul Schrader's *Taxi Driver* begins with an unusually long and memorable word portrait of Travis Bickle, the character played by Robert De Niro. Although Schrader's language seems literary and could be mistaken for backstory, his description of Travis works because of the shockingly intense sense it gives of the man's outer and inner being when we first see him:

TRAVIS BICKLE, age 26, lean, hard, the consummate loner. On the surface he appears good-looking, even handsome; he has a quiet steady look and a disarming smile which flashes from nowhere, lighting up his whole face. But behind that smile, around his dark eyes, in his gaunt cheeks, one can see the ominous stains caused by a life of private fear, emptiness and loneliness. He seems to have wandered in from a land where it is always cold, a country where the inhabitants seldom speak. The head moves, the expression changes, but the eyes remain ever-fixed, unblinking, piercing empty space.

Travis is now drifting in and out of the New York City night life, a dark shadow among darker shadows. Not noticed, no reason to be noticed, Travis is one with his surroundings. He wears rider jeans, cowboy boots, a plaid western shirt and a worn beige Army jacket with a patch reading, "King Kong Company 1968—70."

He has the smell of sex about him: Sick sex, repressed sex, lonely sex, but sex nonetheless. He is a raw male force, driving forward; toward what, one cannot tell. Then one looks closer

```
and sees the inevitable. The clock spring
cannot be wound continually tighter. As the
earth moves toward the sun, Travis Bickle moves
toward violence.
```

Ethan and Joel Coen fittingly take a more casual approach to introducing their central character, the Dude (Jeff Bridges), in *The Big Lebowski:*

```
INTERIOR - RALPHS

It is late, the supermarket all but deserted.
We are tracking in on a fortyish man in
Bermuda shorts and sunglasses at the dairy
case. He is the Dude. His rumpled look and
relaxed manner suggest a man in whom
casualness runs deep.
```

To help you prepare to write your screenplay, make yourself more familiar with your protagonist by writing a brief character biography. This step will help you start fleshing out the bare bones of your adaptation outline; writing the outline should come first, because you need an overall sense of where your story is going, who the character is, and what actions he or she takes before you go into more depth on the character's personality traits and backstory. You need to decide first of all which character is your protagonist (the character primarily responsible for the action of the story). Remember that this is *your* character, who's not necessarily identical with the character as he or she appears in the story you are adapting. Then write a one-page, double-spaced biography of that character. This is not simply a character description but rather an account of the character's life from birth until the time the action of your screenplay begins. This is part of the backstory, information about the story that will help you write the script and may or may not come out during the course of the action of the film in one way or another but should enrich the story by giving it more sense of life and complexity.

Some of the information you may want to include would be the character's full name and year and place of birth; parents' names, occupations, and other facts about the family background and ancestry; the character's siblings and relationships with them and with his or her parents; places where the character has lived; schooling and other training; occupations; significant or formative experiences; other key figures who have influenced the character's life; important interests, traits, and habits; and a physical description. Providing such details (even if they don't all appear in the script) will make your film story seem more real as well as making it easier to read. For instance, giving a name to a character who is unnamed in the source story (as the man is in "To Build a Fire") will help bring him alive on the page. The character biography, unlike a story outline, may be written partly or completely in the past tense.

I learned about writing character biographies from John Ford and his screenwriter Frank S. Nugent. The first of thirteen produced scripts Nugent wrote for the director was the richly textured screenplay for the cavalry Western *Fort Apache* (1948, "suggested by" the short story "Massacre" by James Warner Bellah). That screenplay was my other major influence as a budding screenwriter, after *Citizen Kane,* because Nugent showed me how a film can be novelistic in its depth and do justice to the complexities of history. Nugent recalled how he worked with Ford on *Fort Apache:*

> He made me do something that had never occurred to me before—but something I've practiced ever since: write out complete biographies of every character in the picture. Where born, educated, politics, drinking habits (if any), quirks. You take your character from his childhood and write out all the salient events in his life leading up to the moment the picture finds him—or her.... The advantages are tremendous,

because having thought a character out this way, his actions, his speech, are thereafter compulsory; you know how he'll react to any given situation.

Nugent's minibiography of Lieutenant Colonel Owen Thursday, the deranged martinet played by Henry Fonda in *Fort Apache,* describes the character's earlier life as follows: Thursday "graduated West Point '55...second or third in his class.... Remained in Washington until '69 and was sent as Military Observer to Europe. Saw the Prussian-Austrian War....great student of military affairs. A reputation as a brilliant Cavalry Tactician and a very strict soldier....He had been forcibly impressed with the Prussians...not only by their stern discipline...but also their thesis of the power of frontal attack....In politics is a Republican."

John Wayne's Captain Kirby York is described as "the Washington to Thursday's Braddock. He knows the country. He knows the Indians. York has a sense of humor. He loves and is perfectly satisfied with frontier life. He smokes cigars and drinks bourbon."

(These are excerpts from Nugent's somewhat longer character biographies of Thursday and York, found in Ford's papers. It usually enhances clarity to write in complete sentences.)

Now let your imagination run loose (and do some research) in creating the backstory for your central character.

Biography of Red

by Joseph McBride

Thomas "Red" McGarrity was born on August 4, 1876, in Spokane, Washington. His parents, Pierce and Joy, were Irish immigrants. Pierce worked as a coal miner in Newfoundland before going to the silver mines at Mullan, Idaho. He married Joy Cooper when she ran a beanery for miners. They moved to Spokane to start a freight hauling business. McGarrity Hauling prospered with six wagons and a dozen horses.

Thomas was a quiet, redheaded only child who did not do well in grade school because of his shyness and lack of verbal dexterity. His teachers criticized him for a general lack of imagination. But he had drawing talent and spent most of his time in class sketching horses. Thomas worked as a horse handler at the family's company stable in downtown Spokane. At a local trade school, Thomas was trained for a business career, but he became infatuated with books about adventuring in the Yukon Territory of Canada. His mother warned him of danger, but Thomas left home at nineteen and tried prospecting for gold around Dawson with a boyhood friend. That venture came to bust within nine months.

In the spring of 1902, Thomas took his small savings and traveled back to Dawson, joining a logging camp. The job fulfilled his hopes of emulating what President Theodore Roosevelt called "the strenuous life." Thomas was given the nickname "Red" by his fellow loggers in an expression of camaraderie. But Red was still something of a greenhorn. He scoffed at an Old-Timer who tried to warn him that by taking long hikes alone in the frozen wilderness to scout trails for the following spring's logging, he is risking his life.

8

Exploring Your Story and How to Tell It

Writing the biography of my central character gave me more of a "way in" to the story. Just as I advised you to do, I discovered personal connections to the character as I went about making him my own. In the process of imagining Red's life before we first see him trekking through the Yukon in *To Build a Fire,* I found myself drawing on my family history.

This happened when I wondered how Red came to the Canadian Yukon and why he seems such a greenhorn. Since my mother's family was from the Pacific Northwest, I thought of having Thomas "Red" McGarrity come from the same city, Spokane, Washington. We're descended from Irish immigrant pioneers who worked in the coal and silver mines, and it seemed fitting for this red-bearded fellow to be the son of a silver miner named Pierce, like my grandfather and namesake Pierce Joseph Dunne. Our family was involved in the busing and trucking business, and before that in horse-drawn hauling and transport. My great-grandmother Joy Ward Flynn actually drove a stagecoach in Idaho; she ran a beanery for miners there, as Joy Cooper McGarrity does in Red's backstory. And so I had Red's parents run a hauling business and gave him a fondness for horses. Our Irish family wasn't so newly arrived as Red's parents, but he needed to be more of an adventurer than a settled American of longer standing. I sent Red on his fatal journey into the Canadian wilderness implying that he goes there partly out of boredom with city life and the mundane life of business, partly out of a boyishly romantic infatuation with storybooks, and partly because he wants to live up to his more vigorous father, a more genuine pioneer.

Bearing in mind the fact that *To Build a Fire* is the story of a tragic failure, I interwove Red's character flaws throughout his brief biography. His impractical nature, his nagging sense of inferiority to his father, his lack of imagination, and his idle romanticism are traits that will lead him to his doom. Dramatizing his failings should help us empathize with the man rather than letting us feel superior or contemptuous. I gave Red some problems I share. His bookish personality proves ill suited to the wilderness, and his impracticality makes him slow to recognize danger and distracted when he should be more on guard. Since London's character foolishly mocks the Old-Timer as "womanish" for warning him about the cold, I have Red's mother issue him an earlier warning he disregards with similar thoughtlessness. I thought of giving Red brothers and sisters but decided to make him an only child to emphasize his loneliness and lack of roots, as well as to get away from the cliché of Irish families' prodigious breeding habits. Red remains somewhat boyish in my telling of the story. Previously I'd thought of him as being in his early thirties, but I realized that his inexperience would be more believable and his immaturity more pronounced if he were only twenty-five.

I had to grapple here with London's description of the man as lacking imagination. This does not necessarily mean that he lacks purpose or fails to dream. London, I believe, is referring more to the man's fatal inability to recognize the dangers in his surroundings clearly and quickly enough to survive. "Imagination" in this context means having the sensitivity to know what the dog knows and being able to transcend complacency and understand the deeper imperatives of life and nature. So, after some hesitation, I went with my instincts to give Red a somewhat dreamy, artistic temperament; perhaps this amplification reflects my own personality transforming the original. But if that change shows that Red is, to some degree, imaginative, he is so only in limited and somewhat secondhand ways—sketching repetitively from nature and feeling impelled to lead a life laid out for him in storybooks, especially those of the boys' adventure genre. Red's identification with Theodore Roosevelt, who triumphed over his own weaknesses by leading what he called "the strenuous life," seemed a good way to make my character a man of his times as well as to give him a further streak of inauthenticity.

I was influenced as well by elements of London's own biography—his humble beginnings and rugged early jobs, his love of reading romantic and heroic sagas, his drive toward adventure and wealth, his independence, his failed attempt at prospecting for gold, his artistic nature. But in this cautionary tale, Red is what Jack London might have become if he had lacked London's prodigious and far-ranging sense of imagination. However, one must be careful of not pushing such parallels between a character and his author too far, even when a character is an obvious alter ego such as Hemingway's Nick Adams. A character should not be mistaken for his author, and there is always some degree of artistic distancing involved, even in the most autobiographical fiction. As D. H. Lawrence put it, "Never trust the artist. Trust the tale."

If the protagonist of *To Build a Fire* is to serve as a representative of humankind in all his flaws and strengths, an Everyman, he must become a rounded, highly specific, fully three-dimensional character first. If he is not individualized, he will seem generic, and the process of imagining how he came to his dilemma is essential to bringing him alive on-screen. Naming characters is one of the most important ways of making them seem more real to the reader and making the script easier to follow, which is why "Red" is preferable to "the man."

By the way, I incorporated in my character biography a useful device I picked up from my students. Although a biography tells itself most naturally in the past tense (unlike other forms of screenwriting, which should be in the present tense), I shifted to the present at the very end of the bio ("he is risking his life") to bring Red right to the point at which the action of the story begins. Now I am ready to start fleshing out the story cinematically.

SOME TOOLS OF THE TRADE

Before going any further, get your workplace organized. The traditional method, before computers, for preparing to write a feature screenplay was to get yourself a yellow legal-sized note-pad, a box of index cards, and a corkboard for your wall. Today there are software programs, such as Scrivener, that provide the equivalent of index cards and a corkboard (and still use that terminology), as well as offering many other practical features for use on your computer screen in keeping track of your ideas and managing them efficiently. Just as some writers still prefer writing their first drafts in longhand rather than on a computer, and some famous writers still are faithful to their old manual typewriters, there's no hard-and-fast rule about whether to write with paper or electronically, but most writers today will opt for the latter. One way or another, you need a writing "pad" of some kind for jotting down your ideas and taking notes on structure. The "index cards"—real or virtual—are for break-ing down your story into the key elements of individual scenes, once you have the structure clearly in mind. The "corkboard" is for arranging the "cards" in three acts so that you can see, at a glance, how your film will be put together, where each scene will fit, and how far along you are in writing it.

One advantage of the old-fashioned corkboard and index cards is that you can hang it on your wall and see it as a guide whenever you glance away from your computer screen. I started using a corkboard and index cards while writing my first televi-sion special, when I saw such a board in my producer's office.

If you write for television, displaying the various acts on the wall and showing how they will be interrupted by commercial breaks and other such interludes makes the structure easy to follow. But a computer screen can easily serve the same function almost as quickly and has the added virtue of greater speed and flexibility for making changes. In any case, the constant evolution in structure necessitated by the exigencies of planning a complicated variety program makes it essential to be able to see the evolving pattern before your eyes. I found the process very helpful and carried it over into my feature screenwriting.

WHAT IS A TREATMENT?

The next step in your screenwriting process will be to write the treatment. This is a form you probably haven't heard much, if anything, about before you started looking seriously into screenwriting. No one learns to write a film treatment in a high school or college English class. There's nothing mysterious about it, however. A treatment is a description of the film in narrative paragraph format, giving specific indications of the visual storytelling, characters, and dramatic development. The treatment tells the complete story from beginning to end, describing the settings and characters in detail as well as detailing the story developments, giving a clear sense of the scene-by-scene structure of the film.

With more leisure to tell the story than you had in the highly compressed format of the outline, you can afford to go into more detail about how each scene will play on-screen. It's crucial in the treatment to lay out virtually every scene in order of appearance; that isn't particularly difficult for the short-film format. For our purposes, we'll write a five-page (double-spaced) treatment, which actually is a common length for this form in the world of professional screenwriting. You could also be asked to write one of ten or twenty pages. I've even seen feature treatments running as long as a hundred pages, which seems somewhat absurd. Why not just write the script instead? An exception to this rule were the long treatments written by novelist and screenwriter Graham Greene, who sometimes would start the process of writing an original screenplay by writing a novella about the characters; some of these "treatments" have been published, including *The Third Man* and *The Tenth Man*. As valuable as this step was for a great novelist such as Greene, it's highly unusual. Still, there's no doubt that the more carefully detailed the treatment is, the easier it should be to turn it into a screenplay. Alfred Hitchcock and his wife, screenwriter Alma Reville, usually would write a treatment of about sixty-five pages for each of his films before hiring another writer to flesh out the characters and write the dialogue; but writing such a lengthy treatment was the director's way of being creatively involved in the conception of his films and not the usual way a professional screenwriter works.

For now, a certain compression is still in order for this five-page exercise. How much detail should you go into in writing a treatment? What kind of detail should be included? How visual should it be? As we begin this process, let's explore in more depth all the key points you should remember about cinematic storytelling.

Without skipping over or unduly condensing any part of the film, you should account for virtually all of its structure. That doesn't mean that every bridging moment needs to be included, and you don't have to indicate transitional devices unless you feel it necessary, as I did in my outline by suggesting a series of dissolves to show Red's largely uneventful journeying before his fatal accident. But the general narrative style of your film, and some sense of its visual style, should be included in your treatment, especially if any elements are unusual. You may include a few lines of dialogue for flavor, but a good treatment should focus primarily on the action rather than getting bogged down in dialogue. Generally in this process, the dialogue should come later.

Before we go into further detail on the nuts and bolts of the writing of the treatment, let's discuss some ways of trouble-shooting your story in its present state. We'll see how to fix any structural problems and any awkward dramatic passages, problems with character development, or failure to convey the social setting and period. And we will examine some of the virtues a treatment should possess as a blueprint for a work of visual storytelling. A treatment exists largely to help your reader (and potential purchaser) get a sense of what the film will be. It is more a sales tool, in the best sense, than a literary document. The treatment exists to get people excited about making and seeing your movie.

HOW TO WRITE IN PICTURES

When you're sitting with your yellow pad dreaming up scenes for your movie, it's good discipline to make yourself think of action first and dialogue second. That's what I mean by "writing in pictures." When Robert Towne advised students at the American Film Institute to keep the dialogue "as spare as possible," he added, "You think in terms of trying to advance the narrative not as much with dialogue as with image. Even if the narrative is being advanced while the people are talking, they should not be talking about the narrative." This doesn't mean that dialogue is not always an integral part of cinema—in a later chapter we will discuss in detail how to write good dialogue that complements the visuals—but you should wean yourself from the overdependence most of us have on words at the expense of pictures.

Conceiving your story with plenty of "air" in between the talk is important to make any story breathe on-screen. A movie that's little more than a talkfest is seldom satisfying, though there have been some exceptions, and visually adroit filmmakers such as Quentin Tarantino and Jean-Luc Godard also rely heavily on words. But expressive sequences of purely visual storytelling (what Hitchcock calls "pure cinema") are often the most thrilling and memorable parts of films. Even brief visual interludes between dramatic confrontations can greatly increase the sense of real life going on around the action. In mapping out your structure, one of the crucial elements to consider is how best to alternate short and long scenes, to avoid monotony, give the movie a fluid pace, and to allow each scene precisely the length and emphasis it needs. Thinking visually will help you in rhythmically alternating the length and the style of scenes. Even though an occasional scene may need to be on the longer side, if too many scenes are long-winded, your film will start to seem stodgy and lumbering, a misuse of the medium. Every screen-play, whether an adaptation or not, should concern itself with this musical process, which film editor Walter Murch describes as "finding... visual harmonies, thematic harmonies—and finding them at deeper and deeper levels as you work on the film."

One of film's great virtues is its ability to whisk the audience instantly across vast stretches of time and space. Think of the greatest use of "associative editing" in film history, Kubrick's jump cut in *2001: A Space Odyssey* from the murderous ape throwing a bone in exultation during prehistoric times to the futuristic space station gliding gracefully through the heavens to the tune of "The Blue Danube." In that one breathtaking cut between objects tumbling through the sky in slow motion, the film bridges hundreds of miles of space and hundreds of thousands of years, creating a dark metaphor about mankind's discovery and use of tools.

"Pure cinema" can be seen in its purest form in silent movies. It's instructive for a beginning screenwriter to study silent films to see how stories can be told with a minimum of words (the best silents don't overuse intertitles). The short comedies of Buster Keaton are wonderful examples of how wordless images can be immediately comprehensible for all audiences while at the same time expressing a subtle and complex view of the world. Watch

Keaton's *One Week* (in which Buster and his wife try to assemble a prefabricated house that comes out all wrong) or *The Boat* (in which he builds a boat that sinks with his entire family riding in it) to see how a single situation, spun out for twenty or so minutes of ingenious hilarity, can coexist with a melancholy sense of life's absurdity.

The luxury you have in a feature film for extended dialogue scenes is minimized in the short-film format, since too much dialogue would tend to overbalance the imagery and submerge the relatively minimalist plotline. As a consequence, many of the best short films tend more toward poetry than conventional narrative. Watch Roman Polanski's brilliant short films, made when he was a student in Poland and France, for examples of how the format can be a medium for wordless allegory. In such films as *Two Men and a Wardrobe* and *The Fat and the Lean* (available in a collection of his shorts on the Criterion DVD edition of his first feature, *Knife in the Water*), Polanski takes a simple, cryptic situation involving only a couple of characters and brings out a wealth of philosophical nuances through their eccentric behavior. These witty films present their images without explicating them through dialogue, allowing the viewer to contemplate what they might be telling us about life.

Such films should embolden you to be suggestive and cryptic in your adaptation rather than feeling you need to be overly literal and linear in your storytelling.

DISGUISING YOUR HAND

Even the most poetic short film needs a structure to keep it from flying off in all directions. And at the other extreme, even the humblest thirty-second television commercial dramatizing the use of a product will follow Aristotle's three-act structure: Act 1, You're a guy with bad breath who drives people away at parties; Act 2, A friend at work tells you about a new mouthwash; Act 3, You meet the woman of your dreams at an even fancier party. The fact is that any film with any dramatic content, however short or long or however avant-garde its approach might be, probably will still fall into three acts. Telling a story by setting up a situation, establishing a conflict, and resolving that conflict is so deeply ingrained in us that it's hard to think of ways to avoid such a pattern.

You might want to tell your story backward (as in *Memento,* written and directed by Christopher Nolan from the short story by his brother Jonathan Nolan) or tell parallel stories with the same characters behaving in the different modes of comedy and drama (as in Woody Allen's *Melinda and Melinda*) or double back on part of the plot from an overlapping perspective (as in Quentin Tarantino's *Pulp Fiction,* which he adapted from his and Roger Avary's stories). Viewers have become sophisticated enough, after having seen so many stories unfolding so quickly before their eyes, that they can follow such games when they are played by adroit filmmakers. But somewhere in the midst of such an experiment, no matter how postmodern or outré you are trying to be, you will keep stumbling into Aristotle. The need to sustain audience attention through characters makes the three-act structure virtually inevitable.

So when you examine your outline for purposes of expanding it into a treatment, think harder and more specifically about how and where your three acts fall into place. Draw a simple diagram of the three acts on that yellow pad, with three high points of each act underneath. If some part of your story feels weak and underrepresented, or the opposite—overstuffed with incidents—you may need to adjust that section to rectify the imbalance. If you've left out key elements of the story by veering too far from the original, you may find yourself needing to restore some of the cuts. Scenes that seemed expendable may be indispensable after all. And if you've invented a lot of clever new material but your story now seems unwieldy, examine your scenes with a critical eye for any that seem unnecessary, half formed, or clumsy and for any gaps in the story that might make the audience scratch their heads in confusion.

FINDING YOUR PREMISE

If you're feeling a bit lost in all the complications of your characters' lives and overwhelmed with the problems you are having making individual scenes come to life, asking yourself the basic question "What is the premise?" will force you to step back and take a wider view of what you are writing. Then you will see its contours more plainly.

Your three-act structure does not have to be overly obvious. In fact, it shouldn't be. Unlike in a play, the curtain doesn't come down between acts, and people don't go out into the lobby for cocktails. The transitions between acts in a movie can be almost imperceptible or somewhat disguised. In a 2001 interview praising the storytelling subtlety of William Goldman and Alan J. Pakula in *All the President's Men,* screenwriter-director Steven Soderbergh said, "I've begun to believe more and more that movies are all about transitions. That the key to making good movies is to pay attention to the transition between scenes. And not just how you get from one scene to the next, but where you leave a scene and where you come into a new scene. Those are some of the most important decisions that you make. It can be the difference between a movie that works and a movie that doesn't." The same degree of finesse is needed for conveying your plot. "The more subtle and elegant you are in hiding your plot points," said Billy Wilder, "the better you are as a writer." There are some movies in which the plot has to be laid out explicitly early in the story. A caper movie, a heist movie, a war movie—any movie involving a planned operation—often requires the characters to discuss their plot up front; but almost invariably in such movies, the plot goes awry, and that's part of the dramatic or comedic interest, so we have to understand the plan clearly to appreciate how it falls apart.

A screenwriter is like a cardsharp, cagily concealing his hand, or a magician, disguising his tricks, when he tries not to let the machinery of the premise show. It's better in most films to let the plot creep in slowly while the audience is concentrating on getting to know the characters, the atmosphere, and the setting. You play your cards gradually and carefully; exposing too many to the audience too quickly would force you to fold.

Lajos Egri, in *The Art of Dramatic Writing,* gives some examples of premises from celebrated plays, including Shakespeare's *King Lear* ("Blind trust leads to destruction") and *Othello* ("Jealousy destroys itself and the object of its love"), Henrik Ibsen's *Ghosts* ("The sins of the fathers are visited on the children"), and Tennessee Williams's *Sweet Bird of Youth* ("Ruthless ambition leads to destruction"). We could similarly offer premises for great films: *Citizen Kane* ("Seeking love through possessions is a hollow pursuit"), *The Godfather Part II* ("You can destroy your family in the process of trying to protect it"), or *Schindler's List* ("Who saves one life, saves the world entire").

Although such one-line summations are useful, and no doubt accurate, those premises emerge only gradually onstage or on the screen, and it can be dangerously simplistic to reduce a work of art to a single line, even if it's a great universal truth, such as the line from the Talmud that Ben Kingsley's Itzhak Stern quotes as the premise for Oskar Schindler's mission. A one-line summary runs the risk of turning a film into a homily, a message in a fortune cookie, or, worse, an advertising line (in fact, too many films today resemble extended illustrations of lines dreamed up by the studio marketing department). Any great film, let alone any good film, has a panoply of meanings, and among them will be aspects that qualify and even contradict its central theme. Perhaps, as with *Godfather II,* that theme itself will be a paradox, which Chesterton defined as "a truth standing on its head to attract attention." Life is more complicated than art, and art that aspires to represent life fully can't always be summed up in a one-liner.

But even an ad line can sometimes capture the contradictions that make a great film great. One of my favorites is the ad

line for *Bonnie and Clyde:* "They're young…they're in love…
and they kill people." Sometimes, as Ken Russell did with *The
Music Lovers,* you may sell your movie with a one-line premise
(or "pitch line" or "logline") that rivets the listener's attention
by revealing the essence of the story in a flash. In any case, such
an exercise is invaluable in helping you find the dramatic spine
of your movie, especially if you are feeling somewhat lost in
knowing what it's about. Forcing yourself to define your premise
will reveal the structure of the movie you want to tell. And once
you split that structure into acts, the scenes within those acts
should start falling into place with logical ease.

Defining your premise also will reveal any problems you
may have with your structure by showing how the parts fit or
don't fit. The plot—the motor that drives the narrative, set off
by what's sometimes called "the inciting incident," the source of
the conflict—will also become clearer once you have straight-
ened out the structure. Let's take a look at some famous plots:

- *Citizen Kane:* A newspaper tycoon vainly tries to recapture
  the innocent happiness he knew as a child by heaping up
  useless possessions but isolates himself by treating people
  ruthlessly in his quest for worldly power.

- *The Godfather Part II:* In trying to make his family legitimate, Mafia chieftain Michael Corleone winds up deepen-
  ing its corruption and destroying the lives of his brother and
  sister.

- *Schindler's List:* A businessman who opportunistically joins
  the Nazi Party in World War II decides to spend his fortune
  saving his Jewish workers from the Holocaust.

The inciting incidents that fuel these plots: in *Citizen Kane,*
Kane's mother sells him to a bank; in flashback scenes in *Godfather II,* Vito Corleone, Michael's father, witnesses his mother

being murdered and returns to take revenge; in *Schindler's List*, Oskar Schindler, to his shame, is called "a good man" by an elderly, one-armed Jewish worker who is soon murdered by the Nazis. Complex as the emotional progression of each film is, each springs from an incident that eventually helps the central character define his own purpose, however oblique that incident may seem to the overall plot as it is occurring.

"Know where you're going" is another of the tips for writers offered by Billy Wilder. His insights on structure will help you in troubleshooting your script: "If you have a problem with the third act, the real problem is in the first act.... The event that occurs at the second-act curtain triggers the end of the movie. The third act must build, build, build in tempo and action until the last event, and then—that's it. Don't hang around."

And how do you convey your plot? The best way is to do it through your characters and their actions. Not through their dialogue, tempting though that may be. As Towne says, *They should not be talking about the narrative.* That's one of the most important pieces of advice for any screenwriter to keep in mind. Write those words on an index card and stick it on the wall above your computer. Good dramatic writing doesn't consist of characters telling one another things, but of the audience overhearing characters revealing themselves to one another in ways they may not even intend. That advances the narrative without talking about it directly. Good dramatic writing does not involve characters telling *us* things the writer thinks we need to know. That's a sure sign that the script is in trouble. Trust the audience's intelligence enough to let them piece together the story—and its premise—from the pack of cards you deal them along the way.

The great director Ernst Lubitsch, the master of oblique and elliptical storytelling, advised his protégé Billy Wilder, "Let the audience add up two plus two. They'll love you forever."

TO VERBALIZE OR NOT TO VERBALIZE

But, you may ask, isn't talking about the narrative unavoidable? Sure, in some cases it's necessary. Occasionally a "plot" line of dialogue, or more, can be the right thing for a character to say. In her curtain speech before the intermission in *Gone with the Wind,* Vivien Leigh's Scarlett O'Hara vows, "As God is my witness, as God is my witness, they're not going to lick me. I'm going to live through this, and when it's all over, I'll never be hungry again. No, nor any of my folk. If I have to lie, steal, cheat, or kill. As God is my witness, I'll never be hungry again." That's telling the plot with a vengeance, and it's a thrilling conclusion to the first half of a classic film, but Scarlett's soliloquy is an example of old-fashioned, full-throated theatricality that probably would seem hokey in a movie today. More succinct and allusive, and thus more in keeping with the modern taste in movies, is the way Towne's *Chinatown* memorably wraps up the plot by having Jake Gittes's partner tell him, "Forget it, Jake, it's Chinatown."

Rules about writing are meant to be broken. Each screenplay makes its own rules, depending on the needs of that particular story. Unusual situations may call for surprising solutions. Generally it's best to give characters plenty of room to live and breathe without confiding their thoughts and feelings too explicitly. But though dialogue is usually best when it's subtle and oblique, sometimes there's no better way to convey what someone is feeling than by letting her come out and say it, especially if she is compelled to do so. As Towne writes,

> We tend to believe people when it costs them something to say whatever it is they have to say. It almost takes the form of a mathematical equation: the more it means to a character, the more difficult it is to say. [Gary] Cooper is finally forced by everyone in the courtroom to defend himself in *Mr. Deeds Goes to Town.* [Henry] Fonda struggles manfully to get up

the courage to ask Clementine for a dance [in *My Darling Clementine*]. Then there's Faye Dunaway in *Chinatown:* she has to have the admission of incest with her father literally beaten out of her. I believe her reluctance to speak about it makes it more credible and moving when she does so.

Indeed, Evelyn Mulwray's lines about "She's my sister—she's my daughter.... She's my sister *and* my daughter!" are some of the most powerful and shocking ever uttered on-screen. The fact that they come from such a reserved woman, and that they express a secret no one would want to readily admit, accounts for their great impact.

How much less effective, by contrast, are the endless dissections of feelings and accusations by the 1950s married couple in *Revolutionary Road*. The movie couple played by Kate Winslet and Leonardo DiCaprio constantly yell at us, in numbing detail, their innermost thoughts, making the film resemble an endless Primal Scream session. In effect, they are verbalizing what should be the movie's subtext. Subtext refers to the meanings between the lines. If a movie is operating on less obvious levels than *Revolutionary Road,* it allows us to put the two and two together ourselves rather than insulting us by yelling out the significance of everything and shoving the conclusions in our faces. Richard Yates's source novel is far subtler in dramatizing the couple's interactions.

All the verbose psychodrama in the film, which feels highly theatrical, not only robs the characters of their inner lives but also seems at odds with a time when men and women were stymied by social taboos against overly candid expression of feelings. The most eloquent moments in the film are the silent close-ups of Winslet's despondent housewife, which allow us to explore her tormented face and find our own conclusions in it. That's cinema.

THE JOYS OF SUBTEXT

In a later chapter, we'll explore the various uses of dialogue in movies and how a screenwriter can collaborate with actors by giving them characters to play with expressive subtlety. But for now, as you are mapping out your treatment, it might be a good idea to look at one of the most powerful examples of subtext on the screen, the proposal scene in Frank Capra's *It's a Wonderful Life*. What's remarkable about this scene is its violence. George Bailey (James Stewart) and Mary Hatch (Donna Reed) are clearly destined to be married, but George fights that realization with all his will, knowing that marriage will trap him in his stifling hometown with the responsibilities of family and what he mistakenly considers a dead-end job. Mary, on the other hand, knows that they are right for each other and is stricken by George's inability to accept her love. He accosts her while she's on the telephone with another suitor from New York City, who offers George a job with his plastics company. On one level this kind of opportunity may be the solution George is hoping for, but he is struggling with his deep-seated passion for Mary.

Capra (one of nine writers who worked on the script) films this scene in huge two-shots, with the actors' faces huddled over the telephone as they keenly sense each other's close physical presence. The effect is electric in its eroticism. But George's anger keeps growing throughout the scene until he drops the phone and starts shaking Mary, telling her, "I don't want to get married, ever, to anyone! You understand that? I want to do what *I* want to do! And you're—and you're—." Then he breaks down, draws her close to him, and says with great intensity, "Oh, Mary, Mary!"

This is probably the least orthodox—and most affecting— proposal in film history. It captures George's love for Mary by indirection, to say the least. His recognition of how important his commitment to her might be initially drives him to fury rather than tenderness. The complexity of his emotions and

Mary's progression from seductive amusement to tenderness to alarm and tearful acceptance dramatize the full range of the film's exploration of the dynamics of marriage and the frustrations of a man's inability to break free of his hometown. This is all done largely without any explicit, "on-the-nose" verbal indications. Mary's telling George, ostensibly about the job offer, "He says it's the chance of a lifetime" (she's looking directly into George's eyes at this moment), and George's declaration that "I don't want to get married" are the closest the scene comes to verbalizing this turning point in their lives. Their decision to marry is shown nonverbally, with their embrace.

HIDE THAT BACKSTORY

It's important to avoid being heavy-handed in your exposition. Getting into the story and establishing its terms for the audience generally should be done gradually and gracefully, rather than in a blunt, overly obvious way. Granted, for some stories you might want to follow the hard-boiled writer-director Samuel Fuller's advice to "Grab 'em by the balls" in your opening scene "and never let 'em go." But as Towne and John Huston suggest, you generally can afford to take your time acquainting the audience with the characters and what they represent, since the audience isn't going anywhere, at least not for a while, and they appreciate having the chance to participate in figuring out where the story is going. If it's all spelled out up front, what's the point of telling it at all? Then it would be little more than a news bulletin from your fictional world, not a story.

Similarly, it's advisable to avoid using flashbacks or prologues merely to explain the characters' motives. This amounts to nakedly and crudely putting what should be backstory right up there on the screen. One of the movie clichés I most abhor is starting with a scene of the central character or characters in childhood as a quick and cheap way of providing motivation or a hook for their later behavior. The opening of the execrable *Pearl Harbor* (written by Randall Wallace and directed by Michael Bay) is a case in point, showing the two central characters as boys getting excited over an airplane landing in a field; it's no surprise to find that they grow up to be aviators and wind up taking to the air during the attack on Pearl Harbor. Martin Scorsese's otherwise admirable film *The Aviator* (written by John Logan) has an unfortunate opening with Howard Hughes as a child getting bathed suggestively by his mother, a scene that's supposed to explain his later sexual problems, debilitating germ phobia, and eventual psychosis. That's a lot of weight to put on a flimsy scene, and better ways could have been found to dramatize those traits in Hughes's adult personality.

Such scenes are crutches betraying the filmmakers' insecurity that they have not successfully dramatized their characters. And the implication that some childhood trauma or experience is directly responsible for all that follows usually is pop psychology at its most simplistic. Sometimes, however, such a scene works, as in Clint Eastwood's film of the Dennis Lehane novel *Mystic River,* which starts with a child's abduction. That is valid dramaturgy in Brian Helgeland's screenplay because the childhood scene is actually the catalyst for all that follows; it's what the story is about. But by not being merely an explanatory device, that scene is an exception that proves the rule. The leisurely opening sequences of *Up,* following the main characters from childhood into old age, similarly work as an integral part of the story line. If you want to convey backstory, work it into the story line in that way, by having it emerge in a natural progression. People's pasts do affect their present behavior. You need to find convincing ways of showing how that manifests itself.

In *Only Angels Have Wings,* written by Jules Furthman and directed by Howard Hawks, a group of aviators in South America are joined by a pilot (Richard Barthelmess) with a burned face and a shameful past (he bailed out of a plane leaving another man to die). That backstory is only hinted at in the film. "Yes, and you also accomplish something by showing the attitude of the other people toward that character," the director says in my book *Hawks on Hawks*. "You make whatever they do as important to the story. Because Barthelmess was a pariah when he came in there. But he had a beautiful wife [Rita Hayworth], and it was kinda fun fussing around with the fact that maybe Cary Grant—well, you knew that he had an affair with the girl before, didn't you?"

"How did you go about conveying that?" I asked.

"Well, now, we were making a scene," Hawks explained,

and Rita Hayworth was frightened. She had some lines to read, and she came through the doorway so fast up to where Cary Grant was at a desk that I said, "Hey, hey, wait a minute. This is wrong. Do it the opposite way. Come in, close the door behind you, and lean back and look at him." And I said, "What are you thinking about?" She said, "Well, he's looking at me. I'm a little self-conscious." "OK, say, 'Do you like my hair this way?'" Now, what does that tell you? You know that they've been together. Then she came across and she kissed him. She didn't do much, and I said, "Wait a minute, do a good job of it. And then say, 'I don't know whether you should have done that.' In other words, make it apparent that you did it, but blame *him*." He said to her, "I see you still use the same old goo."

OK, now, you can make up your own mind as to what they were, can't you? You know that they slept together. You know everything. So you've got something. You've got a man coming in with a new wife, so you expect something of it. You don't necessarily have to *do* anything.

YOUR CHALLENGES

As I point out in chapter 2, film at its best can convey thought without words, through images and sounds and the expressions of the actors. There's no greater challenge for a screenwriter than conveying thought without relying on verbalization. So how do you go about doing this in your script and treatment?

Watching the films of Alfred Hitchcock is the best place to start. Studying Hitchcock reminds us of the primal feelings film can stir in us and how those feelings can be inflected with great subtlety. Hitchcock's cinema is intensely subjective. Frequently we are put in the position of a character undergoing a strong emotional experience. Hitchcock will intercut shots of the character's face with what he or she is looking at, as a way of making us understand, concretely, what is on the character's mind, the thoughts that help trigger the emotions. (Hitchcock was a proponent of the Kuleshov effect, which he amusingly demonstrates in a 1964 television interview released on DVD as *A Talk with Hitchcock*.) Hitchcock likes to use subjective tracking shots as a character is walking; he intercuts the character's facial and body language with reverse tracking shots of the exterior situation she is seeing and experiencing. This intercutting immerses us in the scene, almost as a participant, and vividly conveys the thought and emotion involved in the character's encounter with the surroundings.

A characteristic and memorable example of subjective camerawork is the sequence near the end of *Psycho* (written by Joseph Stefano from the novel by Robert Bloch) when Lila Crane (Vera Miles) enters the Bates house to find out what has happened to her sister. As Lila enters the foyer, goes upstairs into the bedrooms of Norman Bates (Anthony Perkins) and his mother, and descends to the fruit cellar, Hitchcock keeps intercutting shots of Lila walking and looking at the creepy décor, and the suspense is almost unbearable. She begins to understand the depth of Norman's psychosis by looking intently at the objects he lives with—the toys in his childish bedroom, a pair of bronzed woman's hands, a mysterious indentation in the bed of his mother's otherwise undisturbed bedroom, and finally the dead mother herself, in a rocking chair in the fruit cellar. Lila winds up face-to-face there with the deranged Norman in woman's garb, holding a knife. Our involvement in Lila's reconnaissance mission, and our sense of her danger, is heightened by the use of subjective camerawork and editing. In true Hitchcockian style, we share the character's perceptions but we also know more than she knows, which increases the suspense. This kind of sequence can be mapped out clearly in a screenplay without using more than a minimum of camera indications, although the fact that the camera is moving with the character can and probably should be mentioned. A treatment would contain a briefer description that captures the overall effect of the sequence.

There are other ways to capture thought on film. The most direct, of course, is through dialogue or narration. Having recourse to such a solution is not only too easy but also relatively uninvolving. Soliloquies usually work better on the stage than on film. Narration can be involving in a film, but the decision to use it should be made with care. "In doing voiceovers," Billy Wilder advised, "be careful not to describe what the audience already sees. Add to what they are seeing." Wilder uses voice-over memorably in *Sunset Boulevard,* which is narrated by a dead man (screenwriter Joe Gillis), a device later imitated in *American Beauty.* Gillis's voice allows him to comment posthumously on what brought him to his death, floating in a silent movie star's swimming pool, and lets him make sardonic remarks on Hollywood, providing social texture and ironically allowing the failed screenwriter to "rewrite" the story of his own life. The kind of narration used in *Sunset Boulevard* is neither redundant nor simply a vehicle for shoveling information to the audience. It provides an attitude, a way of seeing the story that enriches our understanding of the situation. Another example of how integral voice-over narration can be to a film is in *The Diving Bell and the Butterfly,* the film version of the memoir by stroke victim Jean-Dominique Bauby, adapted for the screen by Ronald Harwood; the narration by Bauby (Mathieu Amalric), who cannot speak, offers a moving interior monologue that allows us access to his thoughts and lets him "converse" mentally with the other characters. But if you haven't found a vital reason for using narration, it's best to let the audience intuit what your characters are thinking.

So these are some indications of how you can go about conceiving scenes that convey thought as you run the movie in your head and prepare to write your treatment. There are other styles of filmmaking, but Hitchcock's gets to the essence of the differences between cinema and other forms of artistic expression. Always keep in mind the vital importance of being concrete in telling a story on film. Cinema is more concrete than some of the other media, because it shows photographs in motion and employs its own special properties of editing. But concreteness is important in any art form that is representational and aims to stir the emotions. Hemingway's phrase "the sequence of motion and fact which made the emotion"—so useful to keep in mind while writing screenplays—is a restatement of the artistic principle of the "objective correlative," famously defined by the poet T. S. Eliot in 1919: "The only way of expressing emotion in the form of art is by finding an 'objective correlative'; in other words, a set of objects, a situation, a chain of events which shall be the formula of that *particular* emotion; such that when the external facts, which must terminate in sensory experience, are given, the emotion is immediately evoked."

Another major challenge for a screenwriter, related to the challenge of dramatizing the processes of thought, is how to convey the unseen. What we don't see in a film is often more effective than what we do see. In a suspense film, we (and to some degree the characters) fear catastrophic consequences; in a horror film, the worst anxiety often is our fear of the unknown. The great horror film producer Val Lewton showed the way for other filmmakers by emphasizing the power of suggestion. He believed in subtly suggesting the offscreen presence of danger with the use of shadows, editing, sound, and other suggestive devices. The terror in a Lewton film is amplified by the fact that the monster isn't seen. Classic examples include the swimming pool scene in *Cat People,* in which Jane Randolph is menaced by a beast whose presence is conveyed in shadows and growls, or the scene in *The Leopard Man* when an animal attack on a girl is implied with an interior shot of a closed door, sounds of the struggle outside, and a stream of blood coming from under the door. Steven Spielberg's *Jaws* follows the Lewton tradition by default. Since the mechanical shark built for the film hardly worked, Spielberg had to shoot around it and only suggest the shark's presence in most scenes, which is far more frightening than actually seeing it.

A crucial story element in *To Build a Fire* is the man's insufficient awareness of the danger of the streams deceptively covered with thin coatings of ice and snow. The viewer needs to understand this hidden danger before the man realizes it by stepping into such a stream, the event that leads inexorably to his death. For my treatment, I could solve this problem early in the story by indicating a series of shots of snowbanks, getting closer and closer to a dangerous spot, shown perhaps with glistening water bubbling up and freezing. That sequence of shots could be justified as part of the "atmosphere." I am concerned that it might seem too heavy-handed to punch up the warning in such an obvious way. However, doing so would follow the principle of what Hitchcock called his "bomb theory," defining the difference between suspense and surprise. In the Richard Schickel documentary *The Men Who Made the Movies: Alfred Hitchcock*, Hitchcock explains that if he and another character in a movie are talking about baseball for five minutes, and a bomb explodes, the audience will have a brief shock. On the other hand,

> Tell the audience at the beginning that under the table—and *show* it to them—there's a bomb, and it's gonna go off in five minutes. Now we talk baseball. What are the audience doing? They're saying, "Don't talk about baseball—there's a bomb under there! Get rid of it!" But they're helpless; they can't jump out of their seats up onto the screen and grab hold of the bomb and throw it out. But one important factor—if you work the audience up to this degree, that bomb must never go

off and kill anyone. Otherwise they will be *extremely* angry with you.

I will mull over this kind of premonitory device as I write my treatment and see if I can find a way to make it work effectively. Perhaps I am courting audience anger myself by letting the "bomb" in *To Build a Fire* go off and kill the man, but the alternative would be to contrive a way to let him escape his fate, a solution London tried in his first version of the story before realizing that it was a cop-out.

I'm also thinking of having the dog disclose the information about the hidden streams to the audience. Since the dog is more instinctively aware of natural danger, and since it's closer to the ground, it could be shown gingerly pawing around possible trouble spots as it walks ahead of the man. The dog could bark a warning that the man fails to understand. This would also serve the purpose of building up the contrast between the animal intelligence of the dog and the obtuseness of the human character, a theme of the story that needs to be brought out through sight and sound. Perhaps both options—the bomb theory and the dog—would be worth including. Hitchcock often reiterates key story points visually, with variations, to ensure that the audience fully understands. This becomes part of the visual pleasure of participating in the storytelling.

Step 4

THE TREATMENT

Below is a sample of the beginning of a professional treatment. This is from François Truffaut's treatment for the 1960 film *À bout de souffle/Breathless,* directed by Jean-Luc Godard. For those readers who are surprised to learn that Truffaut was involved in writing this influential film, that's because the film contains no writing credit. Truffaut let Godard use his work without credit, and Godard did not write a complete shooting script. He gave the actors their lines at the time of the shooting, sometimes even shouting lines to Jean Seberg as they were filming amidst busy traffic on the Champs-Élysées. But the treatment demonstrates that *Breathless* should be regarded as being as much a Truffaut film as a Godard film, even if Truffaut doesn't anticipate (at least explicitly) Godard's extensive use of jump-cutting, the film's most influential stylistic device. And the celebrated long bedroom scene was greatly expanded by Godard from one paragraph in Truffaut's treatment. But otherwise the treatment provides a clear blueprint of the film's incidents, structure, themes, and tone.

This treatment is written in the present tense, as every treatment should be. It contains an epigraph, but that is not required; it's simply a literary device that Truffaut includes to help set the tone and theme of the story. The treatment carefully describes the action while establishing the settings and time frames of the different scenes, as you should also do. It is not a requirement to include the setting and time frame of each section of the film on a separate line in boldface, as Truffaut does here, but it's a good idea to flag such major changes typographically. It makes the key transitions in a treatment easier to follow. Truffaut also sometimes uses boldface for the first few transitional words in a section, a device I've also incorporated.

Truffaut's treatment fails to describe the central character (Lucien, whose name was changed in the film to Michel) or "the girl." It is better to include a short but vivid and memorable description of each important character in your story, and to give names to characters.

Specify any changes in time or place in your treatment. Implicitly indicate how scenes will be filmed, but avoid or minimize technical descriptions in your treatment. Basically you are just telling the story here, including every scene except for short transitional scenes. You can include some dialogue if you want, but not very much; save most of that for the screenplay. Make sure again to credit the author and source of your treatment.

À *bout de souffle (Breathless)*
by François Truffaut

"We're going to talk about very nasty things..."
—Stendhal

Marseille, a Tuesday morning.
Lucien is pretending to read *Paris Flirt* at a sidewalk café at the bottom of the Canebière. In reality, he is watching the traffic in front of the Vieux Port.

Near the boats that take tourists to view the Château d'If, a girl signals to Lucien. She indicates a convertible with the insignia "U.S. Army" that is at that moment pulling into a parking spot. The occupants, an American officer, his wife, and their children, go to buy tickets for the Château d'If tour. They are watched by Lucien and the girl, who are nonetheless pretending not to know each other.

As soon as the boat has departed, Lucien approaches the car—a DeSoto convertible. He inspects the car as if he were the owner, checking the tires and oil.

The girl asks Lucien to take her with him but he refuses. Getting behind the wheel, he drives off after hotwiring the car.

Some Hours Later, we see Lucien on the highway. . . .

I'm going to use some of Truffaut's style in my sample treatment for *To Build a Fire*, which follows. Good luck with yours.

To Build a Fire

by Joseph McBride

based on the short story
by Jack London

The Canadian Yukon, January 1902, nine in the morning.

The vast white blankness of the Canadian Yukon Territory extends as far as we can see, toward a hazy horizon. Snow covers the Yukon River and the frozen plains, broken only by low rolling hills and depressions. The dull gray morning light casts a baleful aura over the landscape.

Gradually, a tiny dot appears over a ridge, and then a larger dot. On closer inspection, these are a gray husky dog, leading the way, and a stocky white man with a rough walking stick. Heavily wrapped in a beaver fur coat and

black Russian hat with large earmuffs, mittens,
and Eskimo boots, the man is a little under
six feet tall and looks a bit dandyish. But he
has a brownish-white crust of ice and tobacco
juice covering his trim reddish beard and
collar. Thomas "Red" McGarrity is in his late
twenties, a stolid greenhorn who plods steadily
along the trail, chewing his tobacco and looking
around with some alertness but a lack of
apprehension.

Perhaps he should feel more concerned about
his surroundings; he doesn't realize it is
seventy-five degrees below zero, but the dog seems
instinctively aware of the danger, moving with
great care and efficiency. When Red spits tobacco
juice, it freezes in midair with a sharp,
explosive crackle. He is startled, suddenly
becoming conscious of how cold it actually is.
Red reflexively beats his hands together and
thumps his chest. The dog, safely ensconced in
his fur, looks at him quizzically. The dog trots
ahead, sometimes zigzagging to check soft spots
in the snow with his paws, making sure the ground

is safe. Sometimes the dog leads Red away from
questionable terrain. Red follows, not appearing
to notice. Once the dog halts abruptly, hearing
a crack, and backs away from a patch of sunken
snow. Red becomes alarmed, recognizing the
danger. The dog sits and bites pieces of ice from
his wet paws. Red stops to help, then barks at
the dog to move along, but his voice is blurred
by his muzzle of ice.

As he walks, we hear the voice of an Old-Timer,
a fellow logger, warning Red not to venture into
the winter alone on the trail. We see the old man
a few months earlier at the logging camp, sitting
in a rocking chair by a fire arguing with a
beardless Red, who amusedly calls the man "an old
woman." But the Red who trudges through the snow
looks worried. As he peers into the distance, he
imagines the life awaiting him back at camp: We
see images of the Old-Timer and four burly,
bearded men, all older and more weather-beaten
than Red, eating stew around a hot stove. They
are talking about their plans for spring logging
as the now-bearded Red contentedly plays "Oh, Dem

Golden Slippers" on an accordion while smoking
his pipe.

In the wilderness, Red's face creases with
pain. He looks at his watch (it's a little past
ten), consults a scribbled map at a fork in the
trail and, after some confusion, angles off
toward the west, moving faster and brusquely
ordering the dog ahead. They pass a Native burial
ground, move through a level stretch of woods,
see a mountain range and a deserted cabin in the
distance, and head down an incline toward frozen
Henderson Creek as the midday light brightens a
little. The dog trots along the curves and bends
of the bank, vigilant. Red follows, increasingly
watchful.

At midday, Red finds shelter in a cluster of
rocks under a tree and sits on a log to light a
small fire from brush. It's more difficult than he
expected to pull the matches from his coat. His
hands are stiff. He awkwardly lights the fire and
his pipe, smokes, and rubs the warm bowl against
his freezing cheeks. The dog looks restlessly
around the trail. Red takes his lunch from his

coat, unwrapping biscuits with bacon. He gulps
them down and moves off down the trail again,
waving his arms and thumping his hands with more
vigor. We hear the Old-Timer's voice telling Red
that no one should ever travel alone in the
Klondike after it's fifty below.

Red laughs hollowly, muttering, "Hell—don't I
wish to Christ," as he clomps down an incline.
Suddenly the whiteness under his feet gives way.
His legs plunge straight into a hidden stream.
Red scrambles out, alarmed, soaked to the knees.
He rushes back to the tree, grabs handfuls of
brush and twigs, shaking the tree in the process,
and struggles to build a fire. His hands are
clumsy, but he beats them against his sides to
make them work. He gets the fire going and starts
drying his legs. Above him the snowy branches of
the tree are sprinkling down flakes. Red is busy,
oblivious. Suddenly the branches pour their snow
onto the fire. It abruptly goes out.

**The dog circles fearfully as Red, agitated,
tries to rebuild the fire,** pushing away the snow
and piling more brush from the tree. His hands

are becoming almost useless. He tries vainly to
light some matches. Each one falls into the
snow, unlit, some not even struck. He pounds
furiously on his freezing legs. He yanks the
whole bunch of matches from his coat and strikes
them together with the heels of his bared hands.
He can smell his flesh burning as the bunch
ignites, but at first he can't feel it. He holds
the flaming matches to the kindling, and it bursts
into a fire. He frantically rubs his legs and
feet, starting to get some warmth back into
them. But a large chunk of moss falls from a
trembling branch onto the fire. Red fumbles to
clear it away, but in doing so, he snuffs out
the fire.

The day is gradually darkening as Red sits
desperately looking around for salvation. His
eyes fall on the dog. Dreamlike images flash
before his/our eyes of a man in an Alaskan
blizzard slaughtering a steer with a large axe
and crawling inside its corpse for warmth. Red
laughs hysterically and lurches for the dog. Red
grabs him and rolls around with him, trying to

keep him in his arms, but the dog scurries away, afraid of the man.

Panicked, Red jumps up and starts running wildly along the trail, with the dog bounding ahead. Red runs and runs, falling and rising and falling and plunging forward again. Eventually he takes an abrupt fall and lands headlong in the snow. Sitting immobile, he looks despondent but then begins laughing bitterly at his own foolishness. He mutters almost incoherently, becoming childish in his speech: "Mama—bad boy— bad boy. Next time—do you say me. Daddy come get me. Home now. Now lay me down to sleep. Pray the Lord my soul to keep." He takes great pains to gasp out his final words: "And if I die before I wake—" He mouths silently, "I pray Lord soul take."

Spent of speech, he becomes drowsy and peaceful. He looks around, his eyes sweeping the horizon placidly. Purple twilight is beginning to shade the scene. Red begins imagining his friends finding him dead in the snow. We see a search party of five loggers, his friends from camp,

coming into view and standing in the wind as
snow drifts over his corpse. Red is with them,
moving curiously toward his own dead body. He
kicks it in a gingerly way to make sure he is
dead. The body scarcely budges. We see the Old-
Timer nearby, bundled up in furs, sitting in a
dogsled like an Eskimo, giving Red an accusatory
yet gentle look. Red turns to him and says, "You
were right, old hoss; you were right."

As the sun begins going down, the dying Red is
alone except for the dog, who watches warily from
a distance. Gesturing toward the horizon in vague
supplication, Red sags and drowses into frozen
sleep. The dog waits as twilight darkens.
Eventually he begins whining as he ventures near
the man, catching the scent of death. Night
comes. The dog howls at the stars. Then he trots
away, up the trail in the direction of the camp.
Casting a look back, the dog leaves the man's
frozen corpse behind, his face covered with an
icy mask, his arms vainly outstretched.

Part III

Production

9

Who Needs Formatting?

Now we'll start discussing the practical aspects of getting a screenplay in shape for the production process. Some people resist the idea that a screenplay needs to be written in a standard professional format—or in any particular format, for that matter. They consider this a restriction on their creativity, a way of repressing their individual artistic personality and squeezing it into a conventional mold. If you are entertaining this misguided notion, you need to dismiss it as quickly as possible or find another medium of expression. Like any other art form, but even more so, screenwriting follows certain conventions. The conventions that govern the craft were established long ago and for excellent reasons. They are there to help you.

"It's very much like designing clothes," says screenwriter Akiva Goldsman, who won an Oscar for *A Beautiful Mind*. "The clothing dummy always looks the same. Two arms, two legs, a torso and a head. You can dress it up all you want, but if you don't know what the body looks like, you'll be a terrible clothing designer. And the first thing you have to do is to learn what the body of a screenplay looks like."

Contrary to legend, movies in the early years were not all made "off the cuff." Most silent films had carefully detailed screenplays. But since they did not need to include dialogue, they often resembled treatments more than the screenplay as we know it today. The intertitles were usually written later, in a separate document, by a specialist in title writing. Once movies began to talk in the late 1920s, the standard professional format evolved quickly and logically to deal in a legible way with the combination of images and dialogue that make up a filmable screenplay. If you look at the scripts of such Golden Age classics as *The Grapes of Wrath, Citizen Kane,* or *Casablanca,* you'll see that they look much the same as scripts do today.

Unless you are writing an avant-garde film whose raison d'être is coming up with a new form of cinema, or unless you regard your script simply as private notes for a film you plan to direct with your own money, you will be writing a screenplay that generally resembles other scripts in its layout and its approach to telling a story in cinematic language. Your screenplay will be designed to communicate, and following the standard format will enable you to do so most efficiently. Screenplay conventions can be broken by adept practitioners of the craft for valid creative reasons, and all good scripts have particular problems they solve in unusual ways, but if those conventions are disregarded, chaos will ensue. Someone who writes in blissful or willful ignorance of the professional format will be immediately recognized as unprofessional, and such work will be tossed into the circular file.

So you're only hurting your own cause if you disregard professional script formatting. And beyond such basic commercial considerations, your work will probably suffer if you ignore the format, which is designed to maximize clarity of presentation and readability and to take account of the practical realities of filmmaking. A script that looks professional will do the best possible job of presenting your creative ideas in a way that seems filmable. You want the person who reads it, a potential buyer or an actor or crew member, to be able to visualize the story you want to tell and to do so with a minimum of confusion or complication.

This is not to say that professional screenwriters don't have their own individual styles. Each script you read by a talented screenwriter will have ways of customizing the format that the writer has evolved through practice to express his or her individual taste. Professional screenwriters may seem to ignore some of the basic rules, and some even craft their own alternative formats. After working in the business for several years, I learned a new kind of formatting from a celebrated screenwriter and began using it with satisfying creative results. But however free professional screenwriters become in adapting the standard professional format, you can bet their work will be clearly written and easy to follow. Otherwise they won't last very long in the business.

In this chapter we'll discuss the rationale for the standard format and ways to deviate from it. Let's look at several key format issues as they are reflected in the sample treatment you just read. These basic issues are ones that can throw beginning screenwriters off track, so it's important to understand them at this point in the process. They include how to describe landscape; avoiding camera directions; showing the passage of time and space; describing a character's attire and body language; indicating the use of voice-overs and flashbacks; dramatic foreshadowing; how much dialogue to indicate; how much detail to include in a treatment; and the importance of strong ending imagery.

KEY FORMAT ISSUES

You'll see in my treatment that I described **the landscape** and the sequence of events **without using camera directions,** though I implied that the film first shows Red and the dog in long shot and then moves progressively closer, from medium shots into close-ups. I didn't need to use the technical term "long shot" in the opening because "vast white blankness" and "a tiny dot" imply the use of long shots and let the reader imagine them. Nor did I find it necessary to indicate a close-up of the central character when we first get a good look at him. That's obvious, and indicating a close-up would only irritate the director. But I did use the suggestive language "on closer inspection."

I'll admit I was tempted to use technical terminology when describing Red trekking across varied terrain, in a sequence that needs to have an accelerated sense of movement because it is relatively uneventful. It is important to indicate **the passage of time and space,** so I originally introduced this section by writing, "In a series of quick scenes…," since that sounds less technical than writing "In a series of jump cuts" (or what I wrote in the outline, "A series of dissolves"). But as I revised the treatment, I realized I didn't need technical words at all, only "They pass…," followed by a litany of what Red and the dog walk through and see. I included a note of foreshadowing (a Native burial ground) and a possible place of ignored refuge (a deserted cabin in the distance) to help give meaning as well as variety to the surroundings. But I cut some hifalutin' language from the draft of my opening description ("The landscape is almost lunar in its desolate beauty"), realizing that the metaphor seemed forced, pretentious, and unnecessary. "Just the facts, ma'am," as Joe Friday used to say in *Dragnet.*

For **Red's attire,** I did some research by looking in books on Jack London and the Yukon and by studying historical photographs of trappers, prospectors, and loggers in Alaska's Digital Archives, a website that allows you to search pictures of that period by locations, types of people, and kinds of winter clothing. This research produced a wealth of material that helped me construct a mental image of Red. The developing picture eventually suggested not only a greenhorn but one who "looks a bit dandyish" in his beaver-fur coat and Russian hat. That description, along with Red's youthfulness and his artistic temperament (the accordion), helps me accentuate London's theme that this man is something of a dreamer, ill suited to life in such a punishing landscape.

The **voice-overs** of the Old-Timer and **flashback** images of that wiser man sitting at a fire arguing with Red seemed to fit naturally into the narrative as Red, in the wilderness, belatedly begins to show concern over the cold. I made Red beardless in the flashback to suggest how recently he had arrived in the Yukon Territory. Showing him with his full beard in the later fantasy images of the loggers' camp is shorthand for the passage of time and the development of his character, his attempt to fit in with the hardier, more mature men. I noticed in the London story that the central character consults his watch repeatedly, so I added that detail; **conveying the passage of time** with exactitude helps build a sense of suspense. I paid attention to the effects of **the changing hours on the landscape,** enhancing the sense of foreboding set by the initial description of the "baleful aura" over the land (perhaps too anthropomorphic a phrase, but it seems to work nevertheless). The inexorable progress of time is a powerful element to work into a screenplay. As Red heads toward death, the landscape darkens naturally around him until we end with the dog trotting off into the night, leaving the man's frozen corpse behind.

When I wanted to hear Red speak, I realized I had a bit of a dilemma. London writes, "There was **nobody to talk to;** and, had there been, speech would have been impossible because of the ice-muzzle on his mouth. So he continued monotonously to chew tobacco...." And yet London writes that the man "cursed his luck aloud" and "spoke to the dog, calling it to him; but in his voice was a strange note of fear that frightened the animal, who had never known the man to speak in such a way before." So the story is inconsistent on this point, and I felt I could take enough license to let us **hear the man speak,** but I described his voice as "blurred by his muzzle of ice." When he is dying, I gave him his single prolonged speech in the film, a somewhat incoherent mixture of a child's prayer and address to his parents, as people often resort to when they fear imminent death. (John Ford aficionados may note the similarity of this scene to that of Harry Carey Jr.'s dying monologue in *3 Godfathers,* written by Laurence Stallings and Frank S. Nugent from the novella *The Three Godfathers* by Peter B. Kyne; I couldn't resist one movie homage and couldn't think of a better way to do it.)

Throughout the treatment, I added **fine points of detail** deconstructing Red's belated discovery of his peril and his growing panic as he tries to escape it. The more detail, the better for building up and prolonging suspense; for the screenplay, I will **elongate time** even farther at key moments, particularly in the last section of Red's frantic attempts to avert freezing with fire. Heeding Hitchcock's "bomb theory," I took care to include **foreshadowing of the dangers** of the hidden streams (with the help of the dog scouting soft spots in the snow, skittishly and fearfully) and the snow ominously sprinkling from the tree limbs before it capsizes onto the fire.

In my first draft of the treatment, I had Red's arms fully outstretched as he gestures toward the horizon at the start of **the final sequence.** Then I realized that this posture would anticipate the final image of his frozen, outstretched arms, detracting from its impact. So I changed my first try, "Reaching out his arms toward the horizon in vague supplication, Red remains in that attitude as his body sags," to "Gesturing toward the horizon in vague supplication, Red sags…" Then at the very end, we see "his face covered with an icy mask, his arms vainly outstretched." The suggestion of a further useless gesture of prayer, in the face of the implacable hostility of nature, provides what I hope will be an arresting **final image,** my visual equivalent for London's philosophical ruminations about the indifference of the universe.

For the screenplay, I will go back again to London's story (both the 1902 version and the final 1908 version) for additional detailing and atmosphere to make each scene come fully alive. But as I wrote the treatment, I realized that the script will succeed only if I make the fullest use of **the man's body language** by translating it into cinematic language, as we see him plodding indifferently through the bleak wasteland and then struggling to save himself from his tragic mistakes.

By the way, you'll notice that four times in the treatment I used **the phrase "We see."** Be sparing with those words in screenwriting. In ordinary scenes, the phrase is redundant, since we should see almost everything that happens in a film. But when something imaginary is happening on-screen, as in Red's visions of his friends, it's important to make it clear that "we see" it ourselves. In a film, what is seen in the mind's eye of a character must be made literal, or it will remain only a look in the eye, one that might be hard, if not impossible, to read.

FROM TREATMENT TO SCRIPT

So now that we have the screen story fairly well charted—first things have been dealt with first—what does a script look like?
Not like this:

SCENE:

1. EXTREME LS: a man is turning off the main trail to climb a steep earthbank toward a dim and little-traveled trail. A dog is at his heels.

2. As CAMERA STARTS TRACKING IN, the main TITLE comes onto the screen: To Build a Fire. TITLE HOLDS until the CAMERA is close to the base of the hill, then DISSOLVES off. The man is halfway up the hill.

3. MS from the hill: the man is struggling to make the last step up the hill. He pauses for breath, excusing the act by looking at his watch.

4. CS: the large pocket watch in his hand. It is nine o'clock.

5. MS: the man looks off-screen left toward the spruce timberland and the trail. He takes

off his hat, letting the wind blow through
his hair. Putting the watch back in his pocket
and the hat on his head, he turns to the
right. . . .

That was my first amateurish try with *To Build a Fire* back
in 1967, the script I wrote without the benefit of a book or
course on screenwriting. What I was writing was more a shot
list than a screenplay, notes for the intended director (me), not
a document meant to be shown to others to persuade them to
participate in the filming. Some of the visual ideas aren't bad,
but there's too much information and not enough. We don't need
to know what all the shots will be or their duration; it's tedious
to read the shot designations, and they take us out of the reading experience to try to imagine the editing of the movie. We
don't need to know in which direction the man is turning. This
is mind-numbing detail, and including it makes him seem like a
marionette. This level of detail is not your job. Such micromanaging leaves little room for the actor and director to explore the
character on-screen.

Instead we need some description of the man. So far in my
old script, he's a cipher, not a character. And we need to know
where and when the story takes place. We need a sense of the
atmosphere, the cinematic texture of the story, "the people and
the places and how the weather was." And then we need "the
sequence of motion and fact which made the emotion." By making the script more readable and not simply a sketchy series
of notes, we can give the reader a clear sense of how the film
should look and feel.

Following are some other formatting features that are both
helpful to the reader and essential to the construction of a cinematic story.

HEADINGS

The opening of a professional screenplay should look something like this:

```
EXT. FROZEN LANDSCAPE - YUKON TERRITORY,
CANADA - MORNING (JANUARY 1902)
```

There are other ways to write scene headings, but this is the standard format, the one you need to learn before you begin designing variations. A heading (sometimes called a slugline) goes in ALL CAPS. Don't put headings in italics or boldface or underline them.

The order of description in a heading is logical and is intended to give us a quick sense of where we are (and when). First comes EXT. or INT. (exterior or interior). Then you tell us what kind of setting we are seeing. "FROZEN LANDSCAPE" may seem a bit abstract (compared with PLAIN, FIELD, VALLEY, or other such concrete words), but the particular opening images I've suggested are of a setting that only gradually comes into clear focus (without using that technical term) and gives the overall impression of a mass of overwhelming whiteness. The sky casts a dull glow in this scene, but the effect of snow blindness (or, metaphorically, Red's inability to see the dangers all around him, what London blames on his being "without imagination") is suggested by having the images take a few moments to resolve into view under the MAIN TITLE CREDITS (the standard way to indicate the credits that appear at the beginning of the film, usually just the production company or companies and the names of a few key people; at the end of this chapter, I'll say more about how and why to indicate the credit sequence).

After a dash—rendered in a screenplay heading with a single hyphen—you give us the location. If it's a major city (NEW YORK, CHICAGO, TOKYO), you don't need to give

the country, but if it's a modest-sized city (EUREKA, CALI-
FORNIA) or an area that spans different countries, such as the
Yukon, you need to be more specific. And at the end of the heading comes the time of day (this could also be EARLY MORN-
ING, MIDDAY, AFTERNOON, SUNSET, NIGHT, and so
on). If it is a period film, the year goes in parentheses at the end
of the heading, and the month, if that is relevant.

This is the *full* way to compose a heading. All this detail is
required because the example given here is the first heading of
the screenplay, the one that situates the story in its time and
place. But for subsequent headings in the same location, you can
start simplifying the wording like this:

```
EXT. HILLTOP


TRAIL


WOODS


HENDERSON CREEK


BANK OF CREEK


CLUMP OF TREES


LOG


FIRE
```

Such progressive shortening of headings avoids tedious rep-
etition. Imagine a script of *To Build a Fire* with endless uses of
EXT. before every heading; we know it's all exterior, aside from
the flashbacks and fantasy images of the store and the loggers'
cabin, so it's superfluous to keep saying it. However, when you go
to an interior and back to the wilderness, you need to use EXT.
again to reorient the person reading the script, the one who

may be directing or producing or acting in your film and always needs to know where we are in the story. And when the time of day changes (MIDDAY, EARLY AFTERNOON, SUNSET), put that with the location in the heading, such as "CLUMP OF TREES - MIDDAY," or specify the time interval between scenes, as in "INCLINE - A FEW MINUTES LATER." These time indicators help orient the reader, who might otherwise be confused and have to puzzle out when the scene is happening.

Keep your headings as brief and punchy as possible, to accelerate the reading process. There's an elegant simplicity in such spareness.

METHODS OF SCENE DESCRIPTION

My new draft of the screenplay for *To Build a Fire* continues with scene description under the initial heading:

```
EXT. FROZEN LANDSCAPE - YUKON TERRITORY,
CANADA - MORNING (JANUARY 1902)

Snow and more snow. Nothing but snow. Not even
a rock or a tree. It's hard to make out shapes;
we almost feel snowblind until our eyes start
ADJUSTING to the terrain. The vast white
blankness of the Yukon extends to the distant
horizon. Snow covers the Yukon River and the
frozen plains, broken only by low rolling hills
and depressions. The dull gray morning light
casts a baleful aura over the landscape.

MAIN TITLE CREDITS begin APPEARING out of the
haze.

Gradually, as we MOVE CLOSER to some hilly
terrain,
```

```
A TINY DOT
```

```
appears over a ridge, and then a larger dot.
These are REVEALED as a gray husky DOG,
leading the way, and a stocky white MAN with
a rough walking stick....
```

The words "A TINY DOT," as a heading, are a way of indicating a LONG SHOT of the man without using that term (which in any case would be abbreviated as LS; a medium shot would be MS; a close-up CU; an extreme close-up ECU; and an extreme long shot ELS). Continuing the sentence begun with "A TINY DOT" by placing the rest of it under the heading, with the next word in lowercase, is a lively way of keeping the action flowing and moving the reader's eye rapidly down the page.

The words "ADJUSTING" and "MOVE CLOSER" are camera directions, so those words go in all caps; "APPEARING" goes in all caps because it refers to the credits, but "appears" is in lowercase because it describes a character's action. "ADJUSTING" and "MOVE CLOSER" are relatively nontechnical ways of first indicating a change of focus and then suggesting that we CUT, ZOOM, or TRACK, or that the CAMERA STARTS TRACKING IN. You could use those terms, and you should put them in all caps if you do, but they would start to make the script feel cluttered, as my early effort so laboriously demonstrates.

"REVEALED" is also a camera direction, but it's a more dramatic kind of word than "CUT TO." "REVEALED" is a vivid action word suggesting the impact of our first sight of living creatures in this barren wilderness.

OTHER USES FOR ALL CAPS

The first time characters are introduced in a script—human or otherwise—their names go in ALL CAPS. This is the case whether or not an actual name, a nickname, or a descriptive name is used. When the man's proper name first appears in the script of *To Build a Fire,* that should also go in all caps.

Other words that go in all caps in a screenplay are SOUNDS (such as BANG, SCREECH, EXPLOSION) and transitional devices, including CUT TO, DISSOLVE TO, FADE OUT, FADE IN, and so forth.

Don't put objects in all caps in the description. I see some professional scripts that tell us a character opens a DRAWER, pulls out a CIGARETTE, and takes a SMOKE. Sometimes this distracting typographical mannerism appears in a shooting script for the benefit of the props department, but providing them with an inventory is not really your job when you are writing a spec script. And perhaps some writers think a frequent use of all caps will make a script seem more emphatic, but to me it makes it feel like a comic book or a Dick and Jane reader or that the writer is SHOUTING AT THE TOP OF HIS LUNGS.

A related verbal tic is the overuse of exclamation points and incomplete sentences. With such noisy devices, less usually is more. Be kind to your reader's sensibilities; be confident there's enough excitement in your story that you don't need to hype it so artificially.

TRANSITIONAL DEVICES

You'll notice that I did not begin the script with a FADE IN, even though William Goldman advises in *Adventures in the Screen Trade,* "All screenplays begin with these words." Yes, some writers are fond of that hoary cliché. I've always had an aversion to starting a script this way, because it seems so corny. And it's irrelevant in any case, since the first things we see in a movie are actually the company logo or logos and other elements the writer has no control over; the lawyers and the editor will decide what comes before the first image from the story appears, and whether it fades in or is introduced with a cut or a dissolve from the shot of the Paramount mountain or the latest computer-animated vanity logo of the third executive producer's boutique company.

Whenever you change the location or the time period in a script, you need a transitional device, such as a CUT TO, DISSOLVE TO, or a FADE OUT with a corresponding FADE IN. These devices will signal the reader that such a shift is occurring. If you don't use a transitional device, the reader may have to stop and study what you wrote to orient herself. You don't want that kind of distraction. The only exception to this rule is a montage, which doesn't need transitional devices because they are implicit in that device; a montage is usually written as a numbered list of several scenes, under the heading "MONTAGE" or something more specific, such as "WAR MONTAGE" or "HONEYMOON MONTAGE." Some writers, it's true, dispense with transitional devices, evidently preferring their scripts to look more streamlined (Towne rarely uses them in *Chinatown,* for example), but doing without these helpful tools and still maintaining a logical clarity from one scene to another requires a high degree of professional dexterity.

Most modern films tend to cut from one scene to another rather than using dissolves, which are sometimes seen as old-fashioned devices, though they can be highly expressive. A FADE OUT is an emphatic way of ending a scene, but don't forget the FADE IN unless you want to combine a FADE OUT with a cut by writing FADE OUT/CUT TO (some writers use the words FADE THROUGH TO). Some screenwriters today are fond of embellishing the simple word CUT as HARD CUT or SMASH CUT. Even Steven Zaillian's brilliant screenplay for *Schindler's List* uses the term HARD CUT. But as Gertrude Stein would advise you, a cut is a cut is a cut. The effect of a cut may be intentionally jarring. Hitchcock instructs us on how effective contrast is in cutting, such as cutting from an extreme long shot to an extreme close-up, dramatically "varying the size of the image in relation to its emotional importance within a given episode." But you can convey that effect just as well through your headings and descriptions, without using such hokey language as SMASH CUT.

TYPOGRAPHY AND LAYOUT

A screenplay, unlike an outline or treatment, is single-spaced. The typeface in a script is usually twelve point. Don't use italics, boldfacing, or unusual fonts. Even when a script is generated by a word processor, as most are today, it should look as if it has been typed by a human rather than a machine. This convention dates back to the days when every script was written on a type-writer and then mimeographed for distribution. Some prominent writers, such as Woody Allen, Larry McMurtry, and David Mamet, still use their reliable manual typewriters.

McMurtry is defiant about not entering the electronic age. When he won a Golden Globe Award for the script of *Brokeback Mountain* in 2006, he said, "Most heartfelt, I thank my typewriter. My typewriter is a Hermes 3000, surely one of the noblest instruments of European genius. It has kept me for thirty years out of the dry embrace of the computer." Even though such a quirk may seem to some people impossibly retro and low-tech (I remember how difficult it was trying to make a colleague understand that I wrote most of my screenplays on a sturdy 1940 Royal manual typewriter until I finally could no longer get it repaired in Los Angeles), there's something endearing and authentically human about the traditional handmade look of a typed screenplay.

If, like most of us, you can no longer resist "the dry embrace of the computer," there are numerous software programs that will help you program your screenplay and save you time and trouble with indentations and other settings. (The most commonly used by both professionals and students is Final Draft.)

Just make sure the computer doesn't overrule you and make you write *its* way. Don't try to blame your computer if you find that happening. There's an old saying, "A bad workman blames his tools." You can deprogram most screenwriting software programs to keep them from doing irritating things like putting the word "CONTINUED" at the top and bottom of every page. In a production draft, "CONTINUED" will be added to the tops and the bottoms of pages to help everyone keep scenes straight, but in a spec script, it's needless clutter. And by all means avoid the kind of software program that suggests plot twists. Too much screenwriting is formulaic already without relying on an actual machine for your ideas.

Make sure to use standard margins for your screenplay. The left margin should be somewhat wider than the right: use an inch and a half on the left and an inch on the right. The top and the bottom margins each are one inch. Number each page in the upper right-hand corner. Sometimes the first page of a script is unnumbered, an odd convention, but page two should be numbered accordingly. The title page does not count in the numbering.

Don't number scenes. Only the final shooting script contains scene numbers. Those are added in preproduction by the production coordinator or secretary when the scenes are finalized for shooting and identified by number so that everyone working on the film knows how to refer to them in planning for people, locations, and equipment. Numbering scenes in a spec script is premature and distracting.

Short paragraphs are usually best for screenplays. They make a script look punchy and mimic the look of how scenes are edited together—a strip of film consists of shots joined together vertically. Without saying so, you're implying that each paragraph is a shot or a sequence of shots, a part of a larger unit of the story contained under a scene heading. So there should be a logic to your paragraphing. A change in the kind of action or change of vantage point within a scene usually provides a rationale for shifting to a new paragraph.

And there is nothing deadlier than a screenplay composed of long, long paragraphs. All that uninterrupted gray looks grim on the page and makes the reader's heart sink when he contemplates the task of reading it. Always try to make the reader's life pleasant rather than painful. Do as much of the reader's work for him as possible. You want your reader to be immersed in your story rather than struggling to follow it. Keep that eye moving down the page!

DIALOGUE BLOCKS

Dialogue blocks are indented, usually about three inches from the left side of the page. The name of the character speaking goes above the dialogue block in all caps. Indent the name a few spaces to the right of the dialogue indentation. You can set your computer tabs to make the process of indentation easier; if you are using a computer software program, it will do that job for you.

Don't make the names above dialogue blocks too long. Use only the first or last name of a character. Be consistent with such usage throughout the script. You can refer to a character generically ("WOMAN," "BOY," "COP," "DRUNK"), but naming characters makes them more individualized, allows for easier visualizing, and helps keep them straight in the mind of the reader. If more than one of a group of similar unnamed characters is speaking, label them "WOMAN #1," "WOMAN #2," and so on.

The point of standard and regular indentation of dialogue blocks is to make the script easy to read. The dialogue blocks stand out clearly from the descriptive paragraphs. Scripts that use irregular indentation are cumbersome and confusing to read, as well as unprofessional. You want to make your script reader-friendly, not exasperating to read.

Here's how dialogue blocks are indented in the midst of scene descriptions. This is from Larry McMurtry and Diana Ossana's script of *Brokeback Mountain*:

ALMA JR. blows on her coffee, something on her mind. This is hard for her. . . .

> ALMA JR.
> (apprehensive)
> Me and Kurt . . . we're getting married.

Looks at his oldest daughter.

> ENNIS
> How long you known this Kurt fella?

> ALMA JR.
> (relieved, talks faster)
> About a year. Wedding'll be June fifth at the Methodist Church. Jenny's singing, and Monroe's gonna cater the reception.

A beat.

> ENNIS
> This Kurt fella . . . does he love you?

ALMA JR. is startled—and touched—by the question.

> ALMA JR.
> Yes, Daddy. He loves me.

"QUIZZICALLY"

You'll note the presence of parenthetical directions under some of the character names. These indications of how dialogue should be delivered should be used sparingly. Actors and directors rightfully resent a writer who tries to direct a performance on paper by giving too many dialogue directions. It's not only presumptuous but unrealistic and unhelpful. The actor needs the freedom to develop the characterization within the blueprint of the script.

The best rule of thumb for parenthetical directions is to use them only when a particular rendering of the line is essential to its dramatic meaning, such as "apprehensive" or "relieved" in the scene above. If a line is meant to be spoken "ironically," that alters its meaning, and you can so indicate, although if that is clear from the dialogue itself, spelling it out would be superfluous. For the same reason, indicating that a line should be delivered "sadly," "lightly," "aggressively," "pointedly," or "loudly" may be unnecessary, but if the intended meaning is counterintuitive to what the words of dialogue alone may suggest, you could indicate that the line is to be delivered in a special way ("bitterly," "maliciously," "offhandedly," "teasingly"). But as Hemingway's work teaches us, it's a good rule of writing in general not to overuse adverbs. Adverbs may be a necessary evil in screenwriting, but they still should be used *sparingly* and *judiciously*.

Brief directions of movement can be given parenthetically— "turning to Mary," "looking up," "staring through window," "as he runs away." But if the direction is longer than a phrase, make it a line of description instead. If you must have a parenthetical direction that runs longer, you can break it into two lines, with the second line indented flush with the previous line:

```
              RED
         (walking uphill,
          muttering to dog)
     Go on, boy, go on...
```

Ellipses at the end of a line indicate that it trails off. A dash at the end of a line indicates a more abrupt break in the thought—often an interruption. People in real life interrupt each other frequently and overlap one another's dialogue, so it's good to do so in your screenplay. Fragmenting dialogue in these ways helps give a sense of verisimilitude.

Rather than overrelying on parenthetical directions, it's good to break up dialogue exchanges with lines of description, to give a sense of movement to a scene that otherwise could become talky and static. Long stretches of dialogue with no indications of action can be deadly; they make the script look like a play, and a dull one at that.

I. A. L. Diamond, Billy Wilder's longtime writing partner and a fellow master of witty dialogue, first came to Wilder's attention with a skit written for a Writers Guild awards show. Entitled "Quizzically," it satirically depicts a screenwriting team struggling to find a better word than "quizzically" for a parenthetical direction. The two writers rattle off all the variations they can muster before finally resorting to... "quizzically." When Diamond died in 1988, Wilder nostalgically staged the skit at a Writers Guild tribute to his partner. You can watch him directing Jack Lemmon and Walter Matthau in the skit on the Kino DVD *Billy Wilder Speaks*.

As an aspiring screenwriter struggling with the same kind of problems, you will enjoy watching "Quizzically." Perhaps the true lesson Diamond is offering his fellow screenwriters is that parenthetical directions in a script too often are self-evident, self-indulgent, and absurd. Let the dialogue speak for itself as much as possible. If it's written well, the reader will get your point, and the actors will know how to play it.

FLASHBACKS

A question that often arises with beginning screenwriters is how to indicate a flashback. This is simpler than it may seem. You need to indicate clearly that we're going into an earlier time period. The best way to do so is to use a CUT TO or a DIS-SOLVE TO, followed by a new heading that spells out the place and time:

```
As Red trudges along, his eyes take on a
distant look.

                                CUT TO:

EXT. COUNTRY STORE - DAWSON - NIGHT (A FEW
WEEKS EARLIER)

The Old-Timer, seated in a rocking chair next
to a blazing log fire, is talking with Red, who
is sitting on the floor near the fire.
```

Then when you exit the flashback and return to the main body of the story, use a transitional device and a new heading reiterating the place and time period of that setting:

```
                                CUT TO:

HILLTOP - YUKON WILDERNESS (JANUARY 1902)

Red loses his silly grin and looks somber.
```

Another way to indicate a flashback is simply to label it "(FLASHBACK)" at the end of the heading describing the scene. There's nothing wrong with doing so, but it won't be necessary if you put the time periods in the headings both for the flashback and for the scene that follows the flashback.

Some beginning screenwriters label the opening scene of a script a flashback if it takes place earlier than the main body of the story. But a flashback can only be a flashback if it *flashes back* from a later time period depicted on-screen.

There's a bigger question about flashbacks: Should they be

used at all? Howard Hawks took pride in not using flashbacks. As he said in one of our interviews, "What's good about 'em? If you're not good enough to tell a story without having flashbacks, why the hell do you try to tell them? Oh, I think some extraordinarily good writer can figure out some way of telling a story in flashbacks, but I hate them. Just like I hate screwed-up camera angles." Hawks is being overly strict—where would such classic films as *Citizen Kane, Rashomon, Wild Strawberries, The Man Who Shot Liberty Valance, The Thin Blue Line,* and *Titanic* be without flashbacks?—but a facile overreliance on flashbacks to "explain" character motivations should be avoided resolutely by screenwriters. Beginners especially should guard against that temptation. Use flashbacks only if the story requires them.

NARRATION

If you're using narration, you can put it in dialogue blocks under "NARRATOR" or the name of the character doing the narrating. Put "(VO)" under the name, indented:

```
            NARRATOR
        (VO)
  In the beginning was the Word...
```

"VO" is short for "voice-over," the term for narration from an unseen source. Some writers prefer to put the "(VO)" next to the character's name rather than below it. "(VO)" is different from "(OS)," or "offscreen," which refers to dialogue delivered by a character who's present in the scene but not visible when he or she is speaking. If a character is introduced in a script as an offscreen voice, describe the voice—male? female? how old? sounding like what?

Narrators' dialogue blocks can be interspersed with scene description and other characters' dialogue, as in this scene from

Samson Raphaelson's screenplay for the classic Ernst Lubitsch movie *Heaven Can Wait,* about an old rake named Henry Van Cleve (Don Ameche) reviewing his memories of his amorous escapades:

```
CENTRAL PARK 1874

Nurse is pushing two-year-old Henry in a
carriage.

                HENRY'S VOICE
        I was not even two, and I got involved
        in a triangle. At home, in the
        presence of the family, I was the only
        man in my nurse's life. I was her
        honeybunch, her oogi-woogie-woo. But
        the minute we got to the park—

Big Irish cop comes along.

                COP
        Hello, Bedelia!

                NURSE
        Well, if it isn't Patrick himself! (They
        sit on bench, paying no attention to
        baby. Baby starts crying.) Ah, shut up,
        you little brat! (Baby cries louder.)

CLOSE SHOT OF CRYING BABY:

                HENRY'S VOICE
        No wonder I became a cynic!
```

This wry narration by the older Henry is the kind of voice-over that Lubitsch's protégé Billy Wilder advised is best to use—it adds to what we are seeing, conveying a satirical attitude toward

Henry's past and helping reveal his character. Raphaelson writes "HENRY'S VOICE" for narration rather than using a "(VO)." It's clear from the context that the narrator is Henry as a grown-up, not a baby. But be careful if you use such a character heading for narration, because it could cause confusion if the reader thinks the character is present in the scene but not on-camera. If that is what you intend rather than narration, use "(OS)."

Another way to set narration is in dual columns, with the scene description to the left and the narration to the right. Although this technique is rarely used today other than in scripts for documentaries, using double columns can be an effective and efficient graphic device showing the reader how the film will play with narration. Wilder was fond of double columns, such as in this eloquent excerpt from *Sunset Boulevard:*

NORMA DESMOND'S HOUSE It is a grandiose Italianate structure, mottled by the years, gloomy, forsaken, the little formal garden completely gone to seed.	GILLIS' VOICE It was a great big white elephant of a place. The kind crazy movie people built in the crazy Twenties. A neglected house gets an unhappy look. This one had it in spades.

VARIATIONS

My emphasis on following the basic screenwriting format does not mean that I entirely discourage variations from that format. As I mentioned earlier, after I'd been writing screenplays for several years, I began using a quite different format. By then, I had become adept at conveying cinematic narrative in words and was able to forgo some of the standard conventions without sacrificing clarity of presentation.

When you read screenplays by such modern masters as Coppola, Towne, Paul Schrader, and the Coen brothers, you'll see how they customize their work. "Experimentation is my middle name," Coppola noted when he spoke at San Francisco State University, April 24, 2009. "I have written an original screenplay in prose, double-spaced, as a short story, where I write the dialogue either in present tense or past tense. I have been writing screenplays for so many years that I just now feel comfortable to write it in a screenplay form but take any formatting very liberally, and I do what I want. If I suddenly want to go into a more prose backstory or something, I just put it in parentheses."

Joel and Ethan Coen write in a brisk, stripped-down style, largely doing without the conventional interplay of headings and transitions, instead telling the story in poetic shorthand, as in this sequence from *The Big Lebowski* that finds the Dude (Jeff Bridges) in states of altered consciousness:

```
DUDE'S BUNGALOW

We are looking down at the Dude who lies on
his back on the Persian rug. His eyes are
closed. He wears a Walkman headset. We can just
hear an intermittent clatter leaking tinnily
through the headphones.

In his outflung hand lies a cassette case
labeled VENICE BEACH LEAGUE PLAYOFFS 1987.

The Dude absently licks his lips as we faintly
hear a ball rumbling down the lane. On its
impact with the pins, the Dude opens his eyes.

A blond woman looms over him. Next to her a
young man in paint-spattered denims stoops and
swings something toward the camera.
```

The Dude screams.

The sap catches him on the chin and sends his head thunking back onto the rug.

A million stars explode against a field of black.

We hear the "La-la-la-las" of "The Man in Me."

The black field dissolves into the pattern of the rug. The rug rolls away to reveal an aerial view of the city of Los Angeles at twilight moving below us at great speed.

Sam Hamm is another writer who usually doesn't bother interrupting the flow with a CUT TO, explaining, "I think it's a big waste of time because how the hell else are you gonna get from scene number fifty-one to scene number fifty-two? And besides, with studios keeping close tabs on your page count, you don't want to squander four or five pages' worth of story and dialogue on CUT TO. I try to avoid CUT TO unless I'm drawing attention to the cut, as in: (a) the sort of associative/metaphorical juxtaposition beloved of Russian theorists, or (b) the cheap gag. If you see the line 'Sorry. No way. You will never, EVER get me on that rollercoaster,' followed immediately by a CUT TO—well, I don't have to tell you what comes next."

In his *Taxi Driver* script, Paul Schrader avoids the standard scene headings and substitutes what could be considered chapter titles ("TRAVIS GETS A JOB," "WE MEET TRAVIS," "FURTHER THOUGHTS," "SMALL TALK IN A GREASY SPOON," "THE PUSSY AND THE .44"). Schrader groups related scenes under a snappy, evocative title to point the audience in the thematic directions he wants the story to follow (the titles don't appear on-screen but serve to guide the reader). He often comments on scenes analytically, offering asides to the reader, as in this chapter on Travis's favorite forms of entertainment:

```
MID-AFTERNOON MELODRAMA

Direct cut to pornographic movie: this is the
first time we have actually seen the porno
movie itself. Several actors and actresses are
dallying on screen in whatever manner the
ratings board deems permissible.

Whatever the action, the movie's decor is
strictly Zody's—ersatz landscape paintings,
tufted bedspreads. As in most porno films, the
actors look up occasionally towards the camera
to receive instructions. Studio grunts, groans
and moans of pleasure have been dubbed in.

Action on screen begins to go into slow motion,
the actors and actresses gradually transforming
obscenity into poetry.

CUT to TRAVIS, sitting in his chair in his
apartment, watching afternoon soap opera. He is
cleaning his .38 and eating from a jar of apple
sauce.
```

The Schrader style (which probably influenced the Coens) dispenses with most conventionally "cinematic" devices to tell its story like a punchy, entertaining work of literature rather than a dry blueprint. Eventually I began following the Schrader style in some of my screenplays. While I found that style liberating, supple, and fun to employ, I don't necessarily recommend it to beginning screenwriters. In fact, I hesitated to include this section in the book for fear of influencing writers to start with this style rather than building up to it through experience. Until you have written a few scripts in the basic screenwriting format, dispensing with such conventions as scene headings, transitional devices, and other useful stylistic elements would be ill-advised and dangerous. You run the risk of unintelligibility if you try to write in a freer style before you have learned all the tools of the trade. So I include this note on variations in format for your future reference, with this major caveat.

THE TITLE PAGE

Your title page, the first page inside the covers, should look simple and streamlined. The film's title appears in all caps, centered and underlined a few lines above the midpoint of the page. Below that write, on separate lines, "Screenplay," "by," and your name, and then information about the source material. If you are adapting a published short story of the same title, write "Based on the short story" and "by" and the name of the author, all on separate lines. If another screenwriter has the story credit, write "Based on a story" and "by" and the name of that writer, all on separate lines. All the lines are centered on the page:

<u>TO BUILD A FIRE</u>

Screenplay

by

Joseph McBride

Based on the short story

by

Jack London

If you give your film a different title from that of the source material—say you want to call your adaptation of "To Build a Fire" *Fire and Ice,* from the poem of that title by Robert Frost— include the original title directly under the "Based on" line:

<u>FIRE AND ICE</u>

Screenplay

by

Joseph McBride

Based on the short story

"To Build a Fire"

by

Jack London

TITLES

The title of your film should open up ways of seeing the film. It should also be easy to say and remember. Otherwise people won't mention it to their friends. *Synecdoche, New York,* a surreal movie about life becoming theater, wasn't helped by its tongue-twisting title, even though true Charlie Kaufman fans appreciated the arcane pun both referring to a figure of speech and alluding to a city in eastern New York. There are exceptions to this rule about avoiding esoteric titles—many people in 1960 didn't know how to pronounce *Psycho* (a Wisconsin theater manager told me that some called it "Physico" or "Pissco"), but the film was a huge hit nonetheless. Titles should show some imagination rather than just being a label telling what kind of story it is or what it's about (such as *Going Down the River* or *Leaving Home;* gerunds are the curse of modern titlemaking). Avoid clichés in titles if at all possible. Too many modern films treat the title as a form of short synopsis to ensure that potential moviegoers aren't surprised by the experience. That's a cravenly commercial approach.

A touch of poetry or metaphor would help in a title—as in *Sunset Boulevard, Strangers on a Train, The Last Picture Show, Dances with Wolves,* and *No Country for Old Men.* Reading poems is a good way to think of titles—that's how Margaret Mitchell found *Gone with the Wind* (from Ernest Dowson's "Non Sum Qualis Eram Bonae Sub Regno Cynarae"). The Bible has always been another fertile source for screenwriters. Hemingway thought the best titles were in the book of Ecclesiastes, from which he drew the title for *The Sun Also Rises;* Ecclesiastes gave Henry James the title *The Golden Bowl,* Edith Wharton *The House of Mirth,* and John Grisham *A Time to Kill.* Shakespeare has provided writers with such titles as *The Sound and the Fury, Something Wicked This Way Comes, Brave New World, Pale Fire, The Winter of Our Discontent,* and *What*

Dreams May Come. No modern writer was more brilliant with titles than Tennessee Williams. His richly metaphorical and allusive titles include *The Glass Menagerie; A Streetcar Named Desire; Summer and Smoke; The Rose Tattoo; Cat on a Hot Tin Roof; Suddenly, Last Summer;* and *Small Craft Warnings.*

A title doesn't have to make a great deal of obvious sense if it is striking—*The Silence of the Lambs* is a good example. Titles shouldn't be extraordinarily long, unless there is a valid reason, and even then they will be abbreviated in common reference. Short titles are often the best, as Hitchcock proved with *Blackmail, Sabotage, Rebecca, Suspicion, Notorious, Rear Window, Vertigo, Frenzy,* among others, and as James Cameron showed with *Titanic,* a fitting title for what at the time was the biggest hit in film history. The value of a short, memorable title was demonstrated again by his subsequent box-office champion, *Avatar.*

SOME THOUGHTS ON CREDITS

Although it's not mandatory to do so, you should take the opportunity in your script to indicate how and where in the film the opening credit sequence appears. The screenwriter can suggest how the credits will be integrated into the storytelling; they can serve a variety of useful narrative functions.

The phrase "MAIN TITLE CREDITS" refers to the titles that come early in the film. In most films today, only the principal credits come at the beginning, after the company logos— such as the company or person presenting the film, the other production companies, the stars, sometimes the writer and the director, and the title of the film itself. The order of billing is determined by contracts and guild rules (for example, if the director's credit comes at the beginning, the writer's must as well). Most of the credits today appear at the end of the film, in that seemingly endless crawl. (For anyone serious about film, it's important to pay attention to screen credits, not only to pay respect to your fellow workers in film but also because you can learn so much from this information.)

Indicating where the opening credits appear can be an expressive aesthetic device in your script, punctuating the action in dramatic ways while effortlessly providing information on your story, characters, and themes. If you have an unusual idea for how this should be done, put it into the script, and maybe it will be followed. A celebrated example of a brilliantly metaphorical credit sequence is the one in Stanley Kubrick's *Dr. Strangelove or: How I Learned to Stop Worrying and Love the Bomb.* The credits (by Pablo Ferro) are skywritten over stock footage of two planes refueling in midair ("copulating") to the strains of "Try a Little Tenderness." This outrageous sexual innuendo sets up the film's theme of the interlocking nature of the warlike and sexual impulses. At the same time the credit sequence performs the more mundane task of letting us know that the film will revolve around the B-52 bomber, the perpetually aloft delivery device of nuclear weapons during the Cold War.

You also can provide backstory unobtrusively in your MAIN TITLE CREDITS. The opening credits of *Milk* powerfully establish the repressive world in which gay people lived before activist Harvey Milk (Sean Penn) and others worked to liberate them in the 1960s and 1970s. Newsreel footage of gays and lesbians being arrested in 1950s America provides graphic visual evidence of that repression before the body of the story begins. Even though we don't see much of Milk's life in New York before he leaves for San Francisco, those newsreel scenes also suggest the personal conditions against which he rebelled. The opening chord you strike with a movie helps set its tone and themes. Such decisions about how to open a movie are part of the screenwriter's creative challenge.

Interspersing credits amidst the opening scenes can serve as another way to usher the viewer into the company of your characters. Such a practical use of credits can help give a graceful sense of continuity to otherwise disparate expository scenes. A good example of that technique are the montages of people arriving at Heathrow Airport and various Londoners going about their day in the opening of *Love Actually,* a British ensemble movie written and directed by Richard Curtis. Laying credits over the introductory scenes provides some visual unity and implies a thematic connection among the lives of the eight couples the film will follow. A bit of narration by the prime minister, played by Hugh Grant, adds further cohesion. When one of my students was having trouble figuring out how to give a feeling of linkage to her opening script scenes showing her protagonist's daily routine, I showed her *Love Actually* and suggested she use her credits for a similar purpose. Suddenly her scenes felt more unified and less mundane, while still serving the essential purpose of starting the film with a "day-in-the-life-of" feeling.

There are many other ways to incorporate your opening credits. At one extreme of stylization are the cartoon sequences in the Pink Panther series. The credits of the first entry, *The Pink Panther,* were so popular that they spun off a series of animated shorts featuring the character. But for sheer iconic scene setting and ritualistic invocation of an ongoing character, the partly animated credits of the James Bond series set the gold standard. Accompanied by a brassy theme song, the films typically start with a view through a gunsight, a man in a tuxedo firing a long phallic weapon as the screen turns blood red, and, after a spectacular action sequence, the titles appearing over images of violence and gyrating, seminaked women—an instantly recognizable trademark opening that also serves to give the viewer a visual précis of the Bond ethos.

Other noteworthy examples of credit sequences providing a metaphor for what is to follow include the contents of a child's cigar box in *To Kill a Mockingbird,* setting the 1930s time period and the film's vantage point, with a child's hand crayoning the title card and other key images; the animated double-helix pattern suggesting a whirlpool of obsession spinning out of a woman's eyeball in *Vertigo;* zoom shots into television antennae on tops of houses in *Fahrenheit 451* as a voice reads the credits, since the printed word is banned in that futuristic society. Steven Spielberg's *Catch Me If You Can* begins with an animated introduction to the protean criminal Frank Abagnale Jr. (Leonardo DiCaprio) being pursued by an FBI agent (Tom Hanks) in 1960s pop-art style, providing a foreshadowing of the scenes we're about to see as well as capturing the cinematic ambience of that period. David Fincher's crime thriller *Se7en* starts with a creepy credit collage, filmed and edited in a purposely jarring style, showing the hands of an otherwise unseen serial killer obsessively putting together notebook pages using fragments of words and images cut from printed sources with a razor blade and assembled with tweezers and a sewing needle.

Credits such as these provide a quick guide on how to "read" the movie, its tone and themes and style. Of course, not every credit sequence needs to be clever or fancy. Sometimes plain white lettering on a black screen (as Woody Allen favors for his films) is the simplest way of setting up a movie. Allen usually picks a scratchy old jazz recording to put us into the right mood for his quirky, somewhat retro romances. This personalized approach helps stamp the author's imprint on our consciousness as surely as the nineteenth-century Playbill font and rousing folk music declare a Western the work of John Ford. You can describe the look of your title sequence in a sentence or two, and if you think of a suitable piece of music to put under the opening sequence, mention it in the script.

Or you can simply indicate where the credits appear and hope the filmmakers do them up right.

10

Actors Are Your Medium

Yes, actors are your medium. That statement may surprise some
of you. But the actor is your primary means of expression as a
screenwriter. Stanley Kubrick made this point in a 1960 article for
Sight & Sound entitled "Words and Movies," in which he wrote
that the screenwriter or dramatist "must not think of paper and
ink and words as being his writing tools, but rather that he works
in flesh and feeling.... Writers tend to approach the creation of
drama too much in terms of words, failing to realise that the
greatest force they have is the mood and feeling they can produce in the audience through the actor. They tend to see the actor
grudgingly, as someone likely to ruin what they have written,
rather than seeing that the actor is in every sense their medium."
If you don't give your actors good parts to play, your script will
sink into a morass of dull inexpressiveness. Writing playable parts
will make your script come alive. So how do you do that?

The first thing to realize is that you must have great respect
for actors and for what you call upon them to do. When people
see a film, they mostly follow the actors; when John Ford was
asked how to watch a film, he replied, "Look at the eyes." He
also said, "The secret is people's faces, their eye expression,
their movements." As a result, much of your work as a writer,
and the work of the director, is in the hands of the actors. That
should inspire close and equal collaboration with the people in
front of the camera. But many people who aspire to be filmmakers (a term that encompasses screenwriters) tend to think

of themselves as superior to actors or regard them as a necessary evil: Actors are those silly, overpaid folks who obsess over their hairstyles and trailers and appear in the tabloids getting stoned at trendy nightclubs. Or they are regarded as mere props in the director's mise-en-scène.

Was Hitchcock joking when he declared that actors are cattle? He claimed he was misquoted: "What I really said was, 'Actors should be *treated* like cattle.'" He also said he envied Walt Disney because if Disney didn't like an actor, he could just tear him up. These comments were mostly directorial bravado. Hitchcock actually was a superb director of actors, guiding them skillfully while allowing them a certain degree of freedom within his rigorous visual design. But many filmmakers feel a paralyzing fear in the presence of actors. An insecure director hates actors because he knows they can make or break his film, and a major reason for his insecurity is that he doesn't understand what they do and doesn't know how to speak their language.

The director who admits to revering actors is less common, but when you find one, listen to what he says. "You've got to love actors," said Francis Ford Coppola to the audience at his 2009 talk at San Francisco State University.

Of all the artists [involved in filmmaking], they're the ones who have nothing between them and criticism. If you reject an actor, you're rejecting the person's soul. Although they can be nutty, when they do something beautiful, they do it naked. I have nothing but admiration and respect for them. To me, the cinema is where acting and writing come together. But you've never seen a film where ultimately it's not about where the writing and the acting have collided to make some incredible impression. Rarely if ever is there a movie in which the photography is so great but the acting is nothing much and the story is crappy and yet works. The interesting thing I have learned in the movie business is that many colleagues, for the most part, the film directors that I admire, many of

them (not the ones who began as actors) know next to nothing about acting and are in no position to help an actor. Yet
rarely in a cinema program does anyone know much about
that subject.

When I met Jean Renoir on my first visit to Hollywood in
1970, I asked what advice he had for someone who wanted to
be a director (yes, that was my misguided ambition when I was
twenty-three, before I realized being a writer was a better way
of life). "Try a little acting," Renoir advised. He told me that
having some experience as an actor would help me understand
how actors work. As uncanny luck would have it, four days later
I had my first experience as an actor in a film directed by Orson
Welles. From the first hours of shooting *The Other Side of the
Wind,* I appreciated the wisdom of Renoir's advice. Because I
was an utter neophyte and playing something of a buffoon, a
satirical version of myself, Welles loaded me down with props to
give me things to do, and I struggled so much that Welles reas-
suringly told me the only actor he ever knew who could handle
so many props well was Erich von Stroheim. When I sighed after
the seventh take of one shot went wrong, Welles said, "Now you
appreciate what actors go through." In keeping with Welles's
semi-improvisatory approach to the project, I was allowed to
help write my own part. Welles would discuss with me what
I would say, we would kick ideas back and forth, and then he
would write the scene, which I was expected to follow verbatim.
Being an actor for six years with Welles provided me with
an invaluable education in how actors feel in front of the camera, what they are called upon to do, how they interact with one
another, how they are treated by the director, and what dialogue
is playable and what is not. And not only did I have the opportunity to work under the man I consider the cinema's greatest
director of actors, but I gained invaluable experience by helping
to write my own dialogue and conceive the character. The experience (along with some other forays into acting) enriched my

subsequent work as a screenwriter, sharpening my skills in writing easily speakable dialogue and giving me a far clearer sense of how to construct parts for actors to play. I would recommend that you also follow Renoir's advice to "Try a little acting," even if only in an amateur film or local stage production.

THE WRITER SAVED BY THE ACTOR

Even though they can't work without you, a writer should always be grateful to actors and what they can add to your work. They can make your script seem so much better.

A lesson in what an actor can bring to a part was given to me by Henry Beckman, the fine character actor who appeared in my film *Blood and Guts* as Red Henkel, the manager of the wrestling troupe. Henry brought warmth and humor to the part, for which he won a Canadian Film Award as best supporting actor. Red's most endearing quality is his loyalty. It is displayed when his star wrestler, Dandy Dan, has a heart attack and is forced to retire from the troupe. I had written that in the scene following Dan's retirement, the troupe's bus rolls out with his name painted over. Henry objected, "Red would never do that." How right he was. Dandy Dan's name stayed on the bus for the rest of the movie. After the filming, I sent Henry a letter of thanks for understanding Red better than I had. Henry later told me he had framed the letter and kept it on the wall of his study.

WHAT IS MOVIE ACTING?

Film acting is a widely misunderstood craft. In order to write good parts for actors, a screenwriter should appreciate what screen acting is and is not and how it differs from stage acting. The most common misperception is that the quality of movie acting can be measured by the extent to which the actor submerges his or her personality in the character. The corollary to this assumption is that stars are not really actors because they "play themselves." I believe that the exact opposite is true. The best movie actors "play themselves"; the highest form of movie acting is creating a persona that's indivisible from the role. That's what defines that rare creature, a genuine movie star.

Actors who put on beards, mannerisms, and accents to hide themselves in characters are usually the actors who get the highest praise, because the mechanics show most obviously. Their performances have the veneer of flamboyant stage acting, and audiences often are overly impressed with showiness and virtuosity. But such actors are often second-rate movie performers compared to the great stars who have constructed compelling and recognizable screen personas. Such stars subsume their characters into themselves; that is what makes someone a star. A star is someone who could say, with Walt Whitman, "I am large, I contain multitudes." John Wayne was a far better movie actor than Laurence Olivier, however fine Olivier may have been on the stage. Marilyn Monroe was a splendid movie actor; Helen Hayes ("The First Lady of the American Theater") was not. Gary Cooper could hardly have functioned onstage; the stage would diminish such contemporary stars as Jack Nicholson and Angelina Jolie, but they, like Cooper, captivate viewers on-screen.

It's important for screenwriters not to confuse these two kinds of actors; if you do, you will tend to write parts better suited for the theater than for the screen. This is not to say that some actors can't be good both onstage and on-screen, as Katharine Hepburn, Marlon Brando, Judi Dench, Helen Mirren, and Anthony Hopkins have amply demonstrated. But the demands of the roles are far different in the two media; such versatile actors are able to modulate their performances to the more intimate demands of motion pictures. A screenwriter doesn't have to provide big speeches and opportunities for heavy emoting in order to create a solid screen characterization.

Most of a film performance is simply behaving. An actor

doesn't have to constantly be *doing* something to create a character; instead he or she mostly *inhabits* the character. The actor brings to the performance the basic data of his or her own physique and personality. Alfred Hitchcock, who knew something about the British aristocracy, of whom it was said they "did nothing well," borrowed that expression to describe film acting. He told Truffaut, "When a film has been properly staged, it isn't necessary to rely upon the player's virtuosity or personality for tension and dramatic effects. In my opinion, the chief requisite for an actor is the ability to do nothing well, which is by no means as easy as it sounds. He should be willing to be utilized and wholly integrated into the picture by the director and the camera. He must allow the camera to determine the proper emphasis and the most effective dramatic highlights." Truffaut replies, "This neutrality you expect from your actors is an interesting concept. The point is clearly made in some of your more recent pictures, like *Rear Window* or *Vertigo*. In both films James Stewart isn't required to emote; he simply looks— three or four hundred times—and then you show the viewer what he's looking at. That's all." Well, that's not really all: Stewart's face shows great emotional depths in those two superb performances. But the point about less being more in screen acting is worth keeping in mind when you might be tempted to let your characters start selling their emotions strenuously to the audience rather than just being and doing.

Heath Ledger doesn't need to say much to embody a memorable character in *Brokeback Mountain*. The inhibitions and inarticulateness of the man he is playing, Ennis Del Mar, become key dimensions of this story about gay characters who must keep their sexual preferences hidden in a repressive society. Ledger's subtle facial expressions alternately conceal or reveal his deeper feelings without resorting to words, for he is living "the love that dare not speak its name." This finely modulated performance demonstrates the truth of John Wayne's oft-quoted statement, "The difference between good and bad acting is the difference between acting and reacting. In a bad picture, you can see 'em acting all over the place. In a good picture, they react in a logical way to the situations they're in."

Saying that Ledger "plays himself" as Ennis does not mean that he is identical with the character he is playing. Although Robert De Niro is famous for immersing himself in the occupations of his characters and even put on sixty pounds to play the aging boxer Jake LaMotta in *Raging Bull,* that kind of stunt is not necessary to create a character. Ledger's "playing himself" on-screen in *Brokeback Mountain* means instead that he is finding depths of expression within himself to convey what the character is thinking and feeling. Those depths come out in his facial expressions and body language; dialogue is used by screenwriters Larry McMurtry and Diana Ossana more to help Ennis restrain his deepest feelings than to verbalize them. And an actor of less sensitivity and strength of character might not have successfully embodied Ennis's clandestine personality. But the restraint began with Annie Proulx's conception of the character and the world of scenes she created for him to inhabit.

John Wayne, for the record, denied that he simply played himself on-screen ("It's quite obvious it can't be done"). His definition of his method more subtly defined the important distinction between *being yourself* on-screen and *acting yourself* on-screen: "If you are yourself, you'll be the dullest son of a bitch in the world on-screen. You have to act yourself, you have to project something—a personality." When an actress in his last movie, *The Shootist,* commented on how natural he was, Wayne said, "Natural, hell. Nobody's natural in front of the camera. What she means is that I'm acting natural." Studying the gradual development of Wayne's screen persona before he burst into stardom as the Ringo Kid in John Ford's *Stagecoach* reveals a careful process of evolving his "natural" gestures and mannerisms, postures and methods of movement, the sum total of which transformed Marion Mitchell Morrison into the star we now recognize instantly as "John Wayne."

Within that persona Wayne was able to find a considerable range of inflections, shades, and nuances as he explored different aspects of himself throughout his long film career, in such varied roles as the tyrannical cattle baron Tom Dunson in *Red River,* the paternal U.S. Cavalry captain Nathan Brittles in *She Wore a Yellow Ribbon,* the pacifistic boxer Sean Thornton in *The Quiet Man,* the obsessive Indian hater Ethan Edwards in *The Searchers,* the rowdy and drunken Marshal Rooster Cogburn in *True Grit,* and the gravely valedictory gunfighter J. B. Books in *The Shootist.* Wayne may not have had as broad a range as chameleon actors such as De Niro or Dustin Hoffman have today, but his body of work encompasses an array of characters fully as rich as theirs and with a more strongly individualized screen presence. That accounts for Wayne's enduring appeal as a movie star long after his death.

Today, actors such as Tommy Lee Jones and Tom Hanks have created popular star personas akin to Wayne's or James Stewart's, instantly recognizable images with a wide range of possible variations. The most versatile stars today are allowed, or encouraged, to explore roles that take them farther beyond their established personas than Wayne could do or wanted to do; Stewart, with his constantly evolving and adventurous screen persona, was more akin to one of our contemporary stars. Jones can play, with equal conviction, a Wayne-like sheriff with Texas reticence and old-fashioned integrity in *No Country for Old Men* or an upper-class gay New Orleans Kennedy assassination conspirator in *JFK.* Hanks, perhaps our closest equivalent to Stewart, can portray a childlike, mentally challenged man in *Forrest Gump* or a fatherly schoolteacher turned platoon captain in *Saving Private Ryan.*

Theatrically trained actresses such as Meryl Streep and Cate Blanchett have developed equally strong and diverse cinematic personas. Streep is sometimes mocked for her remarkable facility with accents, but though she inhabits characters of widely varied nationalities and occupations, she is always recognizably

"Meryl Streep," as we have come to expect her to be on-screen. This is not, as some might think, a flaw in her talent, a "mere" signal of theatrical virtuosity. She is a star as distinguished as Katharine Hepburn but one with a wider gallery of characters within her distinctive persona. Streep might seem to undercut my argument that stars always play themselves, but it could be argued that the self she plays is simply richer and more kaleidoscopically varied than that of other contemporary stars and therefore a measure of her greater brilliance. Such actors erase the old distinction between character actor and star. They challenge screenwriters to keeping finding new ways of expanding their familiar personalities.

Writing with a specific star in mind can be a fruitful approach for a screenwriter, even if you don't wind up getting that star to play the role (I. A. L. Diamond joked that you always write for Cary Grant but always wind up with Rock Hudson). Visualizing an actual person playing the part you are writing can help you flesh out the characterization. Your mental casting process can range as widely as you want, over the landscape of actors past and present, from stars to lesser-knowns. I once wrote a screenplay with the rising young actress Amy Irving in mind and kept her picture on the wall above my typewriter for more than a year while I was writing it. When she finally read the script, she said, "Don't do it without me." Although we couldn't raise the money on her name to make the film, thinking of her helped me immeasurably in conceiving a three-dimensional character in the screenplay and when I subsequently developed the story into a novel.

ALLOWING SPACE TO CREATE

Giving the actors space and latitude to participate in creating their characters is one of the primary tasks of the screenwriter, as it is for the director as well. The writer sketches in the basic elements of the character but leaves room for the actor to embellish it, to add nuances, to find other dimensions in concert with the director. Building such freedom into a script is the opposite of the tendency toward micromanagement that can be seen in the work of some aspiring screenwriters, such as my early script for *To Build a Fire.* If you try to anticipate everything a character might do, you're delusional, since so much has to happen before the camera once the cast and the director go to work on location or in the studio. The last thing you should do is to limit their creative opportunities.

That doesn't mean you should be vague in your descriptions of the characters or leave gaping holes in their actions or motivations. The essence of the characters should be clear from the script. Their movements need to be described; their emotions need to be presented clearly. Their moment-by-moment behavior should be indicated, even though it cannot be charted with total precision, except in critical scenes that allow for such close description of behavior, at the rare times in the story when the reader must know exactly, in minute detail, what the character is doing. Generally, however, the script should give the broad outline of the character's actions and hit the dramatic high points, leaving the rest to be filled in by the actor, whose job is to make your blueprint three-dimensional.

PICKING UP HER GLOVE

Let's study an example of what a great actor, working with an eloquent screenplay, can bring to a role, something beyond what is written but clearly stems from the characterization laid out by the writer. In *On the Waterfront,* Marlon Brando makes a celebrated and richly meaningful gesture that emerged from improvisation during a rehearsal on a wintry day on location in a Hoboken, New Jersey, park. As usual in a film, the significance of a gesture depends greatly on its context, and the gesture in turn amplifies the meaning of the context in which it occurs. In Budd Schulberg's story and screenplay (suggested by articles by Malcolm Johnson) for this film directed by Elia Kazan, Terry Malloy (Brando), a waterfront hoodlum, finds himself in the company of a well-mannered young woman, Edie Doyle (Eva Marie Saint), whose dockworker father has sent her to a girls' school run by nuns. Terry is struck by Edie's decency and kindness, a bracing contrast with the crude and violent life he is leading. Terry has just rescued Edie from a dangerous situation, and as they walk through the park, they pass a bum who drops a hint that Terry was complicit in the murder of Edie's brother. Despite her anxious awareness of the threat Terry represents, she is attracted to him all the same. Because he has protected her, she lets down her guard.

Ingmar Bergman once said that a movie star must convey a sense of danger. Some perfectly fine actors lack that sense of danger, so they are unable to become stars. Brando became his generation's most emblematic star—and the actor who changed the face of modern acting—by radiating danger. He did so both in his characters' actions and in the disruptive threat he posed to the old-fashioned norms of well-mannered acting. His notorious "mumbling" was actually a form of more authentic speech than the declamatory style imported to the screen from the stage. His improvisatory gestures came out of a Method awareness of the value of subtext in creating a rounded character by making the subconscious visible.

Towne notes that great stars usually embody paradox and contradiction and that what Brando embodies is the paradox of "the sensitive brute." Such a dual nature helps account for the range of a star's persona and for his or her ability to appeal broadly to movie audiences, crossing boundaries of gender appeal. Kazan, who also directed Brando's breakthrough performance as Stanley Kowalski in Tennessee Williams's *A Streetcar Named Desire,* both onstage and on the screen, said of Brando, "He was such a simple—like a child—but there was so much *violence* in him....I think the trick, the wonderful thing about him, is the ambivalence, again, between a soft, yearning, *girlish* side to him and a dissatisfaction that's violent and can be dangerous." Both of those traits are on display as Terry walks through the park with Edie in *On the Waterfront*.

Schulberg's script doesn't indicate the park setting that adds so much to the scene (his is simply set on a street) but gives numerous indications of how these two characters interact. The dialogue shows their gradual rapprochement. Terry drops his customary bravado to speak more gently and humorously; Edie sheds her aversion and reaches out with empathetic responses. In parenthetical directions in the dialogue blocks, Schulberg has Terry behave "nervously" and speak "evasively" with her, has him say, "Don't be afraid of me. I ain't going to bite you" (in the film, this becomes, "You don't have to be afraid of me, I'm not gonna bite you") and describes him as becoming "increasingly impressed, almost awe-struck." Schulberg describes Edie "glancing at him and then hurrying her steps" while she "gives Terry as wide a berth as possible." But she finds herself "smiling at the way he puts it" and speaking to him "quietly" and "tenderly." When Terry is about to say something coarse, he "looks at her and catches himself, his face registering: I'm with a Nice—Girl."

This well-crafted scene as it appears in the screenplay would be more than enough to create a complex and compelling portrait of two people finding tentative attraction in their differences. But what makes the scene most memorable is a piece of business that's not in the script. Edie wears white gloves, costuming that speaks volumes about her sheltered life and aspirations toward gentility. As they walk into the park, they enter a playground, a choice of setting by Kazan that subtly emphasizes the childlike innocence emerging from Terry's hardened façade. Edie pulls one of the gloves from her pocket and drops it nervously. Terry, without breaking his stride, picks it up. He walks to a children's swing, sits on the seat, and puts the glove on his hand as he talks.

This gesture emerged during a rehearsal when Saint dropped her glove and Brando improvised with it; the director told them to keep it in the film (you can tell it was planned because the scene is done in a tracking shot, which smoothly pauses for a moment so Brando can reach down for the glove). As Kazan pointed out to Jeff Young in their interview book *Kazan: The Master Director Discusses His Films* (which I'd recommend to any writer who wants to understand film acting), Brando's gesture serves a valuable plot function: "I had to somehow answer the question as to why she stays with him. Edie knows that from the point of view of propriety and public opinion, she shouldn't. Even though she wants to. He wants to keep her with him, but he doesn't want to exert any force. He wants to approach her gently. That was a time when Brando saved me. Eve dropped her glove by accident, and he picked it up and put it on his own hand. I could never have thought of that. When she reached for her glove, he got there first so she had to stay with him. At the same time he could play it cool, as though he didn't know he was keeping her. Also, there are all kinds of sexual overtones implicit in the gesture."

Most crucially, the business with the glove is an unconscious sign of Terry's buried sensitivity, his "girlish" way of trying to accommodate her gentility, playfully but with an unspoken seriousness of purpose. Terry's gesture in picking up the glove is seemingly unconscious, a direct line to his inner feelings he cannot express verbally, and when he becomes aware of what he is doing, "he could play it cool" by not expressing his desires in words. Even though Schulberg did not think of this piece of business, Brando's improvisation and Kazan's embrace of it are an outgrowth of what Schulberg wrote about Terry and the dynamics between these characters. The script inspires the actors to inhabit the characters more fully and bring them alive under the tension of the moment; Kazan said the Hoboken location and the cold weather were crucial elements that helped bring reality to their behavior. It may be hard for a writer to imagine all this physical interplay while writing in his study, but you should strive to discover such expressive character touches.

Try to show what the character is thinking and feeling without resorting to dialogue. Thought is most powerfully conveyed through the ways a character acts or reacts and by showing what he or she is reacting to. You can describe the character's thoughts on the page as long as your description doesn't become too abstract and as long as the action gives a clear physical sense of how we will understand the character's thinking process.

TO BUILD A SCENE

Keeping in mind this background about the essence of movie acting, let's see how we would go about conveying Red's thoughts and feelings in the climactic scene of *To Build a Fire*. The basic situation is this: After the snow falls from the tree and extinguishes the fire, Red sits stunned, contemplating his dreadful fate. Simply writing "He sits stunned" would give the actor something to play, but not much. What does it tell the actor about how to play the scene? He has a blank look. What else? The actor would have to come up with something on his own to keep the scene from feeling flat or passing too abruptly. Do you want the poor guy to have to sit out there in the snow rewriting your script? If the writer abrogates responsibility for such a critical part of the story, he's not doing his job properly.

Let's see what could be added to the scene description:

```
He sits stunned. After a few moments he panics.
He wonders if there is any way to escape.
Gradually he becomes aware that the situation
is hopeless.
```

This is somewhat better, but not much. It gives the actor some more nuances or "beats" to play, but it's too abstract and internalized to be easily playable. It needs filling out:

He sits stunned. After a few moments, he looks
around in panic but can see no way of escape.
He seems already frozen in place, unable to
move. His face is a numb mask of fear. Only his
eyes seem alive. He studies his immediate
surroundings with his darting eyes—his numbed
hands and feet, the squashed embers of the
fire, the dog watching with patient wariness.
Red laughs bitterly. He realizes his situation
is hopeless. His face begins to settle into a
resigned expression. He closes his eyes. When
he finally opens them, he seems at peace.

This could be considered micromanaging the performance, but
for such a key scene the actor needs all the help he can get from
the writer. The actor should add more nuances of his own, but
this would give him a solid blueprint to work with.

11

Dialogue as Action

After I went to the first Hollywood screening of John Huston's *The Man Who Would Be King* in 1975, I ran into a studio executive I knew and admired as someone with uncommonly intelligent taste in movies. When I praised the film as a "masterpiece," the executive shook his head and said, "Too talky." Shortly after that, I had lunch with Huston and asked what he thought of that criticism.

"To me," he said, "dialogue can be action; what goes on behind the eyes can be action. It doesn't require flashing sabers."

Between those two arguments lies much fertile ground for exploration by screenwriters. Today the prevailing attitude among studio executives is even more aggressively tilted against so-called "talky" dialogue; the scales have tipped heavily toward wall-to-wall action or slapstick comedy and minimal dialogue, for fear of boring the predominantly youthful audience (presumed by Hollywood to be subliterate) and the increasingly important foreign segment of the marketplace. But the view of dialogue Huston expressed—dialogue as a form of action, a battleground and playground for the revelation of character—has given us most of our best films. If we are trying to explore human nature in our screenplays and not just showing car crashes, explosions, and superheroes, we disregard at our peril the contribution good dialogue can make to a movie.

In *The Man Who Would Be King,* written by Huston and his longtime assistant Gladys Hill from the classic short story by

Rudyard Kipling, Daniel Dravot (Sean Connery) and Peachy Carnehan (Michael Caine) are nineteenth-century British soldiers of fortune who fool the natives of a remote region of Afghanistan into thinking Danny is their hereditary king, the son of Alexander the Great. When they fail, spectacularly, due to Danny's hubris, they have a moment of truth before dying at the hands of his outraged subjects. The following exchange, delivered as they retreat with their rifles while dodging a barrage of stones, may sound "talky" to impatient ears, but it's glorious talk, and its ironically elaborate formality of rhythm and locution, true to the Victorian military setting, helps give the scene a fitting valedictory grace:

> DANNY
> Peachy, I'm heartily ashamed for
> gettin' you killed instead of going
> home rich like you deserved to, on
> account of me bein' so bleedin' high
> and bloody mighty. Can you forgive me?

> PEACHY
> That I can and that I do, Danny, free
> and full and without let or hindrance.

> DANNY
> Everything's all right then.

So what kind of dialogue, then, is actually too "talky"? For a definition I turn to Lajos Egri, who points out in *The Art of Dramatic Writing,*

Art is selective, not photographic, and your point will carry further if unhampered by unnecessary verbiage. A "talky" play is the sign of internal trouble—trouble coming from poor preliminary work. A play is talky because the characters have ceased to grow and the conflict has stopped moving.

Hence the dialogue can only mill around and around, boring the audience and forcing the director to devise business for the actors, in the vain hope of diverting the unfortunate playgoers.

That's all the more true in movies, which provide so much visual data to surround the dialogue, making it less necessary for the dialogue to carry the drama. I usually wait a while in my classes, as I am doing here, to start talking about dialogue. Since we're all accustomed to communicating in speech, most beginning screenwriters have some natural facility for writing dialogue. The harder part of learning screenwriting is learning how to tell stories visually. So I stress the visual in the early weeks of screenwriting classes, as I have done in the previous chapters of this book. Then I start stressing that "writing in pictures" does not mean that cinema is *only* a visual art form or that you should have a disdain for dialogue. Hitchcock's denigration of most movies as being mere "pictures of people talking" has become commonly accepted among modern filmmakers, especially those who don't come from a literary background. But for all the value of silent storytelling, ignoring the importance of talk in pictures is foolish. There are many compelling and memorable scenes in Hitchcock's films that rely primarily on acting and dialogue rather than on virtuosic camerawork.

John Ford, like Hitchcock, came from silent filmmaking. They were part of that early generation of directors who naturally thought in pictures; that training served them well after the talkies arrived, by keeping their films from becoming static talkfests rather than moving pictures. Ford offered a succinct guide to what constitutes good dialogue. He said that talk helps a movie "as long as the dialogue is crisp and cryptic and as long as they're not long soliloquies. Oh, I like talking pictures. They're much easier to make than silent pictures. I mean, silent pictures were hard work—very difficult to get a point over. You had to move the camera around so much." Despite his often-stated aversion to dialogue, and his favorite gag of ripping several pages from the script and telling the producer, "Now we're on schedule," the dialogue in Ford's pictures is always rich and colorful and evocative. Martin Scorsese has said of Frank S. Nugent's screenplay for Ford's 1956 Western *The Searchers* (based on the novel by Alan LeMay), "The dialogue is like poetry! And the changes of expression are so subtle, so magnificent! I see it once or twice a year."

The following dialogue passage from that screenplay, only slightly altered in the filming, demonstrates how Nugent uses poetic dialogue to help convey the character of Ethan Edwards (John Wayne), the obsessive Indian hater who spends five years searching for his kidnapped niece Debbie, with her adopted brother, Martin Pauley (Jeffrey Hunter). At the lowest point in their search, when they have to turn back to civilization empty-handed, the two men are sitting on their horses in falling snow. Martin thinks the search is futile, but Ethan argues with him:

```
                    ETHAN
          Our turnin' back don't change
          anything...not in the long run.
          If she's alive, she's safe...for a
          while...They'll keep her to raise
          as one of their own, till she's of
          an age to...
```

Martin asks if they might still find Debbie, and Ethan declares:

```
                    ETHAN
          An Injun will chase a thing till he
          thinks he's chased it enough...Then he
          quits...Same when he runs...Seems he
          never learns there's such a thing as a
          critter that might just keep comin'
          on...So we'll find them in the end, I
```

```
                 promise you that...We'll find them just
                 as sure as the turning of the earth.
```

Nugent writes that the scene fades to spring, a year and a half later, as the men approach a ranch in Texas, where the search began. The screenwriter thereby indicates one of the film's most stunning visual transitions, a change of seasons almost mystically prompted by Ethan's final line of dialogue. In that powerful scene as played in two-shot against a poetically rendered snowy back-drop, Ethan's implacable determination can be seen in his face—his fierce, stony expression as he sits on his horse while snow falls around them—but his words express the deeper feelings that impel him to keep searching no matter what. The feelings he can't fully express in words, the thoughts he finds unspeakable, are hinted at in the ellipses, such as "till she's of an age to...." There is madness in Ethan's quest (rather than wanting to rescue her, he intends to kill her), stemming from his racist view of Indi-ans and his horror of miscegenation, but there's also an undeni-able epic grandeur to his determination to "just keep comin' on," a trait that finally leads him to rescue the girl and bring her safely home. That aspect of his character, the part that helps us empa-thize with his search even as we stand apart from his racism and violence, is eloquently expressed in Nugent's dialogue.

WHAT MAKES GOOD OR BAD DIALOGUE

The general rule of thumb of movie dialogue is that it should be terse. The screenwriter should not waste words. A screenplay is akin to a poem in its economy of language. But this rule, like all other rules, is made to be broken. Eric Rohmer's films are mostly composed of long and fascinating intellectual conversa-tions, Billy Wilder's love for the colorful rhythms of colloquial American speech pervades his pictures, and one of the principal joys of movies by the Coen brothers is to revel in their quirky, intricate, and hilarious wordplay. The richly textured satire of bland political banalities and doublespeak in the British film *In the Loop* (a spinoff from the TV series *In the Thick of It* written by Jesse Armstrong, Simon Blackwell, director Armando Iannucci, Tony Roche, and Ian Martin) is spot-on in capturing the utter cynicism and elaborate evasions of the truth that surround modern war planning; the film's dissection of the hypocrisies of political speech is reminiscent of George Orwell's classic 1946 essay "Politics and the English Language." Diablo Cody's screenplay for *Juno* delights us with its satirical yet often touching orchestration of contemporary teenage lingo, even if in some scenes she seems to be showing off her own cleverness at the expense of the characterizations. While these films delight in their virtuosic use of language, film dialogue does not have to be rich or ornate to work in conjunction with images. The clever, snappy badinage familiar from 1930s romantic comedies—a style film and television writers still strive to emulate—is not always the best way to write dialogue.

Towne's advice that the narrative should be advanced "not as much with dialogue as with image" and that the characters "should not be talking about the narrative" should usually be your guiding principles for writing dialogue, but still there are times, and not just in caper or other genre movies, when someone just has to explain what's going on to somebody who's in the dark about what's happening, a natural way of letting the audience in on the same points.

A noteworthy example is Frank Capra's comedy-drama *Mr. Smith Goes to Washington,* in which the political secretary played by Jean Arthur, who knows everything about how Washington works, spends much of the movie explaining the United States system of government to the callow and clueless appointed senator played by James Stewart (and, through him, to us). Arthur is such a brilliant actress that she makes these dialogue-heavy scenes dramatically compelling, and she carries much of the film's meaning as she delivers screenwriter Sidney

Buchman's eloquent speeches about the importance of democracy in a time of peril. When I told Arthur I thought she had done some of her best work in the film, she replied, "Well, I had some good lines. It was very impressive, a lot of those speeches. The *story* was the most important thing in…*Mr. Smith*. They were *saying* something."

Sometimes silence or fragmentary speech is just as eloquent on-screen. Simple words and sentences can be more eloquent than complex ones. A single word can be a better line of dialogue than an elaborate speech. And an evocative word used in dialogue doesn't have to be something as poetic as "Rosebud"; the word "yes," ecstatically repeated by Molly Bloom in her closing soliloquy in *Ulysses* ("yes I said yes I will Yes"), is one of the greatest ending utterances in literature, and it plays well even in the otherwise dismal 1967 film version of James Joyce's novel (with Barbara Jefford as Molly). Good movie dialogue can seem deceptively "flat" to read, if the words are the right ones for the context. The opposite can be true as well—fancy dialogue is often more impressive on the page than on the screen.

To learn how to write good movie dialogue, pay close attention to how people talk and how their words express their characters either by revealing or obfuscating their emotions and motives. Listen to how differently different people speak. Learn to reproduce the phrasings and rhythms that make someone's speech individualistic. In a bad screenplay, all the characters talk alike; they all sound like the writer of the script, and the script sounds lifeless.

Along with all the characters talking alike, another tipoff of a bad script is the overuse of character names by other characters in dialogue ("John, why are you doing this?" "I don't know, Jane"). In real life, people don't often use the name of the person they're speaking to, tending to use a name only when unusual emphasis is required, such as when they're angry. Characters who know each other well generally don't need to address each other by name; having them do so usually sounds not only tedious but unnatural. Writers who constantly have characters call each other by name manifest insecurity about whether the audience will be able to tell one character from another without such a crutch. There are many better ways to individualize a character.

A *lack* of dialogue can be more expressive in a film than a line of dialogue, particularly when the line is expected—think of the scene in *Chinatown* when Jake Gittes is told the street address where Evelyn's Chinese servant lives, the place where she will try to hide her daughter. In Towne's screenplay, Evelyn tells Gittes the address and asks, "…do you know where that is?" He replies, "—sure. It's in Chinatown." Gittes, who once worked in Chinatown as a cop, has been doing all he can to avoid going back there in his new life as a private eye, since "Chinatown" represents the chaos he most fears in life. But in the film, after Gittes hears the address, the director, Roman Polanski, simply tracks in to a close-up of Gittes's chagrined face as he says, "—sure"; we supply the words "It's in Chinatown" in our minds, and the scene is much more powerful for keeping the words unspoken.

Generally, as Ford advised, it's best to avoid long speeches (soliloquies) unless there are valid reasons for using them at key moments of the film. We all can recall great speeches in movies—some of my favorites are Stewart's filibuster in *Mr. Smith*, Orson Welles's courtroom oration against capital punishment in *Compulsion*, and Anthony Hopkins's plea to the Supreme Court for the African captives' freedom in *Amistad*—but these lengthy centerpieces, like Molly Bloom's soliloquy in *Ulysses*, are fully earned, integral parts of the story lines, not indulgent digressions or distractions.

Dialogue should not be overly expository or simply a flat statement of fact, but should further the story naturally and reveal dimensions of character that can't be accessed otherwise. This does not mean that characters should simply come out and explain themselves. People don't always say what they mean. They beat around the bush, drop hints, speak evasively, or lie to themselves and others. Often the best dialogue is not "on the nose" but is oblique, indirect, suggestive. I'd been writing screenplays for several years before I realized that my characters were always telling the truth. How much more interesting they became when I started to let them shade the truth or lie.

OBLIQUE DIALOGUE

Good dialogue, in Howard Hawks's view, is "oblique," a technique he said he learned from Hemingway (Hawks was a friend of the writer and filmed his novel *To Have and Have Not,* greatly improving the story in the process). Just as Towne advises that characters "should not be talking about the narrative," Hawks believed in not having characters address issues head-on except in rare instances:

> Noël Coward came to see me once when I was over at Columbia, introduced himself, and said, "What do you call the kind of dialogue that you use?" And I said, "Well, Hemingway calls it oblique dialogue. I call it three-cushion. Because you hit it over here and over here and go over here to get the meaning. You don't state it straight out."

A celebrated example of Hawksian oblique dialogue is the "Who's Joe?" scene in *Only Angels Have Wings,* written by Jules Furthman. A character named Joe has just died in a plane crash. The other fliers, following their stoical code, don't stop to mourn but eat dinner as planned. Their chief, Cary Grant's Geoff Carter, is eating the steak that had been ordered for Joe. A showgirl who has recently joined them, Bonnie Lee (Jean Arthur), is aghast that Geoff would be eating Joe's steak. The scene obliquely shows the fliers' mockery of death and the rough way they teach that lesson to the newcomer. The mood is very Hemingwayesque in its studied indifference to death, a survival stance that masks the men's true emotions:

                    BONNIE
How can you do that?

                    GEOFF
What?

                    BONNIE
Eat that steak.

                    GEOFF
Well, what's the matter with it?

                    BONNIE
It was his.

                    GEOFF
Like, what do you want me to do, have
it stuffed?

                    BONNIE
Haven't you any feelings? Don't you
realize he's dead?

                    GEOFF
Who's dead?

                    LES [SECOND FLYER]
Yeah, who's dead?

                    BONNIE
Joe!

                    GENT [THIRD FLYER]
          (quizzically)
Joe?

                    GEOFF
Well, who's Joe?

                    (239)

LES
Anybody know Joe?

When the men mock her by singing a sentimental song, Bonnie becomes enraged, slaps Geoff, and runs away. He follows her and says, "Yeah, I know he's dead…and he's been dead about twenty minutes, and all the weeping and wailing in the world won't make him any deader twenty years from now. If you feel like bawling, how do you think we feel? Now come on. Go on outside and walk around and stay there until you put all that together."

Another practice Hawks followed when working on a script with his writers was to turn lines around to make them sound fresh and unexpected. I found this technique helpful in improving my scripts, and I am sure you will too. As he told me,

When [Ben] Hecht and [Charles] MacArthur and I used to work on a script, we'd get started around 7:30 in the morning, and we'd work for two hours, and then we'd play backgammon for an hour. Then we'd start again, and one of us would be one character, and one would be another character. We'd read our lines of dialogue, and the whole idea was to try and stump the other people, to see if they could think of something crazier than you could. That is the kind of dialogue we used, and the kind that was fun.…

The first picture we worked on they said, "Oh, we're all through now." I said, "No, tomorrow we start on something new." The fellows said, "What?" I said, "Different ways of saying things." And they had more fun, we had more fun, for about three days saying things in different ways. I'd say, "How do you say this—you've got a line, 'Oh, you're just in love.'" One of them came up with, "Oh, you're just broke out in monkey bites." The audience knows vaguely what you're saying, they like the method of saying it. We go through the entire script in sequence; one of us suggests something, and what you suggest somebody else twists around.

When someone I was advising was writing a screenplay for a Western, I thought it was a good job of work but did not have quite enough period flavor in its dialogue. So I gave her a copy of a dictionary of Western slang and suggested she work in about ten colorful expressions as "different ways of saying things." Without calling too much attention to the quaintness of the lingo, those few twists helped give the script a greater feeling of authenticity.

SUIT THE WORD TO THE CHARACTER

Hamlet, in his speech to the Players, instructs them to

> suit the action to the word, the word to the action; with this special observance, that you o'erstep not the modesty of nature; for anything so overdone is from the purpose of play-ing, whose end, both at the first and now, was and is, to hold, as 'twere, the mirror up to nature; to show virtue her own feature, scorn her own image, and the very age and body of the time his form and pressure.

To that immortal speech, which all filmmakers should keep in mind in creating characters, I would humbly add for the pur-poses of screenwriting, "Suit the word to the character."

Movies tend to be more colloquial than plays; they o'erstep the modesty of nature at their peril. Characters in movies tend not to give speeches but to speak off the cuff. Dialogue in mov-ies generally should be easy for the actors to speak, even if it is hard for the characters to express, and it usually should not be overly literary.

But, again, there are exceptions. There's no more poetic or literary speech in an American film than in Abraham Polon-sky's *Force of Evil,* which he wrote with Ira Wolfert, author of the novel on which it is based, *Tucker's People.* The dialogue is so rich and ornate that the film resembles a modern urban verse play. Polonsky, a novelist, screenwriter, and director who would later be blacklisted, taught screenwriting at the University of Southern California School of Cinema-Television (now the USC School of Cinematic Arts). His love of language was always at the service of his fatalistic moral vision, a view of the world filled with kaleidoscopically complex nuances and ironies. *Force of Evil,* his directing debut, is an uncompromising film noir that uses the numbers racket as a metaphor for the pervasive corruption he saw in American life.

Unburdening himself of conflicted feelings about his own corruption, John Garfield's syndicate lawyer, Joe Morse, speaks with mingled distaste and admiration about his brother, who has made the fatal decision to quit the numbers racket:

```
                    JOE
Don't you see what it is? It's not
natural. To go to great expense for
something you want—that's natural. To
reach out to take it, that's human,
that's natural. But to get your
pleasure from not taking, from
cheating yourself deliberately, like my
brother did today—from not getting,
from not taking—don't you see what a
black thing that is for a man to do?
How it is to hate yourself, your
brother—and make him feel that he's
guilty, that I am guilty. Just to live
and be guilty.
```

This speech is lush, incantatory in its repetitive rhythms, and plays like a soliloquy, even though it takes place while Joe is riding in a taxicab with his mistress, Doris Lowry (Beatrice Pearson). But it's a short soliloquy, not a long one, and it works in the context of the film's overall stylization. The film noir genre rests on its own stylized foundation (think of the elaborate narration typically supplied by haunted detectives or criminals), and Joe Morse is an intellectual reexamining the premises of his life, so Polonsky makes this elaborate form of dialogue play in a way that sounds, if not natural, at least believable in its ironically confessional meditation on morality. Each film makes its own rules, telling you how to "read" it, and we'd be impoverished without Shakespearean films or films by a modern verbal magician such as Abraham Polonsky.

My general caveat against using overly literary dialogue does not mean that all the characters in a screenplay should sound unintelligent or illiterate, but that a person's character often is reflected in the way he or she speaks. If you're going for a wide range of characters, they probably will have a variety of social backgrounds. This is true even within a certain milieu. As *Force of Evil* demonstrates, not every gangster needs to talk like a thug.

Having all the characters in your script speak on the same level of education or in the same style ignores the profound role played by speech in conveying an individual's personality. Being sensitive to such dramatic nuances and varying the levels on which characters communicate will make your script more richly layered as well as more finely textured. Characters' professions also influence the way they talk; it's a good idea in a script to have a doctor or a lawyer or a mechanic use language that stems from their daily occupations. (One exception to the rule of having characters speak in ways appropriate to their backgrounds or professions might be in comedy. Writer-director Preston Sturges gloried in having unlikely characters toss out multisyllabic words for hilarious effect.)

Dialect, especially ethnic dialect, should be used sparingly in a script and usually left to the actors (hopefully you will have Meryl Streep among the cast). But if the setting is multilingual or someone in a script speaks broken English or has a pronounced foreign or regional flavor to his or her speech, that can be indicated in the way the dialogue is written, as long as you avoid

stereotyping. The Coen brothers adroitly capture the idiosyn-
crasies of midwestern speech in *Fargo.* ("Hon? Got the grow-
shries." "Thank you, hon. How's Fargo?" "Yah, real good.")
When I first saw *Fargo,* I found this mockery of my fellow mid-
westerners offensive, but when I went home to Wisconsin and
heard my relatives speaking delightedly about how accurately
their way of talking was captured in the movie, my admiration
for the Coens was renewed. I realized that since the filmmakers are from Minnesota, they have a firsthand knowledge of the
midwestern Scandinavian-and-German-derived dialect, as well
as a genuine affection for these ditzy-sounding characters.

As Ethan Coen wrote in his introduction to the published
screenplay, the story "aims to be both homey and exotic, and
pretends to be true.... Paradoxically, what is closest to home can
seem exotic. We can't read about the South Seas without com-
paring it to Minneapolis, and can't describe Minneapolis, even
to ourselves, without it seeming like the South Seas."

Diablo Cody artfully uses flip, wisecracking dialogue in *Juno*
not only to humorously capture the immature flavor of teenage
life but also, in a deeper sense, to embody the ironic attitude
that pervades the generation she is portraying, their defensive
general avoidance of confronting genuine emotion. In that
sense, many of the film's scenes exemplify the best tradition of
oblique storytelling and dialogue while embedding outbursts of
true feeling within layers of jocularity. When Juno (Ellen Page)
reveals her pregnancy to her friend Leah (Olivia Thirlby) in a
telephone conversation, she has trouble getting her point across.
In the screenplay version of the scene, which contains a few variations from the film, Leah scarcely hears Juno's opening line, "I
am a suicide risk." Even when Juno says, "Dude, I'm pregnant,"
Leah seems in emotional denial.

```
          JUNO
Anyway, yeah, I'm pregnant. And you're
shockingly cavalier.
```

                    LEAH
Is this for real? Like <u>for real, for
real?</u>

                    JUNO
Unfortunately, yes.

                    LEAH
Oh my God! Oh shit! Phuket Thailand!

                    JUNO
That's the kind of emotion I was
looking for in the first take.

                    LEAH
Well, are you going to go to
Havenbrooke or Women Now for the
abortion? You need a note from your
parents for Havenbrooke.

                    JUNO
I know. Women Now, I guess. The
commercial says they help women now.

Leah's casual assumption that Juno plans to have an abortion speaks volumes, obliquely heightening the seriousness of that subject with a satirical twist. And in the film the line is improved by leaving out the words "for the abortion"; the ellipsis heightens Leah's sense that the situation hardly needs discussing. As in the screenplay, Juno's affectless delivery of her joking responses subtly suggests the opposite, that she is concealing her anxiety about the situation, but in the film her face betrays that anxiety.

OVERLAPPING DIALOGUE

The structure of speech is also important in characterization. Someone who speaks in complete sentences unfortunately tends to be unusual today, so that has to be taken into account as well. If a character does so, he or she would seem unusually well educated or unusually formal in manner. Few real conversations proceed without the use of fragmentary phrases, interruptions, and overlapping. Some of this real-life complexity is best left to the actors and the director, but some should be indicated in the script by using dashes at the ends of interrupted lines and, if you want, putting dialogue blocks side by side if two characters are speaking at once.

On the first day of shooting *The Other Side of the Wind,* when Welles was filming a conversation between Peter Bogdanovich and me, the sound man interrupted: "Hold it!" Welles demanded to know what the problem was. The fellow declared, "We have overlapping dialogue!" Welles angrily replied, "We *always* have overlapping dialogue." That was the sound man's last day on the picture. Saying that on a Welles picture would be like someone on a Hitchcock set announcing, "Hold it! We have suspense!" Welles came to movies from theater and radio, and he brought to his first feature, *Citizen Kane* (1941), his characteristically complex orchestration of multiple-character dialogue and elaborately rhythmical patterns of speech. Welles helped change the way people in movies talk, making dialogue more realistic as well as enabling him to have certain phrases stand out from the hubbub for greater emphasis.

But he wasn't the first director to experiment with overlapping dialogue. Howard Hawks had been there before. His 1940 film *His Girl Friday* (based on the great newspaper play by Hecht and MacArthur, *The Front Page*) has some of the fastest dialogue ever heard in movies, and the characters are constantly speaking over one another to hilarious and exhilarating effect.

In one of our interviews, Hawks explained his method of directing overlapping dialogue:

> If you'll ever listen to some people who are talking, especially in a scene of any excitement, they all talk at the same time. All it needs is a little extra work on the dialogue. You add a few words in front of somebody's speech and put a few words at the end, and they can overlap it. It gives you a sense of speed that actually doesn't exist. And then you make the people talk a little faster.

DRAMAS WITHIN DRAMAS

In his great film *The Rules of the Game,* Jean Renoir, playing Octave, exclaims, "On this earth there is one thing that's terrible—it's that everyone has his reasons." Remember that line when you write a screenplay. Every character in your script should have his (or her) reasons. Part of the purpose of writing your character biography is to become so familiar with what the character wants and needs that you can focus her dialogue and actions on those desires and obsessions.

An instructive exercise in learning how to write dramatic dialogue is to write about a young woman trying to persuade a young man to ask her out. Have her try to make the move without coming right out and saying what she wants. Our social interactions are often filled with such oblique exchanges, for people usually don't say directly what they want or what they are thinking. What people say and what they mean are often quite different things. That's even more true in drama than in daily life. As Hitchcock put it, "What is drama, after all, but life with the dull bits cut out." If you are showing two people on a first date having dinner, don't bother showing them ordering the food (unless that becomes a revealing issue between them), but cut right to the meat of their interactions. That should be your main course.

Drama arises from the shadings of the interactions between characters, not so much from overt declarations of intent. In film, which relies so much on looks between characters and other visual context, dialogue can be more oblique than it is onstage, where the dialogue has to carry much more of the show. Even Chekhov's first acts are fairly heavy on character and plot exposition.

Read Chekhov to see how each character is given a vivid individual story line and how the characters often talk at cross-purposes because of their self-absorption. Characters don't always interact smoothly in drama; sometimes they are lost in their own worlds, just as people are in life. But when each character has a purpose, the scenes will come more strongly alive, because the characters will have definition, and their words and actions will have objectives. Characters operating at cross-purposes usually produce the most fertile dramatic conflict.

And always keep in mind the value of subtext. Dialogue can afford to be oblique only if we realize what is going on beneath the surface. We learn that by indirection. We should sense what the characters have on their minds even if they can't verbalize it. The example I gave in chapter 8 from *It's a Wonderful Life* is one of the most moving instances of dramatic subtext. The funniest use of subtext in movies comes in Woody Allen's *Annie Hall,* which he wrote with Marshall Brickman.

When Alvy (Allen) and Annie (Diane Keaton) are suffering through their first date, a situation always fraught with tension, the banal and cautious words they exchange are "translated" with subtitles into their true meanings. When they're out on the terrace of her apartment discussing her photographs, she says defensively, "Yeah, yeah, I sorta dabble around, you know," and the subtitle reads, "[Thinking] DABBLE? LISTEN TO ME. WHAT A JERK." When she goes on about her interest in taking a course in photography, he responds, aware of how pedantic he sounds, "Photography's interesting because, you know, it's, it's a new art form, and a-a set of aesthetic criteria have not emerged yet," but his subtitle asks, "I WONDER WHAT SHE LOOKS LIKE NAKED?"

Annie Hall literally foregrounds its subtext to satirize the part subtext plays in our lives. That sequence is a valuable learning tool for screenwriters. When you write a scene of a first date, a love scene, or any other kind of charged interaction between characters, remember that people's mouths may be saying one thing and their faces something entirely different.

The screenplay for *Sideways,* by Alexander Payne and Jim Taylor from the novel by Rex Pickett, provides a wonderful example of how this works in a romantic comedy-drama. The movie is about two feckless middle-aged men (Paul Giamatti and Thomas Haden Church) taking a trip through the central California wine country, visiting wineries ostensibly to gratify their oenophilia but actually as an excuse for alcoholic indulgence. Along the way they meet a couple of beautiful women who surprisingly take a fancy to them. Miles (Giamatti), a frustrated writer who carries the lengthy manuscript of his hopeless novel in progress in the trunk of his car, is sitting uncomfortably with Maya (Virginia Madsen) while their friends noisily get it on in another room. The talk soon turns from Miles's manuscript to their favorite wines.

When Maya asks, "Why are you so into Pinot?" Miles replies, "I don't know. It's a hard grape to grow. As you know. It's thin-skinned, temperamental, ripens early. It's not a survivor like Cabernet that can grow anywhere and thrive even when neglected. Pinot needs constant care and attention and in fact can only grow in specific little tucked-away corners of the world. And only the most patient and nurturing growers can do it really, can tap into Pinot's most fragile, delicate qualities." It has become clear to Maya, and to us, that Miles is actually describing himself, and what she learns about him turns her on. She soon takes her turn at (unconscious?) self-revelation, telling him, "I do like to think about the life of wine, how it's a living thing." She rhapsodizes about the conditions under which the wine was grown, "what the weather was like," the lives of the winegrowers. And she talks about the novel flavor of each bottle of wine, "Because a bottle of wine is actually alive—it's constantly evolving and gaining complexity.... And it tastes so fucking good."

The camerawork shows the attraction on their faces, giving us increasingly large close-ups as they look intently into each other's eyes. Miles is captivated by Maya's joie de vivre, expressed through her love of the process of winegrowing and her sensual openness, so unlike his repressed emotional state. Before the mood of seduction is broken by Miles's insecurity, the scene vividly demonstrates the way we talk in subtext to express our deepest feelings.

LISTENING

I worked for twelve years as a newspaper reporter. That taught me how to write fast and on any subject I was thrown; it also taught me how to write dialogue and gave me constant practice in that aspect of the craft. Most of all it taught me the neglected art of listening. I interviewed people every day, thousands of people over the years, and I found that the most enjoyable part of the job. It gave me the ability to do something I relished—going up to strangers and talking with them—but would have been too inhibited to do without an excuse. Being able to ring doorbells, stop strangers on the street, and call anyone on the phone in search of a story gives you unlimited license to investigate the full range of human personality. Not only was I learning about all kinds of people, their occupations, and their daily lives, I was also having to listen carefully to how they expressed themselves, edit their words as I wrote them down, and then select and shape the words into meaningful dialogue as I wrote my stories.

This was invaluable training for a screenwriter, and I recommend it to anyone aspiring to write movies or TV shows, although working for a newspaper might not be the wisest choice of even a temporary career anymore. But it's no accident that many of the greatest screenwriters were newspaper reporters first, including Ben Hecht, Frances Marion, Sam Fuller, John Huston, Dudley Nichols, Dorothy Parker, and Frank S. Nugent. Fewer writers today come from a journalistic background (Joe Eszterhas, Nora Ephron, and Rod Lurie are three who have brought their observational skills to screenwriting), but any job that puts you in regular contact with ordinary people is a valuable training ground. Unfortunately, too many young writers and directors come straight from film school into the professional world, knowing little about life beyond watching movies, which is one reason so many films seem derivative.

You don't have to be a reporter, though, to study how people talk. Interview your friends and family about their lives. Chances are they will be delighted to tell you about themselves; it's sad how little interest most people show in their older family members, and it's so gratifying when they make that contact. Videotape the interviews so you can watch and listen to them again. And truly *listen*. Listening is something of a lost art in our frenetic society. The more closely you listen, the more people will open up to you, because they will know you are empathetic.

When I was interviewing people as a reporter, I often thought of how director Leo McCarey loved to talk to ordinary people. Jean Renoir said of him, "McCarey understands people— better perhaps than anyone else in Hollywood." McCarey picked up much of that knowledge through his habit of pumping eccentric characters for their life stories. He said that anyone you meet is interesting for at least a couple of hours. After that, you may have exhausted a person's store of material. But two hours is enough to hear the stories that make someone's life unique. McCarey's films, such as *The Awful Truth, Love Affair,* and *Going My Way,* delight in the colorful unpredictability of human nature. He used his understanding of people to guide actors into moments of rare spontaneity, frissons that build on the dialogue to reveal deeper layers of character. And the best actors will tell you it's crucial in a scene to listen to the other actor or actors rather than just waiting impatiently to say your lines. That's essential in interviewing as well. Instead of concentrating on your questions, concentrate on the answers and let them guide you where to go.

Another important part of your research for a screenplay should be talking with people who are experts in the area you're writing about or who resemble your characters. A student who wrote a script about an elderly Russian woman told me he modeled the character on a lady he knew and had been spending time with, talking about her life. That verisimilitude showed in his script, which had a level of authenticity that book research alone can rarely give.

Most screenwriters will tell you they regularly eavesdrop on people talking in public settings. Whether it's on the bus or the subway, or in a coffee shop, wherever you go, fascinating, even bizarre conversations can be heard, offering you free material for your script. Sometimes newspapers run columns filled with such overheard gems, often hilariously unpredictable. Learning to pay attention to what you hear in public and gathering ideas and phrases and patterns of speech are part of the writer's basic research into the way people talk and behave. Jotting down words and phrases in a notebook is a useful aide-mémoire, although you need to learn how to do so discreetly or you may be accused, like George Bernard Shaw's philologist and phonetician Henry Higgins in *Pygmalion,* of being a police detective.

Here are some of the traits you can listen for in the way people talk:

- Do they have unusual ways of speaking? Listen for their quirky expressions and the idiosyncratic ways they structure their sentences.

- Some people speak more formally, some speak in slang. Some are proper, some are profane.

- Some speak in short bursts, in disjointed phrases, and some are more polished, making it sound as if they think before they talk, speaking in complete sentences.

- Is a person polite? Emphatic? Evasive? Blunt?

- Does a person speak sparely or expansively?

- Can you tell from someone's speech if he's honest or a habitual liar? And what are the signs someone is lying? Reading the transcripts of Richard Nixon's White House conversations is instructive.

- How does someone's emotional state impact her speech? Is the person jovial and hearty or introverted and morose?

- Does someone speak in a pretentious or a casual way? A pretentious person might drop foreign or arcane phrases into his speech to show off his expertise.

- Does a person use antiquated phrases or up-to-date slang?

- Is the person truly knowledgeable or misguided? Is he cheerfully naïve or willfully oblivious?

- Is a person philosophical? Does she expound to herself—or others—on weighty issues? Philosophical dialogue can add depth to a story, as Jean Renoir's films, such as *Grand Illusion* and *The River,* demonstrate. But be careful about trying to squeeze philosophical discussions into your script if they don't seem organic to the material.

Lajos Egri advises, "Sacrifice 'brilliance' for character, if need be, rather than character for brilliance. Dialogue must come from the character, and no bon mot is worth the death of a character you have created. It is possible to have lively, clever, moving dialogue without the loss of a single growing character."

Step 5
THE STEP OUTLINE

Now it's time for your step outline. Not many people know what one is; a step outline is actually quite simple, although it may take some doing to achieve that simplicity. The purpose of such an outline of your screenplay is to break it down into ten steps clearly telling the complete story, with each step detailing a specific section of the film in no more than two or three sentences, including the estimated timing for each section (in parentheses).

On the next page is my step outline for *To Build a Fire*. The division of the story into steps is somewhat arbitrary, as is the limitation of having ten steps, but this serves a useful purpose in enabling you to see the overall structure of the film clearly and in helping you reduce the story to its essential elements.

I always found it invaluable to have a step outline to refer to while writing a screenplay, for quick reference and orientation about where I was intending to go with the story. Deciding on the length of time you allot to each section of the film, even if it is only an estimate at this stage, helps ensure that your scenes don't get out of control and run too long for their overall function in the script.

Describe each important character in your film briefly (very briefly) and indicate the settings and time period (where applicable). Make sure to double-space your step outline. And make sure the title of your script is italicized in the step outline.

Step Outline: *To Build a Fire*

by Joseph McBride, based on the short story
by Jack London

1. In January 1902, Thomas "Red" McGarrity, a
stocky logger in his late twenties, is returning
to his camp in the Canadian Yukon from a
scouting expedition into the wild. Accompanied by
a gray husky dog, Red is a stolid greenhorn who
seems blithely unconcerned about the extreme
morning cold (as MAIN TITLE CREDITS appear). The
dog, however, seems instinctively aware of the
danger. (2:00)

2. Red is startled when he spits tobacco juice
and it crackles in the air, a sign that the
temperature is far colder than anything he has
previously experienced (in fact, it's seventy-five
below zero). The dog zigzags through the snow as

he leads the way, making sure the ground is safe. Hearing a crack, the dog backs away from a patch of sunken snow, and Red becomes alarmed, recognizing the danger. (1:30)

3. As Red walks, we hear the voice of an Old-Timer, a fellow logger, warning Red not to venture into the winter alone on the trail. We see the old man a few months earlier in the logging camp arguing with Red, who calls the man "an old woman." But the Red trudging through the snow looks worried and thinks of the warm and friendly life awaiting him at camp, as we see images of Red and other men at ease around a fire, with Red playing his accordion. (5:00)

4. Red looks pained in the wilderness, checking his watch and a map, brusquely ordering the dog ahead as they angle off to the west. They pass through varied terrain—a Native burial ground, woods, a mountain range with a deserted cabin— and head down an incline toward frozen Henderson Creek. The dog is vigilant. (1:45)

5. At midday, Red finds shelter in a cluster of rocks under a tree and sits on a log to light a small fire from brush, doing so with difficulty, for his hands are stiff. He smokes a pipe and eats his lunch quickly before moving off down the trail. When we hear the Old-Timer's voice telling Red that no one should ever travel alone in the Klondike after it's fifty below, Red laughs hollowly, knowing it's even colder. (2:30)

6. As he clomps down an incline, suddenly the snow under his feet gives way, and his legs plunge straight into a hidden stream. He scrambles out, alarmed, soaked to the knees. He rushes back to the tree, struggling to build a fire, but when he gets the fire going to dry his legs, the branches of the tree pour their snow onto the fire, extinguishing it. (2:00)

7. The dog circles fearfully as Red, agitated, tries to rebuild the fire. But his hands are getting almost useless. He strikes the whole bunch of matches together with the heels of his

hands, getting the kindling to ignite, but after a chunk of moss falls onto the fire, he tries to clear it away and snuffs out the fire. (2:30)

8. Despondent, Red considers killing the dog for warmth, but when he lunges for the dog, his hands are too numb, and the dog leaps away. Red jumps up and runs wildly along the trail in panic, with the dog bounding ahead, but keeps falling and finally takes an abrupt tumble headlong into the snow. He sits in a daze, muttering almost incoherently in a childish mixture of praying and talking to his (unseen) parents. (3:00)

9. Spent of speech, Red becomes drowsy and peaceful as twilight falls. He imagines his friends finding him dead in the snow; we see a search party with Red himself in it, moving curiously toward his own dead body. As the Old-Timer watches from a dogsled, Red tells him, "You were right, old hoss." (2:00)

10. As the sun begins setting, the dying Red is alone except for the dog. Gesturing toward the

horizon in vague supplication, Red sags and

drowses into frozen sleep. The dog catches the

scent of death, howls, and trots away, leaving

behind the man's frozen corpse, his face covered

with an icy mask, his arms vainly outstretched.

(2:00)

12

The Final Script

*T*he time has come to write your screenplay. Congratulations on having most of the work already done. You say you haven't started yet? Well, think again.

By now you should know the original material inside and out, whether it's "To Build a Fire" or another story you've chosen. You've learned the basic principles of screenwriting and studied the professional screenwriting format. And you've outlined your adaptation so thoroughly, in three stages (your adaptation outline, treatment, and step outline), as well as writing your character biography, that you can hit the ground running and turn out the script pages with ease. Or at least much more easily than if you had not done all this preliminary work but were simply staring at that blank computer screen, wondering how to begin.

You may be surprised at how fluidly the writing will emerge from your brain and fingertips now that you have been playing the movie in your head for a few weeks. There's no more exhilarating feeling for a writer than when the story seems to be writing itself. Soon, I hope, that will start happening to you.

You've already seen the opening of my adaptation of "To Build a Fire." I used my treatment and step outline as guides while writing several new drafts of the script. I've also referred back to Jack London's original story as needed, though I tried to let my cinematic imagination take over as I wrote the script and not look at London's words unless I needed some help or wanted to check how he described a certain piece of action or behavior. Reading my new screenplay for *To Build a Fire* should show you how a script looks, giving you a clear sense of the professional screenwriting format. But first, a final checklist.

THE CHECKLIST

The major points of formatting and writing mechanics are covered in the following checklist. When you've drafted your script, double-check it against this list to see if anything still needs fixing.

FORMAT/MECHANICS CHECKLIST

Title page is correctly formatted: _____

Screenplay is of appropriate length: _____

Author and/or original story properly credited: _____

Pages are numbered at top right: _____

Scenes are not numbered: _____

Margins, indentations, and/or spacing are the correct
   widths: _____

Screenplay is single-spaced: _____

Dialogue and/or dialogue headings are correctly indented: _____

No indentation, spacing, layout, and/or printing problems: _____

Where the story is set is adequately indicated: _____

When the story is set is adequately indicated: _____

Production

Important characters are adequately described: _____

No unfilmable backstory material or thoughts are
    included: _____

MAIN TITLE CREDITS are indicated correctly: _____

Scene descriptions are in the present tense: _____

Transitions between scenes are correctly indicated: _____

Enough headings are used: _____

Headings are adequate and correctly formatted: _____

Flashbacks and transitions from flashbacks are correctly
    indicated: _____

Widow lines (isolated scene or dialogue headings) do not appear
    at bottom of page(s): _____

Dialogue that jumps pages is correctly indicated with
    "(CONT'D)" under dialogue on first page, indented, and at
    top of next page, indented under character name: _____

Scene descriptions are not italicized or in ALL CAPS without
    good reason: _____

Cinematic terminology is used correctly: _____

Shot designations are abbreviated rather than spelled out: _____

Shot designations or technical descriptions are used
    sparingly: _____

Character names are in ALL CAPS on first mention: _____

Sounds are given in ALL CAPS: _____

Camera directions are given in ALL CAPS: _____

Scene descriptions are mostly written in complete sentences;
incomplete sentences are used only with good reason: _____

There are no writing errors (e.g., syntax, spelling, grammar,
punctuation): _____

A FINAL WORD ABOUT YOUR SCRIPT

A script for presentation should be bound between separate lightweight cardboard covers (front and back); the covers can be any color as long as they are a single color. Don't print anything on the front cover and don't include a photograph or drawing; that would look amateurish. The script should be three-hole-punched and bound with three metal brads of a strength sufficient to keep the script together. If you don't bind the script adequately, it will fly apart when someone opens it up because the brads will pop out and the pages will cascade all over the floor.

Make sure your brads are not overly long and do not have protruding pointed edges, which can cause cuts. Injuring the reader will not enhance your chances of selling the script.

Good luck—or as we say in showbiz, "Break a leg!"

MY SCRIPT

And here is my complete new screenplay for *To Build a Fire:*

TO BUILD A FIRE

Screenplay

by

Joseph McBride

Based on the short story

by

Jack London

EXT. FROZEN LANDSCAPE - YUKON TERRITORY,
CANADA - MORNING (JANUARY 1902)

Snow and more snow. Nothing but snow. Not even
a rock or a tree. It's hard to make out shapes;
we almost feel snow blind until our eyes start
ADJUSTING to the terrain. The vast white
blankness of the Yukon extends to the distant
horizon. Snow covers the Yukon River and the
frozen plains, broken only by low rolling hills
and depressions. The dull gray morning light
casts a baleful aura over the landscape.

MAIN TITLE CREDITS begin APPEARING out of the
haze. Gradually, as we MOVE CLOSER to some hilly
terrain,

A TINY DOT

appears over a ridge, and then a larger dot.
These are REVEALED as a gray husky DOG, leading
the way, and a stocky white MAN with a rough
walking stick.

RED THE GREENHORN

Heavily wrapped in a beaver-fur coat and black
Russian hat with large earmuffs, mittens, and
Eskimo moccasins, the man is a little under six
feet tall and looks a bit dandyish. But he has a
brownish-white crust of ice and tobacco juice
covering his trim reddish beard and collar.
THOMAS "RED" McGARRITY is in his late twenties,
a stolid greenhorn who plods steadily along the
trail, chewing his tobacco and looking around
with some alertness but a lack of apprehension.

Rubbing his nose and cheekbones with his mittened hand, he casually reaches in his coat pocket for his watch.

THE SMART ONE

The dog, on the other hand, seems instinctively aware of the danger they are facing from the cold. Moving with great care and efficiency, the dog scouts the path ahead of Red, lowering his snout and zigzagging to check soft spots in the snow with his paws, making sure the ground is safe below the white covering.

RIDGE

Red looks at his watch and sees it's nine o'clock. He looks to his side and doesn't see the dog. He thinks the dog must be lagging behind.

> RED
> (angrily)
> Boy!

The dog BARKS up ahead. Now Red notices him. Not appreciating the scouting job the dog is doing, Red HUFFS along to follow him.

> CUT TO:

INCLINE - A FEW MINUTES LATER

The dog and Red head down a slope toward another low ridge, one that winds far into the distance. The trail is only faintly visible under a foot of snow, but it's apparent because the dog promptly dashes up to it and follows its sled tracks westward.

TRAIL

Red seems oblivious to the dog's concern about
the cold. As Red hikes up to the trail, he pauses
for a moment, looking back at the way he came.

DISTANT RIVER

The mile-wide Yukon River, hidden under ice and
snow, rolling in gentle undulations where ice
jams have formed.

RED

turns to survey the terrain ahead ruminatively.
He casually spits tobacco juice. It freezes in
midair with a sharp, explosive CRACKLE. He is
startled, suddenly conscious of just how cold it
is. His hand instinctively goes to a knife he
wears in a sheath at his waist.

Halting at the NOISE, the dog watches Red
reflexively beat his hands together and thump his
chest. Looking fretful at his sign of distress,
the dog turns and trots steadily ahead,
zigzagging as he goes. Red follows in the
distance, swinging his arms as if signaling
unconsciously for help.

                              CUT TO:

WOODS - AN HOUR LATER

A low wind RUSTLES the dense, leafless trees as
Red follows the dog through a dense patch of
woods.

CLEARING

They emerge from the shadows at the edge of the woods. Far away a mountain range dimly shimmers in the gray morning haze. Red studies the sight distractedly.

DOG - MOVING

The dog's alertness has risen as the trail takes a dip through uneven terrain. The dog darts back and forth, sniffing at the snow. Red is ambling along behind him.

CRACK!

The dog halts abruptly, hearing the SOUND, and backs away from a patch of sunken snow.

RED

Alarmed, he recognizes the danger.

SOFT SPOT

The dog darts out of the shallow water. There is ice under the snow, and it has broken to REVEAL a hidden spring.

RIDGE

The dog bounds to safe ground. He bites pieces of ice from his wet paws. Red comes up and tries to help. The dog attempts to shake him off, but Red, insistent, yanks strands of ice from the animal's paws and legs.

> RED
> (sharply)
> Enough o' that, now. <u>Mush!</u>

Red's VOICE SOUNDS strangely BLURRED. The crust
of ice around his mouth makes it difficult for him
to articulate. He looks angered at the effort and
somewhat baffled by his numbness. But the dog
automatically rouses himself at the command,
showing fear of the man and his angry bark.

ALONG THE TRAIL

Red takes the lead this time, half running as he
circles around the soft spot and finds the trail
again, on a slight elevation. The dog suddenly
bounds ahead of him to resume his duty, as
vigilant as before.

RED - MOVING

Red's eyes dart around aimlessly as he plods
determinedly along. His head drops, and he seems
lost in thought. As he walks, we HEAR the VOICE
of an OLD-TIMER, a fellow logger talking with Red
back at the logging camp a few months earlier:

> OLD-TIMER
> (VO)
> You just won't listen. You're so damn
> smart. Think you're still back home
> throwin' snowballs and ridin' your
> toboggan in the park.

Red laughs smugly to himself as he thinks of the
Old-Timer.

> CUT TO:

EXT. COUNTRY STORE - DAWSON - NIGHT (A FEW
MONTHS EARLIER)

The Old-Timer, seated in a rocking chair next
to a blazing log fire, is talking with Red,
who is sitting on the floor near the fire. Both
are smoking pipes. The Old-Timer, a wiry fellow
of about seventy with a scruffy white beard,
keeps struggling with his pipe as he talks
through his teeth. Red, who looks much younger
without a beard, regards him with amused
condescension.

                    OLD-TIMER
        Out here the cold can kill ya, man!
        Gets so damn cold ya better not be out
        there at all, and if ya do, ya better
        know the damn score.

                    RED
                (with juvenile amusement)
        Ah, you're just an old woman. I can
        take care of myself better'n you any
        day.

                    OLD-TIMER
        Go on, perfesser, be a dunderhead, but
        if ya get wet feet and have to build a
        fire when it's sixty, seventy below, you
        better not muck it up or you're a
        goner.

                              CUT TO:

HILLTOP - YUKON WILDERNESS (JANUARY 1902)

Red loses his silly grin and looks somber.

                    (272)

> OLD-TIMER
> (VO)
> Ya can try to run but ya can't git
> away from that kinda cold, no sir, not
> by a long shot you can't.

Fear for the first time shows in Red's eyes. He
picks up his pace to keep up with the dog.

But as Red draws near, the dog skitters ahead on
a downward slant, anxious and alert, nose close
to the ground. Red marches his way forward,
accelerating his pace but still lagging behind.
His eyes peer into the hazy distance, as if he's
looking for something.

                              CUT TO:

EXT. CABIN - LOGGERS' CAMP - NIGHT (FANTASY)

The outline of the long, low log cabin can barely
be SEEN through a veil of steadily falling snow.
Two dogsleds are parked outside.

Cut firewood is piled up under a window, with an
axe stuck in one of the logs. Through the window
a yellow light hazily shines.

                           DISSOLVE TO:

INT. CABIN (FANTASY)

The glow of a blazing fireplace makes the common
area an oasis of heat. The walls and ceiling,
made from rough-hewn logs, give the place a
comfortably close feel. Heavy coats are hung on
hooks around the walls; moose antlers protrude

from one wall. On another is a framed photograph
of actress LILLIE LANGTRY, wearing a low-cut
dress.

Red (now bearded), the Old-Timer, and ANOTHER
MAN, larger and more rugged, are seated in
rocking chairs around the fire, fur blankets on
their laps. Red, eyes closed, is contentedly
PLAYING "Oh, Dem Golden Slippers" on an accordion
while smoking his pipe. The men are wearing
bulky sweaters and denim overalls.

THREE EVEN LARGER MEN, virtually giants, are
seated around a table in the middle of the
room, eating huge steaming bowls of stew. These
men are wearing checked lumberjack shirts
with their overalls; the third also sports a
trapper's fur hat. On a hot stove nearby rests
the stewpot.

Other than the soft-featured Red and the
wizened Old-Timer, all the men are in their
thirties; they have rough-hewn but friendly
faces.

                    LOGGER #1
          There'll be enough to go around. An
          acre or two for each of us.

OLD-TIMER AND RED

The Old-Timer rocks gently, smiling and tapping
his foot to the TUNE of Red's MUSIC. Red's dog
rests at his feet, near the fire. As Red reaches a
jaunty place in the tune, he looks up and grins
at the Old-Timer. There seems a father-son
rapport between the two men.

                    LOGGER #2
                (OS)
        Speak for yourself, Callaway—I can cut
        'em ten times faster'n that.

                    LOGGER #3
                (OS)
        Ah, hell, the Old-Timer can outcut you
        and Sam any day o' the week.

The Old-Timer spits into the fire and guffaws.

                    RED
        I'll say he can!

AROUND THE ROOM

The older men find Red amusingly "green"; teasing
him is their sport.

                    LOGGER #2
        Thought he was "some old woman"!

                    RED
                (embarrassed)
        Ah, I was just a kid when I said that.

The Old-Timer turns toward the men at the table
and points to Red as if to say "That's my boy."
Red pauses in his playing.

                    RED
        He taught me everything I know.

                    OLD-TIMER
        Yeah, but I ain't taught you everything
        I know.

                    (275)

RED AND OLD-TIMER

Affectionate looks pass between them as they
tease each other.

                   RED
   Keep tryin', ol' man. I'm all ears.

               OLD-TIMER
   'Bout time. When you came here you
   thought you wrote the book.

                   RED
   No, I just read it. That's why I came.
   Thought the Yukon was romantic, or
   somethin'.

They all get a good laugh out of that notion.

               LOGGER #1
   Wait till summer for that, kid. Try it
   now, you couldn't get her off ya
   without a axe.

They laugh good-naturedly at the kid's innocence.
Red resumes PLAYING his tune. The other men all
SING along. The song is about dancing, and the
older men's faces become wistful as they think
about women.

Red puffs on his pipe, looking around at his
hearty companions, happy to be safe in their
company.

                            DISSOLVE TO:

RED'S FACE - WILDERNESS (JANUARY 1902)

His face is crusted with ice, creasing with pain.
He feels acutely alone. Thinking about his
friends has sharply increased his sense of
isolation and his apprehension. Panic crosses his
half-frozen features.

He gives a sharp glance at his watch. It's a
little past ten. He pulls a folded map out of his
coat, with some difficulty—his hands are getting
stiff.

MAP

As his hands unfold it, the crudely scribbled map
shows a tangle of lines.

RED

studies the map with consternation.

MAP

As he unfolds it further, it REVEALS a fork in
the trail, with an arrow pointing westward.

RED

checks the trail ahead and sees the fork about a
half a mile off, just as depicted on the map. He
shoves the map back in his coat and angles off
toward the west, moving with a new resolution.
The dog is hesitant, looking around to scout his
way, as if not trusting the man.

>   RED
>   (brusquely)
>   Go on, now! Now!

The dog jumps to his command.

                              CUT TO:

MONTAGE

Red and the dog passing through varied terrain:

(1) A Native burial ground, with mounds poking up through the snow. The dog jumps quickly over the mounds, as if afraid to remain in this place more than a moment. Red has his head down as he walks distractedly.

(2) A stretch of stumps and half-grown trees, planted after the last logging season. Some blackened firewood is scattered amidst the stumps. The dog runs through it and leaves sooty paw prints in the snow up ahead.

(3) A trail with hills beyond it; a deserted cabin at the foot. Red glances over at it wistfully, wondering whether he should seek shelter but rejecting the thought as impractical while he keeps plodding along.

(4) Henderson Creek—frozen and serpentine, winding toward the far horizon. They head down an incline to follow the trail alongside the creek. The dog is vigilant.

MIDDAY REFUGE

Red finds shelter in a cluster of rocks under a tall tree, the largest of a group of spruce

trees. Clusters of clotted snow cover its
branches. Hardly glancing above, Red sits on a
log and gathers sticks and twigs from the
underbrush to put together a small fire. He does
so with difficulty, for his hands are like blocks
of wood. The dog sits at a safe distance,
watching him warily.

Red pulls several wooden sulphur matches from his
inside coat pocket and, after three clumsy tries,
produces a flame. He lights the brush and
gradually gets the fire going, feeding it with
sticks and twigs.

He pulls out his pipe and lights it with a
blazing stick. After a few puffs to calm his
nerves, he takes the pipe from his mouth and
rubs the warm bowl against his freezing cheeks.
He feels a little better.

The dog roams in a circle, looking restlessly
around the trail, anxious to keep moving.

Unbuttoning his coat and pulling off one of his
mittens, Red reaches into his coat to pull out
his lunch. Balancing the pipe on his leg, he
unwraps a piece of rough cloth covering a couple
of biscuits. He opens them to check for the thick
fried slices of grease-covered bacon inside.

Troubled by how numb his exposed fingers feel, he
strikes them against his leg sharply, repeatedly.
He holds them out toward the fire before wolfing
down the biscuits. He hardly tastes them before
he pulls on the mitten again, looking frightened
by the extreme cold.

Clamping the pipe back into his mouth and puffing
to draw the smoke, he jumps up and moves off

down the trail again, scattering the fire with a
kick. The dog yearns back toward the embers,
reluctant to leave. But Red WHISTLES, and the dog
bounds ahead of him, racing in a straight line,
keeping away from the man's anger and fear.

RED

waving his arms and thumping his hands with more
vigor as he hikes. He looks straight ahead as he
bobs up and down on the uneven terrain.

> OLD-TIMER
> (VO)
> If I tole ya once I tole ya a hunnert
> times, no man should ever travel alone
> in the Klondike when it's fifty below.

His voice keeps ECHOING, to Red's dismay. Red's
eyes dart around distractedly, not focusing on
where he walks.

> OLD-TIMER
> (VO)
> Fifty below...fifty below...fifty...

> RED
> (laughs hollowly, muttering)
> Hell, don't I wish to Christ.

> OLD-TIMER
> (VO)
> —and if it's seventy, seventy-five
> below...seventy-five...seventy-five...
> God help him...

Red, mouthing along with the words "seventy-five,"
is clomping down an incline, oblivious to the

ground below his feet. Suddenly the ground
gives way.

THE TRAP

His legs plunge straight into a hidden stream.
Red scrambles out, alarmed, soaked halfway to
the knees.

                  RED
    God damn it all to hell!

HIGHER GROUND

He grabs his walking stick from the snow and
rushes back to the tree, lifting his wet legs as
he scrambles up the hill, stumbling as he climbs,
panting.

THE FIRE

has gone out. Red pushes aside the scattered,
blackened brush and twigs and grabs fresh
handfuls from around the base of the tree to
make a new one, shaking the tree in the process.
He lays a foundation of several larger pieces of
wood on the snow.

Pulling a small shred of birch bark from his
pocket and touching a match to it, he struggles
to build another fire, feeding the flame with
wisps of dried grass and tiny dry twigs. He is
forced to remove his mittens again; his hands
are clumsy and get in his way. As he holds the
flame carefully to the brush, transferring the
burning bark from one hand to the other, he
intermittently beats the free hand against his
side to make it work. He yanks more twigs

from under the tree and feeds them into the
fire.

TREE - FROM OVERHEAD

Above Red the snowy branches of the tree are
sprinkling flakes as he keeps jostling the tree
without thinking.

He gets the fire going well. His hands are
warmer now. Working carefully, he feeds fresh
twigs onto the flame. The dog creeps closer to
the fire for sustenance. Even the animal is
shivering.

THE FIRE

Red puts on his mittens, pulls off his moccasins,
and starts drying his wet legs—the pants and
thick woolen socks are covered with ice. His
moccasin strings and socks are like metal pipes.
It's hard to budge the strings. He reaches for
his sheath knife and cuts them. With fierce
effort, he manages to pull off his socks. He is
moving frantically to knead his bare, frozen feet
and twist them above the fire. As he does so, he
shakes the log on which he sits—the log abuts
the tree.

TREE

The snowy branches of the tree keep dusting the
man below. Red is busy, oblivious. Suddenly one
bough high up in the tree capsizes its load of
snow, falling on the branches below. One branch
after another pours its snow in a white cloud
onto the man and the fire.

THE FIRE

abruptly blotted out.

RED

is terrified. It is as though he has just heard
his own death sentence.

Agitated, he skitters several feet from the tree
and tries to rebuild the fire, pushing away the
snow, working like a demon. This time he is
careful to stay away from the tree, taking the
kindling from flotsam in the open, swinging his
walking stick to dislodge it. He has trouble
bringing his fingers together to pull it out, but
manages to gather twigs by the handful.

THE DOG - MOVING

circles fearfully, studying Red's state of mind
while keeping on high alert. The dog passes back
and forth in front of Red as he strips off his
mittens and vainly tries to light some matches. His
fingers are so inert that he can't manage to strike
one. Each he tries falls into the snow, unlit.

RED ON GROUND NEAR THE LOG

He pounds his numb fingers furiously on his
freezing legs. He struggles to catch hold of
another piece of birch bark in his pocket—it
falls to the ground in front of him. Leaving it
there, he yanks the whole remaining bunch of
matches from his coat.

Trying to separate one from the others, he drops
them in the snow. His inert fingers won't pick

them up. He pulls on his mittens and scoops the bunch of matches into his lap, along with a heap of snow.

Finally, he gets the bunch between the heels of his clumpy hands and carries it to his mouth. He opens his mouth with a violent effort, the ice CRACKING and SNAPPING. He chews at the bunch of matches with his teeth to separate a single match.

The match drops into his lap. Red picks it up with his hands, places it between his teeth, and scratches it against his leg, over and over. Finally it lights. He holds it with his teeth to the piece of birch bark. The burning brimstone makes him COUGH spasmodically. The match falls into the snow and goes out.

DOG'S EYES

narrowing, studying this fumbling man intently to see if he can still succeed in being the fire provider. The dog has his doubts.

MOVING IN ON RED

Removing his right mitten with his teeth, he catches the whole bunch of matches again between the heels of his hands. He scratches the bunch along his leg. It flares into a huge flame—seventy matches at once. He keeps his head to one side to escape the fumes, holding the blazing bunch of matches to the birch bark.

Red's face is glowing with the fire from below. He holds the smoldering bark to the brush and twigs

OS, concentrating his entire being fiercely on that spot.

Smoke rises around his eyes. He can smell his flesh burning as the flames CRACKLE against his right hand, but he can't feel it.

As we MOVE IN CLOSER TO HIS EYES, the pain begins to assault him. His eyes close in agony, but he doesn't let go of the flame.

HIS HANDS

holding the fire against the brush. The small glow begins to spread. It holds, holds, holds—and does not go out. And BURSTS into flame. He jerks his hands apart.

THE PLACE OF FIRE

The dog SIGHS with a release of tension. He stares at Red gratefully and moves closer to the fire. Red drops the matches into the fire and, in deep pain, clutches his hands together and presses them between his knees. The fire rises higher. He holds out his burned hand toward it and winces. Then he lifts his half-frozen feet nearer to the flames.

FEET

glistening with wetness—the legs twisting back and forth in Red's hands. The feet are starting to dry.

DOG AND RED

The dog watches patiently as Red kneads his feet and legs, over and over, with an increasingly

frantic rhythm, keeping them and his hands as
close as possible to the fire without turning
them to ash. He is beginning to feel the warmth
and circulation flow back into his lower
extremities.

RED'S FACE

lightens a bit—maybe all hope is not lost. Maybe
he will make it to camp after all. Maybe...

Just then a large chunk of moss falls from a
trembling branch in front of his eyes, landing on
the fire OS with a sickening SQUISH. A low MOAN
escapes from Red's mouth.

RED'S HANDS

fumble to clear the moss away. But in so doing,
he disrupts the fire. He tries to poke it together
again, but flying twigs gush puffs of smoke and go
out.

The fire fails.

Red's hands drop to his sides.

A FAILED REFUGE - SKY DIMMING

A quiet, motionless tableau: Red sits on the
ground like a statue: "Frozen Man." The dog has
his head in the snow, meditating, ears alert.

Daylight is waning.

Red's body sags and slowly slides, his legs
splayed in the snow.

The dog anxiously scans the sky.

After a few moments of silent despair, Red
GROWLS. He realizes he must put his right mitten
and moccasins back on so his extremities don't
become blocks of ice. He yanks them on
laboriously. Shoving the knife back into its
sheath, he looks around for salvation.

THE DOG

turning to watch him.

RED

His eyes fall on the dog. An idea strikes him.
Red stares madly at the animal.

                    DISSOLVE TO:

ALASKAN BLIZZARD - NIGHT (FANTASY)

In a HOWLING snowstorm so fierce shapes can barely
be DISCERNED, a FARMER in his forties, in
overalls and a fur coat, is out in a field
slaughtering a steer with a large axe. The steer
collapses in a heap. The man HACKS a large rip in
the side of the animal and crawls inside the
corpse for warmth, drawing the bloody hide around
him as the swirling snow covers them from sight.

                    CUT TO:

RED'S CRAZED FACE - DUSK FALLING (JANUARY 1902)

Red laughs hysterically. He sees his salvation
now.

MAN AND DOG

Red suddenly lurches for the dog. The dog is caught off guard. Red grabs him and wrestles him to the ground, rolling around with him, holding him with surprising strength for a man who was virtually inert a few moments ago. Red tries to keep the animal in his arms while reaching with one hand for his knife in its sheath. But his hand is having trouble gripping the knife's handle.

Red flails around with the dog helplessly, his benumbed hands trying to catch hold of the dog's legs, not knowing what else he can do without an axe. But the dog, more nimble in the cold, squeezes out of Red's arms and scurries away, deathly afraid.

Red, his arms dangling, slowly hauls himself to his feet, looking wobbly. Glancing down to assure himself he is actually standing—for his feet have no sensation—he turns slowly from side to side, forlornly surveying this place that soon could be his tomb. He decides he doesn't want to die here.

As if propelled from a cannon, he springs away, running with all his strength down the hill. The dog backs in the opposite direction, shocked by the sight.

RED - RUNNING

He GULPS air greedily as he pushes his body to its limit, pumping his arms ferociously along the trail, his chest HEAVING, his eyes spread wide.

After a few moments, he begins to feel as if he is flying.

He beams in exhilaration as he races along.

BACK AT THE TREE

The dog has turned to watch this strange spectacle with detached curiosity.

SNOWBANK

Starting to GASP, Red loses speed. He slips and tumbles into the snow. He regains his breath and staggers to his feet. He wills himself to run again. In the distance, the dog starts running after him.

                                   JUMP CUT TO:

RED - RUNNING

His BREATHING is more LABORED. His legs are like logs, but he propels them along with great effort. He stumbles again and again but somehow keeps going, his pace slowing agonizingly.

The dog is catching up but keeping a cautious distance.

                                   JUMP CUT TO:

ANOTHER SNOWBANK

Red staggers and collapses headlong into the snow. Half buried, he slowly rises to a sitting position. It is the best he can do. Immobile

again, he looks despondent but begins LAUGHING
bitterly at his own foolishness.

He MUTTERS almost incoherently, becoming childish
in his speech:

> RED
> Mama—bad boy. Next time—do you say
> me. Daddy come get me. Home now. Now
> lay me down to sleep. Pray the Lord
> my soul to keep.

He takes great pains to GASP out:

> RED
> And if I die before I wake—(mouthing
> barely audibly)—I pray Lord soul
> take.

Spent of speech, he becomes drowsy and peaceful.
He looks around, his eyes sweeping the horizon
placidly.

RED'S POV - TWILIGHT

TAKES IN the vast empty wilderness, the dimly
visible trail, and a rise GROWING FAINT in the
purple twilight that is beginning to SHADE the
SCENE. The dog is part of the panorama, sitting
alert, silently watching the man.

RED'S FACE

very happy now as he begins imagining:

> CUT TO:

RED'S POV - TWILIGHT (FANTASY)

A search party of FIVE LOGGERS, the men we saw
in Red's fantasy of the logging camp, COME INTO
VIEW over the rise. They stop, standing in the
wind, staring toward him. Red ("THE OTHER RED")
comes up alongside the group.

THE OTHER RED - OVER HIS SHOULDER

looking at the frozen corpse in the snow. The
Other Red begins to move curiously toward his
own dead body.

RED'S BODY

The Other Red nudges the corpse in a gingerly way
with his foot to make sure he is dead. The body
scarcely budges.

SEARCH PARTY

standing in a circle around the corpse, silently
facing the death of their friend and the
implacable cruelty of nature. At the edge of the
party is the Old-Timer, sitting in a dogsled like
an Eskimo, bundled up in furs.

OLD-TIMER

giving the two Reds an accusatory yet gentle
look.

THE OTHER RED

turns to the Old-Timer sadly:

THE OTHER RED
You were right, old hoss; you were right.

CUT TO:

RED ALONE - SUNSET

Red's friends are gone. He is dying alone in the
snow, except for the dog, who watches from a
distance, waiting calmly for the denouement of
their adventure in survival.

Gesturing toward the horizon in vague
supplication, Red sags and drowses into frozen
sleep.

The dog waits. The sky begins darkening into night.

CUT TO:

OVER RED'S SHOULDER - NIGHT

The dog waiting. Red is motionless. Snow is
drifting around his shoulders and the edges of
his hair and beard.

The dog begins WHINING as he ventures near the
man, catching the scent of death and backing
abruptly away.

DISSOLVE TO:

DOG - NIGHT

HOWLING at the stars that leap, dance, and shine
brightly in the cold sky. Then he moves away, up
the trail in the direction of the camp.

He stops and casts a look back.

TIGHT ON THE MAN'S FACE

His face covered with an icy mask. His eyes look
startled.

DOG

Satisfied that the man is dead, the dog trots
away, leaving the corpse behind.

TABLEAU

of the man sitting motionless in death, his arms
vainly outstretched.

The SKY SLOWLY TURNS BLACK around him.

                              FADE OUT

FADE IN:

END CREDITS APPEAR, white on black, as we HEAR
Red's accordion faintly PLAYING "Oh, Dem Golden
Slippers," MIXED with the SOUND of DRIFTING snow.

13

Epilogue: Breaking into Professional Filmmaking

Now you know how to write a professional-quality screenplay. What do you do next? Unfortunately, there is no easy answer to that question. You may well succeed as a screenwriter, if you are sufficiently devoted to that task, but you should be prepared for the difficulties facing anyone who wants to enter this over-crowded field.

Before I moved to Hollywood to try my luck as a screen-writer, I had the benefit of only one piece of advice—actually just one *word*. Somehow, while living in Wisconsin, I was fortunate enough to meet a recovering screenwriter who was en route to a new life back East. I asked him what advice he had for someone who wanted to become a screenwriter, and he replied, "Chutzpah." Chutzpah is Yiddish for "guts" or "nerve." That was excellent advice indeed, for anyone trying to make it in the film business without chutzpah will face even greater-than-usual odds. Over the course of my subsequent twenty-seven years in Hollywood, I learned a lot more about the business, and I will share some of those hard-earned lessons here. I hope that they will save you years of missteps.

1. The odds against success in the film and television industries are long.

If there were an easy recipe for how to sell a screenplay, the hundreds of thousands (millions?) of people out there who think they want to be screenwriters would all be selling scripts on a regular basis. The reality is that few films are made and that most screenwriters are chronically unemployed. It's not much easier to find work in other branches of the industry, but it's easier to succeed as almost anything than as a screenwriter. Billy Wilder said that if he had a child who wanted to make movies in the modern film industry, he'd advise him to become a stuntman, a special-effects creator, or a lawyer, because that's where most of the jobs are. Wilder was only half joking. If you learn one of the technical crafts, or get your law degree, you will be much more hirable than if you were to show up in Hollywood clutching a bunch of screenplays. The independent field is actually a more promising route for aspiring writers or directors to follow (we'll get to that option in due course), but it's always a struggle to succeed in any branch of the film business. Even people who make it usually have to endure a few tough years before they start selling scripts.

Screenwriting is such a ridiculously overcrowded field because so many people mistakenly believe the media hype that it's easy to write and sell a script—anybody can write one, and it's a quick way to strike it rich. But the field is overrun with naïve aspirants, including thousands of film-school graduates clutching their diplomas hopefully. Or should I say clutching their diplomas *hopelessly*? A film school diploma, at best, might open a few doors with alumni of your school who happen to be working in the business. Otherwise it won't help you much in finding a job. (Though once you have a job, the skills you learned at school will be valuable.) A completed screenplay probably will be most valuable as a calling card to get you in the door to see someone who will ask, "So what else do you have?" That's if you're lucky enough to find a producer who will read the script or a hungry young agent who might take a chance on representing you for a few months.

The misconception about what a snap it is to write and sell screenplays is pushed by unscrupulous authors to sell copies of their how-to books. It's also a myth strenuously promoted by

Hollywood in order to lure more suckers to town every year. Every so often, the fact that some screenwriter has sold a script for millions of dollars is widely publicized to hide the fact that about half of all *professional* screenwriters actually are out of work in any given year.

According to a document the Writers Guild of America issued to explain its reasons for striking in 2007, these are the hard facts: "Most writers are middle-class; 46% did not even work last year. Of those who do work, one quarter make less than $37,700 a year and 50% make less than $105,000 a year. Over a five-year period of employment and unemployment, a writer's average income is $62,000 per year." That average, it should be noted, factors in the considerably higher sums earned by some of the fortunate half of the Writers Guild membership who actually find work, and even those who do so are often unemployed. For the large pool of unemployed writers, including those uncounted hordes who still haven't managed to make it into the WGA, a job grilling hamburgers might be a more sensible survival option than screenwriting.

I always warn aspiring screenwriters about the dangers they will face so that, if they choose to plunge into the shark tank anyway, they will do so with their eyes wide open. And I do so to make sure that, before making the decision to enter this daunting profession, they ask themselves the question I posed at the start of this book, "Do I want it badly enough, and why?" If you don't want it badly enough to put up with all the mishegoss you will encounter, and if your reasons for wanting it aren't sensible, I hope you will give it a miss and go into some less torturous line of work. And if you think I'm overly blunt in discouraging aspiring writers who don't have what it takes to survive with their talent intact, you ought to hear what Flannery O'Connor said on the subject:

Everywhere I go I'm asked if I think the universities stifle writers. My opinion is that they don't stifle enough of them.

There's many a bestseller that could have been prevented by a good teacher. The idea of being a writer attracts a good many shiftless people, those who are merely burdened with poetic feelings or afflicted with sensibility....It is a fact that if, either by nature or training, these people can learn to write badly enough, they can make a great deal of money, and in a way it seems a shame to deny them this opportunity; but then...I believe that these people should be stifled with all deliberate speed.

Enough with the dire warnings. Now how *do* you make a living in the film business?

2. *Get a job.*

That's not advice aspiring filmmakers like to hear. But it is crucial to success in the film business. Have a "day job" to pay the rent while you are writing screenplays or knocking on doors. That way you will avoid desperation and the appearance of desperation while you are pounding the pavement in Hollywood, London, Paris, Hong Kong, or other centers of the film industry. Find another set of skills that will keep you afloat and provide you with options. Even people who become established in the industry need another source of income to provide security from the vagaries of the film business. "I always wanted to make personal films, but those of you who are with me in that, you've got to get a day job," said Francis Ford Coppola in his April 2009 speech at San Francisco State University. "The film business isn't even a business. One minute you're on top of the world, one minute you're a jerk, they love you, they hate you. At least if you're making films that are personal and practicing in an art form that you love, then you can figure out how to make a living."

One of the most sensible people in the film industry, Harrison Ford, made his living as a carpenter in his early years, before he became known as Han Solo and Indiana Jones. When

Ford showed up for acting auditions in his carpenter's outfit, with an apron filled with tools and speckled with sawdust, people were impressed that he was a regular guy with an actual profession. He would tell them things like, "I've got forty-five minutes before I have to go build a roof for someone in the Valley." Hollywood people would feel flattered that this hardworking, no-nonsense fellow was giving them his time. He wasn't like the thousands of actors and writers hanging around Hollywood waiting pathetically for the phone to ring, keeping their lives on hold to stay at the beck and call of producers. Such subservience becomes self-perpetuating since it demonstrates a willingness to grovel. People in Hollywood (or anywhere else) don't respect grovelers. Harrison Ford eventually started getting acting jobs, but he enjoyed carpentry so much he kept doing it for fun.

If you can't build a roof, find something else you can do to put food on the table. Be realistic about your life. Dreams are wonderful, but you can't eat them. So even if you are willing to do whatever it takes to survive in show business, you would be well advised to have a day job that pays the bills while you are trying to sell your first scripts. Actress Carol Burnett told students at an American Film Institute seminar that you need a day job (as she had as a hat-check girl in a women's tearoom during her early days in New York) so you don't "look desperate" when you're looking for work in show business. But she told them not to give more than "five years of dedicated work going for it," because after that long it would be unlikely they would get their big break.

3. Location, location, location—Hollywood or bust?

Today's film business is decentralized. Novelist William Faulkner, who famously preferred working at home in Oxford, Mississippi, but as a screenwriter was compelled to spend more time in California than he wished, would be pleased to know that a screenwriter no longer is expected to live and work in Hollywood or any other film capital. You can live in Kalamazoo, Michigan, or Ames, Iowa, and make your own movies if you want. Many independent filmmakers are scattered throughout the country, happily working in a less frenetic, less incestuous atmosphere than they would face in Hollywood, where everyone seems to have a script in his back pocket and almost all conversations are about what movies grossed how much over the weekend. Your sense of values can easily become skewed in such an environment, and the constant awareness of cutthroat competition is debilitating.

Stanley Kubrick left Hollywood for rural England in the early 1960s and worked in London and elsewhere in the U.K. for the rest of his career because he found the atmosphere in Hollywood so poisonous. Even though he conceded that "Hollywood is best" as a production center, he said,

> I don't like living there.... When I lived there people would ask how it's going and you know that what they hoped to hear was that you were behind schedule or had trouble with the star.... You read books or see films that depict people being corrupted by Hollywood, but it isn't that. It's this tremendous sense of insecurity. A lot of destructive competitiveness. In comparison, England seems very remote. I try to keep up, read the trade papers, but it's good to get it on paper and not have to hear it every place you go. I think it's good to just do the work and insulate yourself from the undercurrent of low-level malevolence.

It was much harder for a filmmaker to function outside of Hollywood when Kubrick made his move—he didn't leave until he was well established and could set up his productions in England, using American financing—but in today's world, with the Internet and other new forms of communications and distribution, a filmmaker is no longer tethered to the former heart of the industry. My friend Sam Hamm, the screenwriter of *Batman* and other major films, lives in San Francisco. When I asked how that works in terms of running his career, he said it's easy to go to meetings in Los Angeles—he just hops on the plane in the morning and comes back the same night. "Scarcity creates value, or at least the illusion of value," Sam said. "When I was starting out, my agent cleverly told executives that I was coming to L.A., taking four or five meetings in a two-day window. They could have one of those slots or wait until my next trip down. Which sounds crazy, but it worked—he somehow convinced the execs that my time was more valuable than theirs, and believe me, it wasn't." Sam knows he's a lucky exception; most writers will want to spend at least a few years in Hollywood to make contacts and establish themselves before they contemplate a long-distance career. "But it's nice to live among civilians, instead of industry types," he said. "I don't have to talk about grosses and deals with my neighbors. Most of them have no idea what I do for a living." If you don't want to live in L.A. but still want to write mainstream, major-studio films, you may want to follow that same two-step procedure of first establishing yourself in Hollywood and then moving elsewhere.

Before taking the plunge of moving to Hollywood, or as an alternative to that lifestyle, you can make your own film on video, anywhere you want, and distribute it yourself on DVD or post it on the Internet, as I have been urging my students to do for years. Some have done just that, writing and directing low-budget shorts and features and promoting them on the Web and in film festivals. If you don't want to be a director or think you're not ready to direct but have written a script you'd like to see filmed independently, find a collaborator you can work with to help bring your picture to the screen. (When I say "independently," I mean in the true sense of the word, not the way studios define it, as a low-budget branch of their operations.) If you find a partner to direct your script, both of you will have what's known as a "calling-card film."

Anyone who wants to succeed as a filmmaker needs a calling-card film, a vehicle to show people what you can do. Steven Spielberg spent ten years making 8 mm and 16 mm films before he made his breakthrough with the highly polished, fully professional *Amblin',* the short subject he wrote and directed in 35 mm in 1968. The twenty-one-year-old filmmaker made it because he was having trouble getting people in Hollywood to look at his amateur films. His mentor, Universal film librarian Chuck Silvers, was one with the foresight to look at them, and he was mightily impressed, but he told Spielberg he had to make a 35 mm film to get other people's attention in the industry. Spielberg found an aspiring producer, Denis Hoffman, who was willing to invest about $20,000 in a short. Sidney J. Sheinberg, then head of television for Universal, saw *Amblin'* at the urging of Chuck Silvers and the next morning offered Spielberg a seven-year contract to direct for television.

Today you don't need to shoot on 35 mm or even on film to produce a professional-looking piece of work. New technologies, such as inexpensive digital cameras and DVD burners, have democratized filmmaking to a large extent, making it possible for anyone to make and distribute her own movie for relatively little money. If you get your hands on a good digital video camera, you can produce a film with sufficient technical quality. If you can't afford to buy your own camera, rent one or, better yet, make friends with someone who owns one and let that person be your cinematographer (if he or she is qualified). My late friend Gary Graver, Orson Welles's cinematographer, was working in video toward the end of his career. I asked Gary a few years ago how cheaply he could make a feature on video. He thought for a few moments and said, "Under a thousand dollars."

Putting together that kind of budget is within anybody's means. You don't need millions of dollars to make a movie, only a camera, a good script, and a couple of good actors. Your movie won't have fancy "production values" or CGI effects, but it can tell a gripping story, and that's what it's all about. For guidance on how to make a no-budget movie, read Robert Rodriguez's delightful book *Rebel Without a Crew: Or How a 23-Year-Old*

Filmmaker with $7,000 Became a Hollywood Player, his diary of the making of *El Mariachi.* Rodriguez managed to get that 1992 feature in the can for only about $7,000, and it ultimately was released by Sony with some success. With music fees and post-production expenses to transfer the 16 mm footage to 35 mm for theatrical release, the final production cost of *El Mariachi* was a lot higher, but that doesn't negate Rodriguez's inspiring example of how cheaply one can make a movie.

Rodriguez offers an amusing demonstration of his cost-cutting and time-saving techniques in a supplement on the *El Mariachi* DVD, *The Robert Rodriguez Ten Minute Film School.* He tells us that he wouldn't even buy a can of paint, because

> if you want to make a movie for a really low budget, you can't spend on anything. You have to *refuse* to spend. I mean, that's just basically how you do it. You refuse to spend on anything. You start spending a little bit, you start that money hose going, and you just can't stop it. Think of a creative way to get around your problem.

Don't pay your cast and crew, but give them percentages in case the picture makes a profit; feed your company (frugally), but borrow equipment and props rather than paying for them; shoot in real locations you beg, borrow, or steal; do your homework and rehearse with the actors ahead of time so you won't waste time on location deciding how to shoot your setups. Most importantly, write a script that minimizes your limitations and maximizes your strengths. As Rodriguez tells us, aspiring filmmakers who attempt to compete with Hollywood production values are doomed to failure:

> No matter how hard they tried, with their limited funds they could never make their demo as slick as Hollywood. They'd come off looking like cheaper imitations. So go the opposite way. Why try and make a slick-looking film when you have no

money? Don't even try. Make a movie that Hollywood could never make no matter how much money they have. Tell a story they'd never risk, or make a movie that goes for the throat the way they'd never do, because they are too mainstream. Fill your film with great ideas, which they can't come up with no matter how much money they have. They can't make their movies more creative with money. Only more expensive. The creative person with limitless imagination and no money can make a better film than the talentless mogul with the limitless checkbook every time.

If you produce a no-budget feature that people might enjoy seeing, you can set up your own website and sell DVD copies. A film with some kind of attractive story hook or one that gets favorable reviews at film festivals might actually earn a modest profit through online sales. I was pleased to read that Spike Lee, while talking with film students at his alma mater, Atlanta's Morehouse College, urged them to follow this same path. He advised them to bypass the whole prohibitively expensive system of commercial financing and distribution and just make their own films on DVD to sell directly to the public. You can put clips of your film online and even consider marketing the film for Internet viewing in its entirety, now that the technology to do so is becoming more viable. If you can get the film shown in festivals, many of which are looking for good independent films, that will bring you public exposure and attention from producers, distributors, and other people scouting for new talent. Festival reviews can be quoted on your website, and you can send your DVD around to other critics who might like the film and offer you a blurb.

And once you have your calling-card film in hand, you can use it to gain entrée to potential buyers of your next project. Having something concrete to show people, whether it's a film or a completed screenplay, is worth any amount of talk. But what do you do if you want to try the more conventional route first? What if you don't want to direct but simply want to write and sell screenplays to the major studios or to independent producers who make films for wide distribution? And what if all your film ideas are too ambitious to be filmed on a shoestring?

4. *Make your own breaks.*

The catch-22 of selling screenplays in Hollywood is that you can't sell a script without an agent, but you can't get an agent until you've sold a script. Fortunately, there are ways around this maddening conundrum. Although agents will be more willing to pay attention if you have a producer or director interested in your script (that's how I got my first agent in Hollywood, though we didn't last long together), some agents are actively looking for new talent and are willing to read your script. If you can get a recommendation from a fellow writer to his or her agent, that would be ideal, but you can get your work to agents' attention on your own if necessary. "The best way to get an agent is to send the manuscript to every agent ten times," says screenwriter-director Ron Shelton, whose films include *Bull Durham* and *White Men Can't Jump*. "That's how I got an agent. I spent three years sending my script to everyone who would read it and knocking on doors. I sent it everywhere. Everyone in town is always looking for something they can sell. Get a list of the agencies that read unsolicited manuscripts."

However, don't ever show your screenplay to an agency that charges a reading fee; that usually will be some sort of scam, and your money will be wasted. It might be necessary to pay a fee to enter your script in a screenwriting competition, whether through a film festival or some other organization, but those contests are worthwhile in helping call attention to your talent and elevating you above the crowd. A prize or honorable mention from a screenwriting competition will look good on your résumé and get you in the door with agents.

Sometimes agents appear at public events in the Los Angeles area—on panels or at schools—as a way of making themselves accessible to aspiring writers. Some directors and producers also make the rounds of such venues; one director I know used to make a habit of hanging around University of Southern California film screenings to meet writers who might be willing to write a spec script for him. The Writers Guild discourages writing on spec, but if you're a writer who hasn't sold anything, you might want to consider taking a shot at such an opportunity (my first produced screenplay, *Blood and Guts,* was written on spec for director Paul Lynch, who worked closely with me on its development). Whenever you write on spec, always be sure to register each stage of your written material with the WGA and get a collaboration agreement in writing up front to protect yourself. One former student of mine, who failed to take such precautions, was burned by a producer who talked him into rewriting a script on spec and then sold it to a studio without him.

Have a portfolio of material ready to sell when you arrive in town—two or three feature-length scripts and several other ideas (on varied subjects) in treatment form, all registered, all neatly presented. Keep a paper trail of all the contacts you make with your scripts or treatments, including notes on telephone and other conversations as well as delivery confirmations and correspondence. Constantly generate new ideas. Always have a project in the works. Write every day. Read widely to find material and enrich your knowledge of the world. Be persistent with material you believe in, but don't just keep flogging the same screenplay if it isn't selling. Having a variety of scripts and stories to offer people gives you a greater chance of appealing to different tastes and navigating the vagaries of the marketplace.

It may be reassuring to know that screenwriter Ed Solomon believes the process of finding an agent for your script ultimately comes down to the question of quality: "I hate to say this, but if your script is genuinely good it will attract agents like a magnet. The sad truth is that most scripts probably aren't that good."

5. *Don't pitch your ideas if you can help it.*

The pitching process, in my opinion, is one of the most insidious parts of the Hollywood racket. A producer or studio executive will call in ten or fifteen writers, mention the skeleton of a story idea, and ask the writers to embellish it on the spot. Then he will take the writers' ideas and turn them over to the writer he actually wants to hire. This is nothing but legalized idea theft. You can protect yourself from it by handing over your ideas in writing (and making the other party sign a receipt) or by avoiding pitching altogether. You don't have to pitch scripts to be a successful screenwriter, as William Goldman attests: "I have only tried one 'pitch' in my life and that was for friends, and I was so awful I quit halfway through."

Once I "sold" a project based on a three-word pitch about how I would write a biopic of a certain figure in modern American history. Before I could go on, the producer said, "I'll do it!" I also lined up an Academy Award–winning director to make the film, but the project ultimately fell apart for reasons largely beyond our control. If I had to do it all over again, however, I would avoid the scores of pitch meetings I attended, most of which were a waste of time. I realized later that, like Goldman, I wasn't particularly good at pitching; I do my best work on the page, not off the top of my head, and I suspect that's true of many, if not most, writers. That's why we become writers, because we're better at typing than talking. The scripts I did sell were not pitched ahead of time. But there are some screenwriters with the gift of glibness who can spitball story ideas and wow their listeners with their ability to ad-lib. More power to them.

Screenwriter Akiva Goldsman, whose credits since *A Beautiful Mind* include *Cinderella Man, The Da Vinci Code,* and *I Am Legend,* has this advice to offer on pitching:

> I don't rehearse, but you certainly need to know your story
> well before you can pitch it. I'm lucky that I'm social because

it's true that pitching is a social art. Relationships are irrelevant, because you can go into a room with someone you have a relationship with and not sell it. To all the introvert writers who have a tough time pitching, my advice is to not worry about pitching. Concentrate on the writing, because you won't get to pitch unless you've written well in the first place. If you're lucky and get called in to pitch, get a best friend or a producer who'll help you practice. You don't have to be a great pitcher if you're a great writer. I know brilliant writers who are terrible in rooms.

A few years ago, long after my last pitch meeting, I had an epiphany. I finally understood how the pitching process worked. When I would pitch, I would concentrate all my energy on how to tell the story. But another component of the process had always eluded me. Whenever I went in to tell the story, I was all revved up and ready to start in, but the producer or executive invariably would launch into a ten- or fifteen-minute spiel about what he had done over the weekend (unfortunately, it was usually a he). And usually what he had been doing was something like hunting or sailing or watching football, subjects I had trouble feigning interest in, especially when I was so impatient to get down to what I thought was the business of the meeting. I never quite understood why all that small talk was necessary. At the time I put it down to the egotism of powerful men with too much leisure time. But years later I suddenly realized that it was *then,* during that period of small talk, that you sell your story or strike out with it. In those ten or fifteen minutes, the essence of the meeting occurs. The small talk is the producer's way of seeing if he'd like to spend months having beers with you while you work on the movie together.

If I were newly arrived in Hollywood today, I'd avoid the whole mishegoss and just write the damn screenplay. As I found, you stand a better chance of selling a story when you write it all out and show *that* way how you see the movie. And though they may still mess with it in the long run, you stand a somewhat better chance of telling the story your way if you don't let them get their fingers in it too early in the process by trying to tell you how to "improve" your story, as often happens in pitch meetings.

But if you must pitch a story, don't just submit it orally. Idea theft is the dirty secret of Hollywood. It's rampant. As I was advised to do by the Writers Guild after a particularly blatant instance of theft (more on that in a moment), bring a written outline of your story to the pitch meeting and get a signed receipt before the meeting starts. If the producer won't sign for it, immediately leave the office with your outline in hand. Or if that kind of assertiveness makes you uncomfortable, send the outline to his or her office by FedEx the day before the meeting, so you can get a signature of receipt (faxing it would also work). Proving access is essential to protect your material if you submit it to someone. If possible, have your agent in the room when you discuss a story with a potential buyer.

Screenwriter Joe Eszterhas adds this advice: "You can do a few things to protect yourself, but not many.... If you are about to have a meeting with a studio executive, a development person, a producer, a director, an assistant to any of the above, or an agent to pitch a story, as soon as you get home from the meeting, write a memo describing the details of the meeting as well as the details of the story or stories that you pitched. Same drill as before: Put the memo in an envelope, send it to yourself in the mail, and don't open it when it comes back to you. Besides these things, there's not much you can do if you're ripped off except sue." Or as our fellow Writers Guild member Jay Leno advises, "You have to write faster than they can steal."

You may think we are exaggerating the need for such precautions, but the last time I went into a pitch meeting, I spent a couple of hours giving a producer ideas for his upcoming television special, and my guard was down because the producer had told my agent he would hire me for the show. As it happened, the producer simply stole my ideas rather than hiring me, and I was unable to stop him from using them on the show because I had not submitted anything in writing. I filed a complaint with the Writers Guild, to no avail; my agent (whom I later fired) refused to cooperate with the hearing, preferring to preserve his relationship with the powerful producer over his relationship with me.

So you may not be able to protect yourself entirely if you go in to pitch your ideas, but if you take these precautions, you may stand a fighting chance. Opinions differ, however, on how trusting you should be of the process and how far you should go to protect yourself. Screenwriter Sam Hamm disagrees with the idea of delivering a written copy of your story when you pitch it. He tells me,

> I don't think it's a bad idea to write a memo detailing exactly what you pitched to a producer or an executive, as long as you mail it to yourself or register it with the WGA. But I don't believe in leaving paper. It fixes the pitch in stone and gives the higher-ups something to react against. ("Oh, look, on p. 2, he's wearing an argyle sweater. I HATE argyle sweaters"— which is a goofy exaggeration, but believe me, an exec who wants to turn you down will seize on ANY excuse to turn you down.) The producer will either be taking his own notes or will have a factotum in the meeting taking notes for him. That record will contain the give-and-take between writer and producer—including the "good ideas" the producer comes up with on the spot, the stuff he doesn't like and wants to lose or fix, the stuff he does like and wants to play up. The revised version, the POTENTIAL version that you plant in the producer's head, if you're lucky, will be the one that he pitches to the studio. And that's the one you want him to pitch, because without his enthusiasm the studio will not buy it.
>
> If you can somehow get the other guy to think that your vision is his vision (as with the director!), you're halfway to

making the sale. Paper makes the vision less fluid, less plastic. It just gets in the way.

As for the possibility of idea theft, Sam advises writers to go into meetings without worrying about that to an incapacitating degree:

Yes, you will meet crooked producers who will take your brilliant ideas if you let them. You will sometimes discover that your brilliant ideas have also occurred to other writers— sometimes even before they occurred to you. The lesson? Ideas are cheap. Anyone can have them, and anyone can swipe them—but if you learn your craft and develop an individual voice, no one will be able to swipe your execution.

6. Is compromising necessary? Bend but don't break.

Paul Schrader once said that knowing when to walk out of the room is essential to keeping your integrity in the film business. There are some moments when the stakes are too high for compromise. Hopefully you will recognize them when they present themselves, not in retrospect, but in such a contentious business, it's hard to avoid some regrets over the times when you should have just said no. You'll usually feel better afterward when you do.

And yet there are many other times when cooperation and collaboration are called for. A producer's or director's idea of how to improve your story may actually make it better. You can't be so wedded to your ideas that you refuse to listen. Once you sell the project or are hired to work on the script and start working with other people, that kind of collaboration is simply inevitable. You may have to give in on small matters to prevail on a few large issues. Filmmakers in the Golden Age of Hollywood often would write in lines and pieces of business they knew would never get past the censors, hoping this would distract the censors from other lines and scenes they really wanted to keep in the movie. Often that kind of game works with studios, producers, and directors. And often a subtle diplomacy is called for; there are no clear guidelines for how to practice such diplomacy, although studying Machiavelli or Henry Kissinger might give you some tips.

When I was working on the script of *Rock 'n' Roll High School,* the director, Allan Arkush, suggested combining two characters (the demure but rebellious student Kate and a boy science genius) into one. Responding in a knee-jerk way, I said I didn't think it would work, but Allan asked me to consider the idea, and I soon realized it would help the film a great deal by building up Kate's character. But when Allan objected to blowing up the school at the end of the film, claiming it "would make the students unsympathetic," I resisted on that crucial point and, fortunately, won my argument.

Billy Wilder gave me an excellent piece of advice when I was a young writer that I wished I had followed more assiduously. He recommended that I find a more experienced director with whom to collaborate, as he had done early in his Hollywood career with the great Ernst Lubitsch. Not only can the more experienced director offer you the benefits of his wisdom and expertise, he can also help you sell your project and navigate through the shark-infested waters of the system. The same can be true if you find a writing collaborator who's more experienced than you are and more skilled at selling projects. Collaboration ideally can provide a team with a complementary set of skills, both creative and practical. But collaboration should not mean capitulation. A writer without a backbone is begging to have his or her work mutilated or trashed. The fine line between bending and breaking is ultimately a matter of personal taste and convictions. If you care deeply about your work, you will not make such moves or decisions lightly. And if you don't care about your work, why are you a writer?

Perhaps the most vexing problem with filmmaking is that the people who care the most about their work are at something of a disadvantage. More cynical people have the advantage of not caring. A cynic, Oscar Wilde tells us, is "a man who knows the price of everything, and the value of nothing." Cynics will exploit your sense of caring and try to turn it into a disadvantage through mockery and other power plays. The only people who can sustain a career in the movie business are the ones who somehow can work out the difficult balance between caring and not caring. These people are able to survive painful losses in the hopes of earning occasional victories. One such screenwriter is Ron Bass, whose credits include *Rain Man, The Joy Luck Club, My Best Friend's Wedding,* and *Amelia.* Even this prolific writer admits,

> It's a very hard business…you're failing all the time as a screenwriter. The odds of anything getting liked are so small, and to get it made, they're even smaller. Even a wonderful script that everyone loves won't get made for all kinds of reasons. Even if it gets made, they may screw it up in making or marketing it, and it may flop.…[Y]ou're always being criticized and rejected. And yet, if you don't remain vulnerable to that, you're hurting yourself. Those who can harden their hearts to it and say, "To hell with them, I don't care what they say, I know I'm right" can become arrogant and lack the openness that maybe they don't have all the answers, maybe they're not doing such a great job and the criticism is correct.

Such pragmatism may enable you to survive the slings and arrows of a screenwriting career, but you'll have to decide for yourself whether the sacrifices are worth it.

7. Don't try to figure out what's "commercial."

Does anybody know what's commercial? If people think they do, they're fooling themselves. The world, and audiences' tastes in movies, change so rapidly that even the savviest producers and directors and writers can only guess at what people will be interested in seeing when a film finally reaches the screen. If any of us knew for certain what movies people would want to see in the future, we'd be running a studio and doing a much better job of it than those who do. David Picker, who once ran United Artists, honestly admitted that if he had said yes to the projects he said no to, and vice versa, his track record would have been about the same. Even the overreliance on sequels and remakes in today's Hollywood, while designed to prevent failure, does not offer anything more certain than diminishing success. Anyone wanting to do something more original should know that its chances of commercial success are entirely a crapshoot.

We've discussed this before, but it bears repeating as you prepare to enter the marketplace with your ideas: The dumbest thing you can do as a screenwriter is to imitate the current success or trend, because the film you copy will seem old hat a couple of years from now, when some other film will be the big hit. Today's trend will be long gone by the time your script is made (if it is at all). The sequels and remakes will be churned out by writers with longer track records than yours. The fact is that the really big hits, the most groundbreaking and influential films, the ones that inspire everyone to want to copy them, are usually the projects that seem so dodgy in script form (because they are truly new) that they have trouble getting financed and are turned down by most of the studios. Today that's even true of many films that win the Oscar for best picture, since those tend to be risk-taking projects by definition.

Writing what you truly care about will increase the likelihood that you will write well and (as Hemingway would put it) truly. Of course, good and true writing is no guarantee of success, especially in the film business, but people, even the most hardened cynics, are more likely to respond to work that comes from the heart than to work that comes from reading the trades and trying to second-guess the marketplace.

William Goldman's cardinal rule about moviemaking is worth keeping in mind whenever you are tempted to listen to self-styled experts trying to tell you what kinds of scripts to write or not to write. Never forget these reassuring words:

NOBODY KNOWS ANYTHING.

Here's a glaring and rather comical example: I acquired my first Hollywood agent shortly after I moved to Los Angeles in July 1973. Among the pieces of advice he gave me at our initial meeting was not to write about teenagers or write comedies, because those kinds of films (he said) were hard to sell. Just a week later, George Lucas's *American Graffiti* came out. That comedy about teenagers became one of the biggest hits in film history, grossing more than $115 million in domestic theatrical box-office receipts on a production cost of only about $700,000. Ever since then, film companies have been churning out teenage comedies, usually with success. So much for advice from a supposed expert on how to sell screenplays.

8. Do other forms of writing.

If you do nothing but write screenplays, you put yourself at a disadvantage by limiting your professional options and making yourself vulnerable to the ups and downs of the marketplace. But if you also write books (nonfiction or fiction), plays, and/or articles, you will have an identity and a career outside the field of screenwriting. The advantages are manifold: greater respect, greater opportunities, more clout, and, above all, more personal satisfaction.

Unfortunately, Hollywood has a habit of taking "mere" professional screenwriters for granted by treating them with a mixture of familiarity and contempt. If you do nothing but write screenplays, you will face this demeaning attitude no matter how successful you may become at that craft. But if you have a broader writing career that brings you validation from the world beyond Hollywood, you will find yourself treated with far more respect by your fellow filmmakers.

Furthermore, if you can sell a story first in another medium, it is much easier to sell that story as a film, especially if it is off-beat or controversial. Almost 300,000 books are published each year in America (a figure that does not include print-on-demand and short-run books), and only about 600 feature films are released theatrically each year in the United States (that figure does not count several thousand features that are made but aren't distributed). Your chances of getting a novel published, if it is well written, are greater than your shot at having an original screenplay produced and distributed. Novels, nonfiction books, and magazine articles are often optioned or purchased as film material. That outside validation works wonders on film companies when they decide whether to purchase a story you have written.

Even if your book is never made into a film, you will see your work in print and earn some money from it. And options can be a lucrative source of income. I know a successful novelist who hasn't yet had a film made from his work but earns a good, steady income each year from the renewal of options on his books. Such an income in turn will help finance your writing of more books and screenplays. If your book happens to be successful, you will not only earn royalties but will also find that its purchase price for filming will escalate. So if you have a good idea for a movie, whether it stems purely from your imagination or is based on actual events, see if you can write it first as a book, and then you will stand a better chance of selling it to the movies. You may or may not be hired to adapt your own book for the screen, but you will stand a fair chance of doing so.

And the more unconventional your screenplay idea is, the more necessary it may be to seek such validation elsewhere before filmmakers will take a chance with it.

9. Have a life.

Don't become consumed by the film business—have interests and friends outside the business. You won't have anything worth writing about if you don't have a life. And if you do nothing but work, you will become so depressed that all your effort eventually will become counterproductive, and you'll have nothing to fall back upon when things get tough.

So value your family and loved ones. Read widely. Travel. Explore.

10. And remember what's most important about writing—

—not the money, not the fame, not the perks, but the craft, the joy of writing. That's all that can stand the test of time. And ultimately, through all the highs and lows of a professional career, it is the love of your craft that will sustain you as a writer.

Appendix A

The Basic Steps in the Screenwriting Process

- Conception

  Getting original ideas from life experiences, history, news events, your imagination, and other such sources, or adapting preexisting literary material;

  Or being hired by a film company to write a screenplay based on existing material—rewriting a script, writing a script based on an idea proposed by a filmmaker or a production company, and so on

- Obtaining rights to material (if necessary)

  Taking an option on or purchasing literary material, making other legal agreements with real people portrayed, and so on.

- Taking notes, fleshing out your idea

- Writing a synopsis (for yourself) or treatment (to show or submit)

- Registering your synopsis or treatment with the Writers Guild of America, West, or using another method of protecting the idea (such as sending it to yourself by registered mail or copyrighting it with the Library of Congress)

Appendix A

- Step outlining
  on paper and/or on index cards; display on a board or a computer program for easy reference

- Writing and revising the screenplay (usually 100–120 pages for a feature-length film)

- Registering the screenplay (see above)

- Selling the screenplay
  through an agent, personal approaches to filmmakers, festival and other competition entries, or so on.
  Or raising the funds to make the film yourself on film or digitally

- Rewriting the screenplay
  if required by the purchaser or desired by yourself to make improvements

- Production and postproduction of the film; publicity process
  The screenwriter is often excluded from these stages but should fight for continuing involvement

Appendix B

"To Build a Fire"
by Jack London

This version of the story first appeared in
The Century Magazine, New York, August 1908

*D*ay had broken cold and gray, exceedingly cold and gray, when the man turned aside from the main Yukon trail and climbed the high earth-bank, where a dim and little-travelled trail led eastward through the fat spruce timberland. It was a steep bank, and he paused for breath at the top, excusing the act to himself by looking at his watch. It was nine o'clock. There was no sun nor hint of sun, though there was not a cloud in the sky. It was a clear day, and yet there seemed an intangible pall over the face of things, a subtle gloom that made the day dark, and that was due to the absence of sun. This fact did not worry the man. He was used to the lack of sun. It had been days since he had seen the sun, and he knew that a few more days must pass before that cheerful orb, due south, would just peep above the sky line and dip immediately from view.

The man flung a look back along the way he had come. The Yukon lay a mile wide and hidden under three feet of ice. On top of this ice were as many feet of snow. It was all pure white, rolling in gentle undulations where the ice jams of the freeze-up had formed. North and south, as far as his eye could see, it was unbroken white, save for a dark hairline that curved and twisted from around the spruce-covered island to the south, and that curved and twisted away into the north, where it disappeared behind another spruce-covered island. This dark hairline was the trail—the main trail—that led south five hundred miles to the Chilcoot Pass, Dyea, and salt water; and that led north seventy miles to Dawson, and still on to the north a thousand miles to Nulato, and finally to St. Michael, on Bering Sea, a thousand miles and half a thousand more.

But all this—the mysterious, far-reaching hairline trail, the absence of sun from the sky, the tremendous cold, and the strangeness and weirdness of it all—made no impression on the man. It was not because he was long used to it. He was a new-comer in the land, a *chechaquo,* and this was his first winter. The trouble with him was that he was without imagination. He was quick and alert in the things of life, but only in the things, and not in the significances. Fifty degrees below zero meant eighty-odd degrees of frost. Such fact impressed him as being cold and uncomfortable, and that was all. It did not lead him to meditate upon his frailty as a creature of temperature, and upon man's frailty in general, able only to live within certain narrow limits of heat and cold; and from there on it did not lead him to the conjectural field of immortality and man's place in the universe. Fifty degrees below zero stood for a bite of frost that hurt and that must be guarded against by the use of mittens, ear flaps, warm moccasins, and thick socks. Fifty degrees below zero was to him just precisely fifty degrees below zero. That there should be anything more to it than that was a thought that never entered his head.

As he turned to go on, he spat speculatively. There was a sharp, explosive crackle that startled him. He spat again. And again, in the air, before it could fall to the snow, the spittle crackled. He knew that at fifty below spittle crackled on the snow, but this spittle had crackled in the air. Undoubtedly it was colder than fifty below—how much colder he did not know. But the temperature did not matter. He was bound for the old claim on the left fork of Henderson Creek, where the boys were already. They had come over across the divide from the Indian Creek country, while he had come the roundabout way to take a look at the possibilities of getting out logs in the spring from the islands in the Yukon. He would be in to camp by six o'clock; a bit after dark, it was true, but the boys would be there, a fire would be going, and a hot supper would be ready. As for lunch, he pressed his hand against the protruding bundle under his jacket. It was also under his shirt, wrapped up in a handkerchief and lying against the naked skin. It was the only way to keep the biscuits from freezing. He smiled agreeably to himself as he thought of those biscuits, each cut open and sopped in bacon grease, and each enclosing a generous slice of fried bacon.

He plunged in among the big spruce trees. The trail was faint. A foot of snow had fallen since the last sled had passed over, and he was glad he was without a sled, travelling light. In fact, he carried nothing but the lunch wrapped in the handkerchief. He was surprised, however, at the cold. It certainly was cold, he concluded, as he rubbed his numb nose and cheekbones with his mittened hand. He was a warm-whiskered man, but the hair on his face did not protect the high cheekbones and the eager nose that thrust itself aggressively into the frosty air.

At the man's heels trotted a dog, a big native husky, the proper wolf dog, gray-coated and without any visible or temperamental difference from its brother, the wild wolf. The animal was depressed by the tremendous cold. It knew that it was no time for travelling. Its instinct told it a truer tale than was told to the man by the man's judgment. In reality, it was not merely colder than fifty below zero; it was colder than sixty below, than seventy below. It was seventy-five below zero. Since the freezing-point is thirty-two above zero, it meant that one hundred and seven degrees of frost obtained. The dog did not know anything about thermometers. Possibly in its brain there was no sharp consciousness of a condition of very cold such as was in the man's brain. But the brute had its instinct. It experienced a vague but menacing apprehension that subdued it and made it slink along at the man's heels, and that made it question eagerly every unwonted movement of the man as if expecting him to go into camp or to seek shelter somewhere and build a fire. The dog had learned fire, and it wanted fire, or else to burrow under the snow and cuddle its warmth away from the air.

The frozen moisture of its breathing had settled on its fur in a fine powder of frost, and especially were its jowls, muzzle, and eyelashes whitened by its crystalled breath. The man's red beard and mustache were likewise frosted, but more solidly, the deposit taking the form of ice and increasing with every warm, moist breath he exhaled. Also, the man was chewing tobacco, and the muzzle of ice held his lips so rigidly that he was unable to clear his chin when he expelled the juice. The result was that a crystal beard of the color and solidity of amber was increasing its length on his chin. If he fell down it would shatter itself, like glass, into brittle fragments. But he did not mind the appendage. It was the penalty all tobacco chewers paid in that country, and he had been out before in two cold snaps. They had not been so cold as this, he knew, but by the spirit thermometer at Sixty Mile he knew they had been registered at fifty below and at fifty-five.

He held on through the level stretch of woods for several miles, crossed a wide flat of nigger heads, and dropped down a bank to the frozen bed of a small stream. This was Henderson Creek, and he knew he was ten miles from the forks. He looked at his watch. It was ten o'clock. He was making four miles an hour, and he calculated that he would arrive at the forks at half-past twelve. He decided to celebrate that event by eating his lunch there.

The dog dropped in again at his heels, with a tail drooping discouragement, as the man swung along the creek bed. The furrow of the old sled trail was plainly visible, but a dozen inches of snow covered the marks of the last runners. In a month no man had come up or down that silent creek. The man held steadily on. He was not much given to thinking, and just then particularly he had nothing to think about save that he would eat lunch at the forks and that at six o'clock he would be in camp with the boys. There was nobody to talk to; and, had there been, speech would have been impossible because of the ice muzzle on his mouth. So he continued monotonously to chew tobacco and to increase the length of his amber beard.

Once in a while the thought reiterated itself that it was very cold and that he had never experienced such cold. As he walked along he rubbed his cheekbones and nose with the back of his mittened hand. He did this automatically, now and again changing hands. But rub as he would, the instant he stopped his cheekbones went numb, and the following instant the end of his nose went numb. He was sure to frost his cheeks; he knew that, and experienced a pang of regret that he had not devised a nose-strap of the sort Bud wore in cold snaps. Such a strap passed across the cheeks, as well, and saved them. But it didn't matter much, after all. What were frosted cheeks? A bit painful, that was all; they were never serious.

Empty as the man's mind was of thoughts, he was keenly observant, and he noticed the changes in the creek, the curves and bends and timber jams, and always he sharply noted where he placed his feet. Once, coming around a bend, he shied abruptly, like a startled horse, curved away from the place where he had been walking, and retreated several paces back along the trail. The creek he knew was frozen clear to the bottom—no creek could contain water in that arctic winter—but he knew also that there were springs that bubbled out from the hillsides and ran along under the snow and on top the ice of the creek. He knew that the coldest snaps never froze these springs, and he knew likewise their danger. They were traps. They hid pools of water under the snow that might be three inches deep, or three feet. Sometimes a skin of ice half an inch thick covered them, and in turn was covered by the snow. Sometimes there were alternate layers of water and ice skin, so that when one broke through he kept on breaking through for a while, sometimes wetting himself to the waist.

That was why he had shied in such panic. He had felt the give under his feet and heard the crackle of a snow-hidden ice skin. And to get his feet wet in such a temperature meant trouble and danger. At the very least it meant delay, for he would be forced to stop and build a fire, and under its protection to bare his feet while he dried his socks and moccasins. He stood and studied the creek bed and its banks, and decided that the flow of water came from the right. He reflected awhile, rubbing his nose and cheeks, then skirted to the left, stepping gingerly and testing the footing for each step. Once clear of the danger, he took a fresh chew of tobacco and swung along at his four-mile gait.

In the course of the next two hours he came upon several similar traps. Usually the snow above the hidden pools had a sunken, candied appearance that advertised the danger. Once again, however, he had a close call; and once, suspecting danger, he compelled the dog to go on in front. The dog did not want to go. It hung back until the man shoved it forward, and then it went quickly across the white, unbroken surface. Suddenly it broke through, floundered to one side, and got away to firmer footing. It had wet its forefeet and legs, and almost immediately the water that clung to it turned to ice. It made quick efforts to lick the ice off its legs, then dropped down in the snow and began to bite out the ice that had formed between the toes. This was a matter of instinct. To permit the ice to remain would mean sore feet. It did not know this. It merely obeyed the mysterious prompting that arose from the deep crypts of its being. But the man knew, having achieved a judgment on the subject, and he removed the mitten from his right hand and helped tear out the ice particles. He did not expose his fingers more than a minute, and was astonished at the swift numbness that smote them. It certainly was cold. He pulled on the mitten hastily, and beat the hand savagely across his chest.

At twelve o'clock the day was at its brightest. Yet the sun was too far south on its winter journey to clear the horizon. The bulge of the earth intervened between it and Henderson Creek, where the man walked under a clear sky at noon and cast no shadow. At half-past twelve, to the minute, he arrived at the forks of the creek. He was pleased at the speed he had made. If he kept it up, he would certainly be with the boys by six. He unbuttoned his jacket and shirt and drew forth his lunch. The action consumed no more than a quarter of a minute, yet in that brief moment the numbness laid hold of the exposed fingers. He did not put the mitten on, but, instead, struck the fingers a dozen sharp smashes against his leg. Then he sat down on a snow-covered log to eat. The sting that followed upon the striking of his fingers against his leg ceased so quickly that he was startled. He had had no chance to take a bite of biscuit. He struck the fingers repeatedly and returned them to the mitten, baring the other hand for the purpose of eating. He tried to take a mouthful, but the ice muzzle prevented. He had forgotten to build a fire and thaw out. He chuckled at his foolishness, and as he chuckled he noted the numbness creeping into the exposed fingers. Also, he noted that the stinging which had first come to his toes when he sat down was already passing away. He wondered whether the toes were warm or numb. He moved them inside the moccasins and decided that they were numb.

He pulled the mitten on hurriedly and stood up. He was a bit frightened. He stamped up and down until the stinging returned into the feet. It certainly was cold, was his thought. That man from Sulphur Creek had spoken the truth when telling how cold it sometimes got in the country. And he had laughed at him at the time! That showed one must not be too sure of things. There was no mistake about it, it *was* cold. He strode up and down, stamping his feet and threshing his arms, until reassured by the returning warmth. Then he got out matches and proceeded to make a fire. From the undergrowth, where high water of the previous spring had lodged a supply of seasoned twigs, he got his firewood. Working carefully from a small beginning, he soon had a roaring fire, over which he thawed the ice from his face and in the protection of which he ate his biscuits. For the moment the cold of space was outwitted. The dog took satisfaction in the fire, stretching out close enough for warmth and far enough away to escape being singed.

When the man had finished, he filled his pipe and took his comfortable time over a smoke. Then he pulled on his mittens, settled the ear flaps of his cap firmly about his ears, and took the creek trail up the left fork. The dog was disappointed and yearned back toward the fire. This man did not know cold. Possibly all the generations of his ancestry had been ignorant of cold, of real cold, of cold one hundred and seven degrees below freezing point. But the dog knew; all its ancestry knew, and it had inherited the knowledge. And it knew that it was not good to walk abroad in such fearful cold. It was the time to lie snug in a hole in the snow and wait for a curtain of cloud to be drawn across the face of outer space whence this cold came. On the other hand, there was keen intimacy between the dog and the man. The one was the toil slave of the other, and the only caresses it had ever received were the caresses of the whip lash and of harsh and menacing throat sounds that threatened the whip lash. So the dog made no effort to communicate its apprehension to the man. It was not concerned in the welfare of the man; it was for its own sake that it yearned back toward the fire. But the man whistled, and spoke to it with the sound of whip lashes, and the dog swung in at the man's heels and followed after.

The man took a chew of tobacco and proceeded to start a new amber beard. Also, his moist breath quickly powdered with white his mustache, eyebrows, and lashes. There did not seem to be so many springs on the left fork of the Henderson, and for half an hour the man saw no signs of any. And then it happened. At a place where there were no signs, where the soft, unbroken snow seemed to advertise solidity beneath, the man broke through. It was not deep. He wet himself halfway to the knees before he floundered out to the firm crust.

He was angry, and cursed his luck aloud. He had hoped to get into camp with the boys at six o'clock, and this would delay him an hour, for he would have to build a fire and dry out his foot-gear. This was imperative at that low temperature—he knew that much; and he turned aside to the bank, which he climbed. On top, tangled in the underbrush about the trunks of several small spruce trees, was a high-water deposit of dry firewood—sticks and twigs, principally, but also larger portions of seasoned branches and fine, dry, last year's grasses. He threw down several large pieces on top of the snow. This served for a foundation and prevented the young flame from drowning itself in the snow it otherwise would melt. The flame he got by touching a match to a small shred of birch bark that he took from his pocket. This burned even more readily than paper. Placing it on the foundation, he fed the young flame with wisps of dry grass and with the tiniest dry twigs.

He worked slowly and carefully, keenly aware of his danger. Gradually, as the flame grew stronger, he increased the size of the twigs with which he fed it. He squatted in the snow, pulling the twigs out from their entanglement in the brush and feeding directly to the flame. He knew there must be no failure. When it is seventy-five below zero, a man must not fail in his first attempt to build a fire—that is, if his feet are wet. If his feet are dry, and he fails, he can run along the trail for half a mile and restore his circulation. But the circulation of wet and freezing feet cannot be restored by running when it is seventy-five below. No matter how fast he runs, the wet feet will freeze the harder.

All this the man knew. The old-timer on Sulphur Creek had told him about it the previous fall, and now he was appreciating the advice. Already all sensation had gone out of his feet. To build the fire he had been forced to remove his mittens, and the fingers had quickly gone numb. His pace of four miles an hour had kept his heart pumping blood to the surface of his body and to all the extremities. But the instant he stopped, the action of the pump eased down. The cold of space smote the unprotected tip of the planet, and he, being on that unprotected tip, received the full force of the blow. The blood of his body recoiled before it. The blood was alive, like the dog, and like the dog it wanted to hide away and cover itself up from the fearful cold. So long as he walked four miles an hour, he pumped that blood, willy-nilly, to the surface; but now it ebbed away and sank down into the recesses of his body. The extremities were the first to feel its absence. His wet feet froze the faster, and his exposed fingers numbed the faster, though they had not yet begun to freeze. Nose and cheeks were already freezing, while the skin of all his body chilled as it lost its blood.

But he was safe. Toes and nose and cheeks would be only touched by the frost, for the fire was beginning to burn with strength. He was feeding it with twigs the size of his finger. In another minute he would be able to feed it with branches the size of his wrist, and then he could remove his wet footgear, and, while it dried, he could keep his naked feet warm by the fire, rubbing them at first, of course, with snow. The fire was a success. He was safe. He remembered the advice of the old-timer on Sulphur Creek, and smiled. The old-timer had been very serious in laying down the law that no man must travel alone in the Klondike after fifty below. Well, here he was; he had had the accident; he was alone; and he had saved himself. Those old-timers were rather womanish, some of them, he thought. All a man had to do was to keep his head, and he was all right. Any man who was a man could travel alone. But it was surprising, the rapidity with which his cheeks and nose were freezing. And he had not thought his fingers could go lifeless in so short a time. Lifeless they were, for he could scarcely make them move together to grip a twig, and they seemed remote from his body and from him. When he touched a twig, he had to look and see whether or not he had hold of it. The wires were pretty well down between him and his finger ends.

All of which counted for little. There was the fire, snapping and crackling and promising life with every dancing flame. He started to untie his moccasins. They were coated with ice; the thick German socks were like sheaths of iron halfway to the knees; and the moccasin strings were like rods of steel all twisted and knotted as by some conflagration. For a moment he tugged with his numb fingers, then, realizing the folly of it, he drew his sheath knife.

But before he could cut the strings, it happened. It was his own fault or, rather, his mistake. He should not have built the fire under the spruce tree. He should have built it in the open. But it had been easier to pull the twigs from the brush and drop them directly on the fire. Now the tree under which he had done this carried a weight of snow on its boughs. No wind had blown for weeks, and each bough was fully freighted. Each time he had pulled a twig he had communicated a slight agitation to the tree—an imperceptible agitation, so far as he was concerned, but an agitation sufficient to bring about the disaster. High up in the tree one bough capsized its load of snow. This fell on the boughs beneath, capsizing them. This process continued, spreading out and involving the whole tree. It grew like an avalanche, and it descended without warning upon the man and the fire, and the fire was blotted out! Where it had burned was a mantle of fresh and disordered snow.

The man was shocked. It was as though he had just heard his own sentence of death. For a moment he sat and stared at the spot where the fire had been. Then he grew very calm. Perhaps the old-timer on Sulphur Creek was right. If he had only had a trail mate he would have been in no danger now. The trail mate could have built the fire. Well, it was up to him to build the fire over again, and this second time there must be no failure. Even if he succeeded, he would most likely lose some toes. His feet must be badly frozen by now, and there would be some time before the second fire was ready.

Such were his thoughts, but he did not sit and think them. He was busy all the time they were passing through his mind. He made a new foundation for a fire, this time in the open, where no treacherous tree could blot it out. Next, he gathered dry grasses and tiny twigs from the high-water flotsam. He could not bring his fingers together to pull them out, but he was able to gather them by the handful. In this way he got many rotten twigs and bits of green moss that were undesirable, but it was the best he could do. He worked methodically, even collecting an armful of the larger branches to be used later when the fire gathered strength. And all the while the dog sat and watched him, a certain yearning wistfulness in its eyes, for it looked upon him as the fire provider, and the fire was slow in coming.

When all was ready, the man reached in his pocket for a second piece of birch bark. He knew the bark was there, and, though he could not feel it with his fingers, he could hear its crisp rustling as he fumbled for it. Try as he would, he could not clutch hold of it. And all the time, in his consciousness, was the knowledge that each instant his feet were freezing. This thought tended to put him in a panic, but he fought against it and kept calm. He pulled on his mittens with his teeth, and threshed his arms back and forth, beating his hands with all his might against his sides. He did this sitting down, and he stood up to do it; and all the while the dog sat in the snow, its wolf brush of a tail curled around warmly over its forefeet, its sharp wolf ears pricked forward intently as it watched the man. And the man, as he beat and threshed with his arms and hands, felt a great surge of envy as he regarded the creature that was warm and secure in its natural covering.

After a time he was aware of the first faraway signals of sensations in his beaten fingers. The faint tingling grew stronger till it evolved into a stinging ache that was excruciating, but which the man hailed with satisfaction. He stripped the mitten from his right hand and fetched forth the birch bark. The exposed fingers were quickly going numb again. Next he brought out his bunch of sulphur matches. But the tremendous cold had already driven the life out of his fingers. In his effort to separate one match from the others, the whole bunch fell in the snow. He tried to pick it out of the snow, but failed. The dead fingers could neither touch nor clutch. He was very careful. He drove the thought of his freezing feet, and nose, and cheeks, out of his mind, devoting his whole soul to the matches. He watched, using the sense of vision in place of that of touch, and when he saw his fingers on each side the bunch, he closed them—that is, he willed to close them, for the wires were drawn, and the fingers did not obey. He pulled the mitten on the right hand, and beat it fiercely against his knee. Then, with both mittened hands, he scooped the bunch of matches, along with much snow, into his lap. Yet he was no better off.

After some manipulation he managed to get the bunch between the heels of his mittened hands. In this fashion he carried it to his mouth. The ice crackled and snapped when by a violent effort he opened his mouth. He drew the lower jaw in, curled the upper lip out of the way, and scraped the bunch with his upper teeth in order to separate a match. He succeeded in getting one, which he dropped on his lap. He was no better off. He could not pick it up. Then he devised a way. He picked it up in his teeth and scratched it on his leg. Twenty times he scratched before he succeeded in lighting it. As it flamed he held it with his teeth to the birch bark. But the burning brimstone went up his nostrils and into his lungs, causing him to cough spasmodically. The match fell into the snow and went out.

The old-timer on Sulphur Creek was right, he thought in the moment of controlled despair that ensued: after fifty below, a man should travel with a partner. He beat his hands, but failed in exciting any sensation. Suddenly he bared both hands, removing the mittens with his teeth. He caught the whole bunch between the heels of his hands. His arm muscles not being frozen enabled him to press the hand heels tightly against the matches. Then he scratched the bunch along his leg. It flared into flame, seventy sulphur matches at once! There was no wind to blow them out. He kept his head to one side to escape the strangling fumes, and held the blazing bunch to the birch bark. As he so held it, he became aware of sensation in his hand. His flesh was burning. He could smell it. Deep down below the surface he could feel it. The sensation developed into pain that grew acute. And still he endured it, holding the flame of the matches clumsily to the bark that would not light readily because his own burning hands were in the way, absorbing most of the flame.

At last, when he could endure no more, he jerked his hands apart. The blazing matches fell sizzling into the snow, but the birch bark was alight. He began laying dry grasses and the tiniest twigs on the flame. He could not pick and choose, for he had to lift the fuel between the heels of his hands. Small pieces of rotten wood and green moss clung to the twigs, and he bit them off as well as he could with his teeth. He cherished the flame carefully and awkwardly. It meant life, and it must not perish. The withdrawal of blood from the surface of his body now made him begin to shiver, and he grew more awkward. A large piece of green moss fell squarely on the little fire. He tried to poke it out with his fingers, but his shivering frame made him poke too far, and he disrupted the nucleus of the little fire, the burning grasses and tiny twigs separating and scattering. He tried to poke them together again, but in spite of the tenseness of the effort, his shivering got away with him, and the twigs were hopelessly scattered. Each twig gushed a puff of smoke and went out. The fire provider had failed. As he looked apathetically about him, his eyes chanced on the dog, sitting across the ruins of the fire from him, in the snow, making restless, hunching movements, slightly lifting one forefoot and then the other, shifting its weight back and forth on them with wistful eagerness.

The sight of the dog put a wild idea into his head. He remembered the tale of the man, caught in a blizzard, who killed a steer and crawled inside the carcass, and so was saved. He would kill the dog and bury his hands in the warm body until the numbness went out of them. Then he could build another fire. He spoke to the dog, calling it to him; but in his voice was a strange note of fear that frightened the animal, who had never known the man to speak in such a way before. Something was the matter, and its suspicious nature sensed danger—it knew not what danger but somewhere, somehow, in its brain arose an apprehension of the man. It flattened its ears down at the sound of the man's voice, and its restless, hunching movements and the liftings and shiftings of its forefeet became more pronounced; but it would not come to the man. He got on his hands and knees and crawled toward the dog. This unusual posture again excited suspicion, and the animal sidled mincingly away.

The man sat up in the snow for a moment and struggled for calmness. Then he pulled on his mittens, by means of his teeth, and got up on his feet. He glanced down at first in order to assure himself that he was really standing up, for the absence of sensation in his feet left him unrelated to the earth. His erect position in itself started to drive the webs of suspicion from the dog's mind; and when he spoke peremptorily, with the sound of whip lashes in his voice, the dog rendered its customary allegiance and came to him. As it came within reaching distance, the man lost his control. His arms flashed out to the dog, and he experienced genuine surprise when he discovered that his hands could not clutch, that there was neither bend nor feeling in the fingers. He had forgotten for the moment that they were frozen and that they were freezing more and more. All this happened quickly, and before the animal could get away, he encircled its body with his arms. He sat down in the snow, and in this fashion held the dog, while it snarled and whined and struggled.

But it was all he could do, hold its body encircled in his arms and sit there. He realized that he could not kill the dog. There was no way to do it. With his helpless hands he could neither draw nor hold his sheath knife nor throttle the animal. He released it, and it plunged wildly away, with tail between its legs, and still snarling. It halted forty feet away and surveyed him curiously, with ears sharply pricked forward.

The man looked down at his hands in order to locate them, and found them hanging on the ends of his arms. It struck him as curious that one should have to use his eyes in order to find out where his hands were. He began threshing his arms back and forth, beating the mittened hands against his sides. He did this for five minutes, violently, and his heart pumped enough blood up to the surface to put a stop to his shivering. But no sensation was aroused in the hands. He had an impression that they hung like weights on the ends of his arms, but when he tried to run the impression down, he could not find it.

A certain fear of death, dull and oppressive, came to him. This fear quickly became poignant as he realized that it was no longer a mere matter of freezing his fingers and toes, or of losing his hands and feet, but that it was a matter of life and death with the chances against him. This threw him into a panic, and he turned and ran up the creek bed along the old, dim trail. The dog joined in behind and kept up with him. He ran blindly, without intention, in fear such as he had never known in his life. Slowly, as he plowed and floundered through the snow, he began to see things again—the banks of the creek, the old timber jams, the leafless aspens, and the sky. The running made him feel better. He did not shiver. Maybe, if he ran on, his feet would thaw out; and, anyway, if he ran far enough, he would reach camp and the boys. Without doubt he would lose some fingers and toes and some of his face; but the boys would take care of him, and save the rest of him when he got there. And at the same time there was another thought in his mind that said he would never get to the camp and the boys; that it was too many miles away, that the freezing had too great a start on him, and that he would soon be stiff and dead. This thought he kept in the background and refused to consider. Sometimes it pushed itself forward and demanded to be heard, but he thrust it back and strove to think of other things.

It struck him as curious that he could run at all on feet so frozen that he could not feel them when they struck the earth and took the weight of his body. He seemed to himself to skim along above the surface and to have no connection with the earth.

Somewhere he had once seen a winged Mercury, and he wondered if Mercury felt as he felt when skimming over the earth.

His theory of running until he reached camp and the boys had one flaw in it: he lacked the endurance. Several times he stumbled, and finally he tottered, crumpled up, and fell. When he tried to rise, he failed. He must sit and rest, he decided, and next time he would merely walk and keep on going. As he sat and regained his breath, he noted that he was feeling quite warm and comfortable. He was not shivering, and it even seemed that a warm glow had come to his chest and trunk. And yet, when he touched his nose or cheeks, there was no sensation. Running would not thaw them out. Nor would it thaw out his hands and feet. Then the thought came to him that the frozen portions of his body must be extending. He tried to keep this thought down, to forget it, to think of something else; he was aware of the panicky feeling that it caused, and he was afraid of the panic. But the thought asserted itself, and persisted, until it produced a vision of his body totally frozen. This was too much, and he made another wild run along the trail. Once he slowed down to a walk, but the thought of the freezing extending itself made him run again.

And all the time the dog ran with him, at his heels. When he fell down a second time, it curled its tail over its forefeet and sat in front of him, facing him, curiously eager and intent. The warmth and security of the animal angered him, and he cursed it till it flattened down its ears appeasingly. This time the shivering came more quickly upon the man. He was losing in his battle with the frost. It was creeping into his body from all sides. The thought of it drove him on, but he ran no more than a hundred feet, when he staggered and pitched headlong. It was his last panic. When he had recovered his breath and control, he sat up and entertained in his mind the conception of meeting death with dignity. However, the conception did not come to him in such terms. His idea of it was that he had been making a fool of himself, running around like a chicken with its head cut off—such was the simile that occurred to him. Well, he was bound to freeze anyway, and he might as well take it decently. With this newfound peace of mind came the first glimmerings of drowsiness. A good idea, he thought, to sleep off to death. It was like taking an anesthetic. Freezing was not so bad as people thought. There were lots worse ways to die.

He pictured the boys finding his body next day. Suddenly he found himself with them, coming along the trail and looking for himself. And, still with them, he came around a turn in the trail and found himself lying in the snow. He did not belong with himself any more, for even then he was out of himself, standing with the boys and looking at himself in the snow. It certainly was cold, was his thought. When he got back to the States he could tell the folks what real cold was. He drifted on from this to a vision of the old-timer on Sulphur Creek. He could see him quite clearly, warm and comfortable, and smoking a pipe.

"You were right, old hoss; you were right," the man mumbled to the old-timer of Sulphur Creek.

Then the man drowsed off into what seemed to him the most comfortable and satisfying sleep he had ever known. The dog sat facing him and waiting. The brief day drew to a close in a long, slow twilight. There were no signs of a fire to be made, and, besides, never in the dog's experience had it known a man to sit like that in the snow and make no fire. As the twilight drew on, its eager yearning for the fire mastered it, and with a great lifting and shifting of forefeet, it whined softly, then flattened its ears down in anticipation of being chidden by the man. But the man remained silent. Later the dog whined loudly. And still later it crept close to the man and caught the scent of death. This made the animal bristle and back away. A little longer it delayed, howling under the stars that leaped and danced and shone brightly in the cold sky. Then it turned and trotted up the trail in the direction of the camp it knew, where were the other food providers and fire providers.

Selected Bibliography

Aristotle, *The Poetics of Aristotle,* trans. by S. H. Butcher, Macmillan, London and New York, 1902.

George Bluestone, *Novels into Film,* The Johns Hopkins Press, Baltimore, 1957.

Stephen E. Bowles, Ronald Mangravite, and Peter A. Zorn, Jr., *The Screenwriter's Manual: A Complete Reference of Format and Style,* Pearson, Boston, 2006.

Charles Brackett, Billy Wilder, and D. M. Marshman, Jr., *Sunset Boulevard* (screenplay), introduction by Jeffrey Meyers, University of California Press, Berkeley, 1999.

John Brady, *The Craft of the Screenwriter: Interviews with Six Celebrated Screenwriters,* Simon & Schuster/Touchstone, New York, 1981.

Diablo Cody, *Juno* (screenplay), introduction by Cody and foreword by Jason Reitman, Newmarket Press, New York, 2007.

Ethan Coen and Joel Coen, *Fargo* (screenplay), introduction by Ethan Coen, Faber and Faber, London, 1996.

———, *The Big Lebowski* (screenplay), Faber and Faber, London, 1998.

Selected Bibliography

Joel and Ethan Coen, *Barton Fink & Miller's Crossing* (screenplays), introduction by Roderick Jaynes (the Coens), Faber and Faber, London, 1991.

Cameron Crowe, *Conversations with Wilder,* Knopf, New York, 1999.

Tom Dardis, *Some Time in the Sun: The Hollywood Years of F. Scott Fitzgerald, William Faulkner, Nathanael West, Aldous Huxley, and James Agee,* Scribner, New York, 1976; revised edition, Penguin, New York, 1981.

Robin Eggar, "Woody Allen on *Vicky Cristina Barcelona,*" *The Sunday Times* (London), January 11, 2009.

Lajos Egri, *The Art of Dramatic Writing: Its Basis in the Creative Interpretation of Human Motives,* introduction by Gilbert Miller, Simon & Schuster, New York, 1946, and 1960 Touchstone edition (earlier version published as *How to Write a Play,* Simon & Schuster, 1942).

Joe Eszterhas, *The Devil's Guide to Hollywood: The Screenwriter as God!,* St. Martin's Press, New York, 2006.

Rob Feld, "Q&A with David Koepp," in Josh Friedman and Koepp, *War of the Worlds: The Shooting Script,* introduction by Koepp, Newmarket Press, New York, 2005.

Syd Field, *The Screenwriter's Problem Solver: How to Recognize, Identify, and Define Screenwriting Problems,* Dell, New York, 1998.

————, *Screenplay: The Foundations of Screenwriting, A Step-by-Step Guide from Concept to Finished Script,* Dell, New York, 1979; Delta revised edition, Bantam Dell, New York, 2005.

John Gassner and Dudley Nichols, eds., *Twenty Best Film Plays,* Crown, New York, 1943.

Selected Bibliography

William Goldman, *Adventures in the Screen Trade: A Personal View of Hollywood and Screenwriting,* Warner Books, New York, 1983; paperback edition, Warner Books, 1984, includes Goldman's screenplay *Butch Cassidy and the Sundance Kid.*

————, *Which Lie Did I Tell?: More Adventures in the Screen Trade,* Pantheon Books, New York, 2000.

Ben Hecht, *A Child of the Century: The Autobiography of Ben Hecht,* Simon & Schuster, New York, 1954.

Ernest Hemingway, *Ernest Hemingway on Writing,* edited by Larry W. Phillips, Simon & Schuster/Touchstone, New York, 1984.

Patricia Highsmith, *Plotting and Writing Suspense Fiction,* revised updated edition, St. Martin's Griffin, New York, 2001.

Julian Hoxter, *Write What You Don't Know: An Accessible Manual for Screenwriters,* Continuum, New York, 2011.

Karl Iglesias, *The 101 Habits of Highly Successful Screenwriters: Insider Secrets from Hollywood's Top Writers,* Adams Media Corporation, Avon, Massachusetts, 2001.

Stephen King, *On Writing: A Memoir of the Craft,* Scribner, New York, 2000.

Bill Krohn, *Hitchcock at Work,* Phaidon Press, London, 2000.

Stanley Kubrick, "Words and Movies," *Sight & Sound,* vol. 30, Winter 1960/61.

Eric Lax, *Conversations with Woody Allen: His Films, the Movies, and Moviemaking,* Knopf, New York, 2007.

Jack London, "To Build a Fire," *Youth's Companion,* Boston, May 29, 1902 (first version); the revised version was published in *The*

Century Magazine, New York, August 1908, and in London's collection *Lost Face,* Macmillan, New York, 1910.

Rick Lyman, "Watching Movies with Steven Soderbergh: Follow the Muse; Inspiration to Balance Lofty and Light" (on *All the President's Men*), *New York Times,* February 26, 2001.

Herman J. Mankiewicz and Orson Welles, *Citizen Kane* (screenplay and dialogue transcription of film), *The "Citizen Kane" Book,* introduction by Pauline Kael, Little, Brown, Boston, 1971.

Joseph McBride, "Bread and Dreams: Young Screenwriters" and "'Nothing Will Ever Stop Hitch,'" *Daily Variety,* 42nd Anniversary Issue, October 1975.

————, "John Huston Finds that the Slow Generation of *King* Has Made It a Richer Film," *Variety,* December 16, 1975; reprinted in Robert Emmet Long, ed., *John Huston: Interviews,* University Press of Mississippi, Jackson, 2001.

————, *Hawks on Hawks,* University of California Press, Berkeley, 1982.

————, ed., *Filmmakers on Filmmaking: The American Film Institute Seminars on Motion Pictures and Television,* volumes 1 and 2, J. P. Tarcher, Los Angeles, 1983.

————, "The Patient Englishman" (Anthony Minghella interview), *Mr. Showbiz,* February 11, 1997.

————, "Riskinesque: How Robert Riskin Spoke Through Frank Capra and Vice Versa," *Written By,* December 1998–January 1999; reprinted in Jason Shinder and Peter Bogdanovich, eds., *The Best American Film Writing 1999,* St. Martin's Griffin, New York, 1999.

————, "The Pathological Hero's Conscience: Screenwriter Frank S. Nugent Was the Quiet Man Behind Director John Ford," *Written By,* May 2001.

———, *What Ever Happened to Orson Welles?: A Portrait of an Independent Career*, University Press of Kentucky, Lexington, 2006.

———, "Who Is John Huston? The Riddle of Adaptation and Authorship," *Oxford American*, April 2007.

———, "The Screenplay as Genre," in Greil Marcus and Werner Sollors, eds., *A New Literary History of America*, Harvard University Press Reference Library, Belknap Press, Cambridge, MA, 2009.

———, "'A Pavane for an Early American': Abraham Polonsky Discusses *Tell Them Willie Boy Is Here*," in Andrew Dickos, ed., *Abraham Polonsky: Interviews*, University Press of Mississippi, Jackson, 2012.

Joseph McBride and Todd McCarthy, "Going for Extra Innings" (Billy Wilder interview), *Film Comment*, January–February 1979; reprinted in Robert Horton, ed., *Billy Wilder: Interviews*, University Press of Mississippi, Jackson, 2002.

Patrick McGilligan, ed., *Backstory* (series of interviews with screenwriters), five volumes, University of California Press, Berkeley, 1991–2009.

Alexander Mackendrick, *On Film-making: An Introduction to the Craft of the Director*, edited by Paul Cronin, foreword by Martin Scorsese, Faber and Faber, London, 2004.

Larry McMurtry, "Properties, Projects, Possibilities" (column), *American Film*, June 1976.

———, *Film Flam: Essays on Hollywood*, Simon & Schuster, New York, 1987.

Larry McMurtry and Diana Ossana, *Brokeback Mountain* (screenplay), from the short story by Annie Proulx, in Proulx, McMurtry, and Ossana, *Brokeback Mountain: Story to Screenplay*, Scribner, New York, 2005.

Frank S. Nugent, *The Searchers* (screenplay), Turner Classic Movies and ScreenPress Publishing Limited, Suffolk, U.K., published as a supplement to *Sight & Sound,* December 2002.

Flannery O'Connor, "The Nature and Aim of Fiction" and "Writing Short Stories" in O'Connor, *Mystery and Manners: Occasional Prose,* selected and edited by Sally and Robert Fitzgerald, Farrar, Straus & Giroux, New York, 1969.

———, *The Habit of Being,* letters selected and edited by Sally Fitzgerald, Farrar, Straus & Giroux, New York, 1979.

Michael Ondaatje, *The Conversations: Walter Murch and the Art of Editing Film,* Knopf, New York, 2002.

Alexander Payne and Jim Taylor, *Sideways: The Shooting Script* (based on the novel by Rex Pickett), Newmarket Press, New York, 2004.

Samson Raphaelson, *Three Screen Comedies by Samson Raphaelson: Trouble in Paradise, The Shop Around the Corner, Heaven Can Wait* (screenplays), introduction by Pauline Kael, The Wisconsin Center for Film and Theater Research, University of Wisconsin Press, Madison, 1983; includes Raphaelson's essay "Freundschaft: How It Was with Lubitsch and Me," first published in *The New Yorker,* May 11, 1981.

Jean Renoir, *Renoir on Renoir: Interviews, Essays, and Remarks,* translated by Carol Volk, Cambridge University Press, Cambridge, 1989; originally published as *Entretiens et propos,* Éditions de l'Etoile, Cahiers du Cinéma, Paris, 1979.

Jean Renoir and Charles Spaak, *Grand Illusion* (screenplay), translated by Marianne Alexandre and Andrew Sinclair, Lorrimer, London, and Simon & Schuster, New York, 1968.

Robert Rodriguez, *Rebel Without a Crew: Or How a 23-Year-Old Filmmaker with $7,000 Became a Hollywood Player,* Dutton, New

York, 1995; and the Plume edition (including "The Ten-Minute Film School" and the screenplay for *El Mariachi*), New York, 1996.

Paul Schrader, *Taxi Driver* (screenplay), Faber and Faber, London, 1990.

Budd Schulberg, *On the Waterfront: The Final Shooting Script,* Samuel French, New York, 1988.

Tom Stempel, *FrameWork: A History of Screenwriting in the American Film,* foreword by Philip Dunne, Continuum, New York, 1988; third edition, Syracuse University Press, Syracuse, 2000.

William Strunk Jr. and E. B. White, *The Elements of Style,* fourth edition, foreword by Roger Angell, Longman, New York, 1999.

Robert Towne, *Chinatown and The Last Detail: Screenplays by Robert Towne,* with the introduction "On Moving Pictures," Grove Press, New York, 1997.

François Truffaut, *Hitchcock,* with the collaboration of Helen G. Scott, Simon & Schuster, New York, 1967, originally published as *Le Cinéma selon Hitchcock,* Paris, Robert Laffont, 1966; revised paperback edition, *Hitchcock/Truffaut,* Éditions Ramsay, Paris, 1983, and Simon & Schuster/Touchstone, New York, 1985.

——, "The Original Treatment" for the 1960 film *À bout de souffle (Breathless),* directed by Jean-Luc Godard, *L'Avant-Scène Cinéma,* March 1968; translated by Dory O'Brien for *Breathless* (includes transcription of film), edited by Dudley Andrew, Rutgers University Press, New Brunswick, NJ, and London, 1987.

Mark A. Viera, *Irving Thalberg: Boy Wonder to Producer Prince,* University of California Press, Berkeley, 2010.

Franklin Walker, *Jack London and the Klondike: The Genesis of an American Writer,* The Huntington Library, San Marino, California, 1966.

Selected Bibliography

Orson Welles and Oja Kodar, *The Other Side of the Wind* (screenplay), in *The Other Side of the Wind,* edited by Giorgio Gosetti, Cahiers du Cinéma and Festival International du Film de Locarno, Paris and Locarno, 2005.

Nathanael West, *The Day of the Locust,* Random House, New York, 1939; reprinted in West, *Nathanael West: Novels and Other Writings,* Library of America, New York, 1997.

Billy Wilder and Raymond Chandler, *Double Indemnity* (screenplay), based on the novel by James M. Cain, introduction by Jeffrey Meyers, University of California Press, Berkeley, 2000.

Billy Wilder and I. A. L. Diamond, *The Apartment* (screenplay), Faber and Faber, London, 1998; previously published in *The Apartment and The Fortune Cookie: Two Screenplays,* Praeger, New York, 1971.

Jeff Young, *Kazan: The Master Director Discusses His Films; Interviews with Elia Kazan,* Newmarket Press, New York, 1999.

Acknowledgments

When I began teaching full-time more than a decade ago, my biggest surprise was realizing how much a teacher learns from his students. This book would not exist had it not been for my lively experiences teaching beginning and advanced screenwriting courses at San Francisco State University (and before that at the now-defunct New College of California in San Francisco). My heartfelt thanks go to all my students for our fertile discussions of the craft and for their challenging questions and feedback and their diligent work as screenwriters. Helping them learn how to write scripts has taught me as much about the craft as I have learned from my own work as a screenwriter, and I have been able to apply those lessons to a wider audience through this book. Although I enjoyed teaching myself how to write screenplays back in the 1960s, there were many times when I wished I'd had the benefit of a mentor to guide and warn me about all the challenges ahead. I hope this book will serve that purpose for the aspiring screenwriters who read it.

For the privilege of teaching screenwriting and film studies at San Francisco State, I thank Stephen Ujlaki, former chair of our Cinema Department and now dean of the Loyola Marymount University School of Film and Television in Los Angeles, who has always been unfailingly encouraging and supportive of my work, and my colleague Steven Kovacs, who headed the search committee that hired me. I first met Steve Kovacs on the chilly night in December 1978 when we were blowing up Vince

Acknowledgments

Lombardi High School for the ending of *Rock 'n' Roll High School* and he was the New World Pictures executive benignly supervising our creative mischief. Both Steves have been exemplary in the way they combine their academic careers with their work as professional filmmakers, and they share my convictions about the value of studying both the practical and the theoretical aspects of this popular art form, and about the critical importance of sound writing skills. They have helped me make a smooth transition from freelance writing and part-time teaching to a full-time career in academia.

I thank San Francisco State for granting me a sabbatical leave to write this book, and Steve Ujlaki and Jenny Lau for their support in that process, as well as our president, Robert A. Corrigan; John M. Gemello, our retired provost and vice president for academic affairs; Kurt Daw, our former dean of the College of Creative Arts; Ronald Compesi, our former interim dean; our dean of Humanities, Paul Sherwin; and Marilyn Verhey, our retired dean of faculty affairs. Marilyn also provided kind support and expert guidance to me as I was on the path to tenure. My other colleagues at San Francisco State have also given me heartening encouragement, including our new chair, Daniel Bernardi, and I have benefited greatly from discussions of writing and teaching with such esteemed friends and mentors as Larry Clark, Jim Goldner, Jim Kitses, Martha Gorzycki, Warren Haack, Scott Boswell, and Julian Hoxter, our screenwriting coordinator and the author of the entertaining and insightful 2011 guidebook *Write What You Don't Know: An Accessible Manual for Screenwriters.* At New College, Daniel Cassidy and Esther "Hetty" O'Hara recruited me to teach screenwriting and film studies in the Irish Studies Department. Hetty remains a pillar of strength in my life. Danny is sorely missed by his many friends.

Early in my writing career, when I was still in Wisconsin, I learned foundational lessons about filmmaking from Professors Richard Byrne and Russell Merritt and from my friends William Donnelly and Michael Wilmington, as well as from the anonymous screenwriter who taught me the importance of "chutzpah." My original screenwriting models were Herman J. Mankiewicz and Orson Welles, whose screenplay for *Citizen Kane* I was fortunate to find at the State Historical Society of Wisconsin (now the Wisconsin Historical Society) in Madison, in the collection of Welles's attorney L. Arnold Weissberger. Running the Wisconsin Film Society gave me access to a print of *Kane* that I used as my cinematic textbook, as well as many other films and a remarkable audience that included many future filmmakers, most notably Errol Morris. Madison was also a fertile breeding ground for film scholars, and I have kept up my friendships with Patrick McGilligan, Douglas Gomery, Gerald Peary, David Bordwell, and others. I appreciate David's enthusiastic and generous encouragement of this project at key points in its development, which helped inspire me to finally write the book. And I thank Lea Jacobs and Ben Brewster for bringing me back to the campus to speak in 2010 on writing biographies of film directors.

When I went to Hollywood, I benefited from the kindness and generosity of fellow screenwriters and film buffs George Kirgo and Julie Kirgo, his daughter. George, who for a time served as president of the Writers Guild of America, remained my friend until his untimely death, and I treasure my ongoing friendship with Julie (and our collaboration when she wrote the documentary *Becoming John Ford* with director Nick Redman, for which she recruited me as a consultant and interviewee). Julie was a student in the first film course I ever taught, International Film Directors, an opportunity I was given by Gary Shusett at Sherwood Oaks Experimental College in Hollywood, in the days when Syd Field was also getting his start there as a screenwriting teacher.

Since we only had two film courses at the University of Wisconsin–Madison when I was a student in the late 1960s, I had to create my own curriculum by watching films day and night on campus and spending many years in Hollywood and elsewhere seeking out filmmakers I admired so I could pump them with questions about the crafts of writing and directing. I am especially grateful for the generosity of Orson Welles (who let me collaborate on my own dialogue in *The Other Side of the Wind,* my first professional work in film), Howard Hawks, Jean Renoir, Allan Dwan, Samuel Fuller, Abraham Polonsky, Rouben Mamoulian, Paul Schrader, Robert Towne, Terrence Malick, Gavin Lambert, Edward L. Bernds, John Sanford, Billy Wilder, Philip Dunne, John Huston, Alfred Hitchcock, and François Truffaut. D. W. Griffith (who advised screenwriters to "Think in pictures!") was long gone before I came to Hollywood, but I was fortunate to be able to discuss him and that formative period of filmmaking with Lillian Gish. My editor at *Daily Variety* in Hollywood, Thomas L. Pryor, and my fellow film critic and business writer Arthur D. *"Murf."* Murphy gave me the equivalent of a graduate education in the byzantine realities of the film business. Comments by Francis Ford Coppola on screenwriting and other aspects of writing and filmmaking are from his April 24, 2009, appearance at San Francisco State University, sponsored by the Cinema Department under the auspices of Steve Ujlaki. My heartfelt thanks to Coppola for permission to use his sagacious quotes and to his assistant, Adriana Rotaru, and longtime aide Tom Luddy, as well as to Steve, for helping facilitate the permission.

I am grateful to Roger Corman and Jon Davison for giving me my start in professional screenwriting. Directors Joe Dante and Allan Arkush and the erudite story editor Frances Doel provided me with exciting creative opportunities at Corman's New World Pictures. George Stevens Jr. was my writing partner and producer on five American Film Institute Life Achievement Award specials, my most rewarding experiences as a scriptwriter. Jeff Berg, the Hollywood agent par excellence, expertly guided my screenwriting career in a crucial period and shared his wisdom about the business. Henry Beckman taught me a critical lesson about the importance of actors in the writing process. Working with producer-director-editor Harrison Engle on several projects has been a fertile experience in collaboration.

Writers I never met but who have profoundly inspired me include Ernest Hemingway, Graham Greene, and Nathanael West and screenwriters Michael Wilson, Frank S. Nugent, Robert Riskin, and Sidney Buchman.

Other screenwriters I have been fortunate enough to interview over the years include Jay Presson Allen, Ingmar Bergman, Jeffrey Boam, I. A. L. Diamond, Edward Dryhurst, Julius J. Epstein, Bob Gale, Theodor S. Geisel (Dr. Seuss), Carl Gottlieb, Albert Hackett, Ian McLellan Hunter, Willard Huyck, Lawrence Kasdan, Gloria Katz, William Link, Rod Lurie, John Lee Mahin, Richard B. Matheson, Paul Mazursky, John Milius, Anthony Minghella, Carlton Moss, Allen Rivkin, Neil Simon, Oliver Stone, Tom Stoppard, and Gore Vidal. Others who have educated me on the intricacies of the movie business include reporter and biographer Bob Thomas; studio executive and producer Mike Medavoy; MGM story editor and film historian Samuel Marx; actress Fay Wray (Robert Riskin's widow) and screenwriters Victoria Riskin and David Rintels; and assistant director Louis Race. Authors Jerzy Kosinski and Barry Farrell were extraordinarily generous in encouraging my screenwriting ambitions.

I thank the four publishers' representatives who approached me in my office at San Francisco State during a six-month period to ask me to write a book on screenwriting. I took their enthusiasm as a further sign that I should finally begin work on *Writing in Pictures,* which had been germinating in my mind for years.

Every film historian owes an enormous debt to the Margaret Herrick Library of the Academy of Motion Picture Arts and Sciences and to its stellar staff of librarians, headed by Linda Harris Mehr and also including Sandra Archer and Barbara Hall. When it was harder to access screenplays than it is today, the Academy library's Howard Prouty provided me with Nugent's screenplay adaptation of Alan LeMay's novel *The*

Searchers, and Robert Gitt (then of Dartmouth College Films, later of the UCLA Film and Television Archive) gave me a copy of Welles's screenplay adaptation of Booth Tarkington's Pulitzer Prize–winning novel *The Magnificent Ambersons.* The University of Wisconsin Memorial Library was a major asset to my early research, and the Wisconsin Historical Society and its Wisconsin Center for Film and Theater Research have long been a priceless resource for my work as a film historian. I thank Barbara Kaiser and Ben Brewster for their diligent curatorship of my own collection of book manuscripts, screenplays, and other papers, and Maxine Fleckner Ducey for her always helpful assistance with my research. I learned a great deal about writing when I worked on my Frank Capra biography with copy editor Virginia Clark. My late parents, Marian Dunne McBride and Raymond E. McBride, who were both newspaper reporters, guided my early steps as a writer.

I am grateful to the publications that have printed my articles and interviews about screenwriting, especially *Written By,* the magazine of the Writers Guild of America, West, which has run my profiles of screenwriters Robert Riskin, Michael Wilson, Marguerite Roberts, Frank S. Nugent, Gavin Lambert, Abraham Polonsky, Billy Wilder, and Rod Lurie. I have been professionally sustained on numerous occasions over more than thirty years by my membership in the Writers Guild and encouraged by my WGA Award for *The American Film Institute Salute to John Huston* and my four other WGA nominations for AFI Life Achievement Award shows.

Other publications that have printed my pieces on screenwriting include *The New York Review of Books; Film Comment; Film Quarterly; Sight & Sound; American Film; Cineaste; Oxford American; CreativePlanet.com;* and *The Real Paper* (Boston). I am grateful to David Thomson and Greil Marcus for inviting me to write the section on screenwriting for the 2009 Harvard University Press book *A New Literary History of America,* edited by Marcus and Werner Sollors. For asking me to host discussions with screenwriters and directors, thanks to David Shepard of the Directors Guild of America; Ronald Haver of the Los Angeles County Museum of Art; Gary Abrahams and Gary Essert of the Los Angeles International Film Exposition (Filmex); the UCLA Film and Television Archive; the Los Angeles Cinematheque; and the Los Feliz Theater, Hollywood.

I always benefit enormously from sharing ideas with my friends and fellow film scholars Jonathan Lethem, Bill Krohn, Patrick McGilligan, Jonathan Rosenbaum, Janet Bergstrom, Peter Tonguette, Leonard Maltin, F. X. Feeney, Glenn Frankel, Fred Lombardi, Steve Mayhew, Joe Dante, and Sam Hamm. Sam has visited my classes several times to speak about screenwriting and is always treated like a rock star by the students. He was especially helpful to me in the process of writing this book by generously sharing his thoughts and advice on screenwriting and how it can be taught. I am grateful to Sam for reading the manuscript and generously offering valuable comments and suggestions for improving it. My former student Conal Chan, who is now a Hollywood screenwriter, also gave me helpful suggestions for this book. Two of the most delightful people in the world of film are Harry Carey Jr., actor and writer, and his wife, Marilyn, and knowing them has enriched my life. Lou Race has been my friend and colleague for almost forty years now, and he and his wife, Judy, always make my visits to Los Angeles a pleasure.

I miss Maurice L. Muehle greatly. Maury was my attorney from the late 1980s until his death in 2009. By helping me surmount many obstacles, he enabled me to succeed in my goals as an author. Maury was a kind and faithful friend, as well as a dazzling legal mind and invaluable counselor, and I always enjoyed our wide-ranging conversations on the law and literature.

Richard Parks of the Richard Parks Agency has always been a bulwark of support for my career, and it is a pleasure to deal with a man of such consummate intelligence, taste, integrity, and diplomacy. Richard's loyalty and wise counsel make my writing career possible. His work is ably supported by Barbara Levy of the Barbara Levy Literary Agency, London, and Camilla Ferrier of the Marsh Agency, London.

I am grateful to Zachary Wagman of Vintage/Anchor for acquiring *Writing in Pictures* and for his enthusiastic appreciation of my approach to screenwriting and his sensitive editing of the manuscript. After Zack moved to another editorship at the Crown Publishing Group division of Random House, Diana Secker Tesdell inherited this project, sharing Zack's enthusiasm and offering me similarly expert guidance in a seamless transition. I am pleased to find myself in such good hands with both of my editors at Random House. Amy Ryan improved the book with her astute copyediting. Walter Donohue, who acquired the book for Faber and Faber in the U.K., has always been supportive of my work and has published several of my earlier books as well; I also thank Walter for facilitating permissions to quote from screenplays.

Ruth O'Hara has always been there for me personally and professionally. I value her brilliant and generous insights into film, teaching, and everything else. She and our son, John McBride, have taught me much of what I know about teaching. Discussing film, politics, and economics with John always leaves me feeling much smarter. John also provided expert technical support for this book and created my website, josephmcbridefilm.com. My daughter, Jessica McBride, a fine writer and teacher, and granddaughter, Anne Bucher, bring joy to my life. The rest of the McBride and O'Hara clans are also wonderfully supportive and intellectually energizing.

Life with my beloved partner Ann Weiser Cornell is an endless delight. With her warmth and wisdom, she sets a constant model for me to emulate with her indefatigable creative enterprise as a stellar teacher and writer. She has contributed many important ideas to this book, including detailed editing suggestions that have greatly enhanced my work. By contributing to my teaching on a daily basis, and by her example, she has helped me better understand how to communicate my love of the craft of writing.

Joseph McBride
Berkeley, California
September 2011

Index

(355)

Index

Index